BRITISH IMMIGRATION POLICY UNDER THE CONSERVATIVE GOVERNMENT

British Immigration Policy Under the Conservative Government

ASIFA MAARIA HUSSAIN
University of Glasgow, UK

Routledge
Taylor & Francis Group

LONDON AND NEW YORK

First published 2001 by Ashgate Publishing

Reissued 2018 by Routledge
2 Park Square, Milton Park, Abingdon, Oxon OX14 4RN
711 Third Avenue, New York, NY 10017, USA

Routledge is an imprint of the Taylor & Francis Group, an informa business

Publisher's Note
The publisher has gone to great lengths to ensure the quality of this reprint
but points out that some imperfections in the original copies may be
apparent.

Disclaimer
The publisher has made every effort to trace copyright holders and
welcomes correspondence from those they have been unable to contact.

A Library of Congress record exists under LC control number: 2001090209

ISBN 13: 978-1-138-73449-4 (hbk)
ISBN 13: 978-1-138-73448-7 (pbk)
ISBN 13: 978-1-315-18723-5 (ebk)

Contents

List of Figures

List of Tables

x

Preface

Under Margaret Thatcher the Conservative party imposed a very tough immigration regime whose impact manifested itself into very serious negative consequences for immigrants from the Indian sub-continent, a region which made up thirty two per cent of all nationalities accepted for settlement in 1980. The exact reason for the tough stance on immigration is open to debate but there is no doubt that it was driven by a combination of political, economic, and nationalistic reasons. The cumulative impact of this tough approach was to cause the break-up and separation of families, which in turn caused suffering and distress among families. The strict approach also saw vigorous procedures to ensure that potential immigrants satisfied the criteria laid out and these were detested by the individuals who had to endure them. The controversial nature of the immigration controls and their impact on individuals was such that it attracted a great deal of criticism and generated much heated political debates.

There were a number of reasons why I chose this particular study, not all of which I can explain in great detail here. Firstly the Conservative party's immigration policy provided an intriguing example of a tough immigration regime in practice, regarded not surprisingly as one of the strictest in Western Europe during its time. Its severe controversy generated some fascinating debates, and had profound effects on the lives of many individuals.

Secondly this research was of interest to me as there has been no research done specifically on the *impact* on individuals of immigration policy under Thatcher, especially in relation to Scotland. Although it has to be said that as a native Scot giving the study a Scottish flavour gave me personal pleasure.

Glasgow has been chosen as the geographical focus of the study for a number of reasons. Firstly, it has a large community from the Indian sub-continent living there, giving me easier access to conduct a survey and to do individual interviews for case studies. Secondly, since there is a large immigrant population, there are many organisations which have been around since the late 1970s and early 1980s based in Glasgow. These organisations could give me comprehensive knowledge of the problems faced by immigrants in the 1980s. Thirdly, the appellate authority is based in Glasgow which allowed me to sit through the appeal cases on immigration, and write about them when analysing individual cases. This gave me personal experience in the manner in which immigration appeal cases are conducted. Thus many of the political actors involved in the immigration procedures were near enough based in Glasgow i.e. Immigration Police, Adjudicators and Scottish Labour MPs. In other words choosing Glasgow was also a case of convenience that provided me with distinct advantages to undertake my work.

The conventional view expressed by most writers that the Conservative approach to immigration from the Indian sub-continent was discriminatory, harsh and unnecessarily strict, is I believe largely sustained by the findings of this book.

To set out my argument the book is divided into a number of chapters. Chapter 1 basically introduces the topic of this study, and reviews some of the most important contemporary literature in this field. Chapter 2 describes and analyses the legislative machinery which was at the heart of the Conservative party's enforcement of its immigration policy. Chapter 3 looks at the various organisations in Glasgow which had the task of protecting immigrant rights, and which had to tackle the legal impediments imposed by government laws by taking on the role of pressure groups.

Chapters 4 and 5 are dedicated to a comprehensive look at the impact on individuals of immigration policy during the Thatcher period, and what deductions can be made about the nature of such a policy. Chapter 6 provides the official view which allows the argument to be balanced. Chapter 7 examines the political perceptions from an MP's viewpoint on the question of immigration. The final chapter simply summarises and concludes the main findings of this work.

The book draws on a rich source of particularly primary sources including official Parliamentary documents and laws, and others which are far too extensive to list here. A considerable amount of fieldwork was involved. To start with all the parties involved in the immigration arena in were interviewed. This included the opinions of the civil servants performing their duties as immigration officials. A survey was conducted on people from the Indian sub-continent living in areas of Glasgow, and the experience of individuals who provided extremely interesting cases was looked at. I interviewed immigration officials in Glasgow about their involvement in immigration and opinion on Conservative immigration policy. I attended regular sittings at a number of immigration cases. A visit to London was made to interview officials from the Home Office and Foreign and Commonwealth Office to get an opinion of how they handled their work, and the criticisms that were levelled against them. Scottish Conservative and Labour MPs were also interviewed to attain some insight into whether they considered the Conservative Immigration policy as discriminatory and if they themselves saw any flaws in the immigration procedures. By interviewing parties from all sides a balanced argument could then be pursued. This work represents the first attempt at tackling in detail the impact of Conservative immigration policy on individuals in Scotland. Most of the sources and information appearing in chapters three, four, five and six are therefore new. However, it has to be stressed that immigration is a UK wide issue and therefore the effects of the immigration regime are applicable to the rest of the United Kingdom.

Acknowledgements

I must express a debt of gratitude to a number of people without whose support it would have been very difficult to pursue such a sensitive study.

Firstly I would like to express my thanks to certain members of the academic staff in the Department of Politics at Glasgow University, who were kind enough to offer me advice and general help on matters or questions which arose from this study. They were: Peter Fotheringham; Bill Miller; and Richard Crook.

I would also like to express my sincere thanks to various officials and individuals in the immigration arena who provided me with useful sources, and some of whom allowed me to interview them. They were: Masood Nabi, former Senior Counsellor at the Immigration Advisory Service who allowed me to keep constant liaison with his organisation; Jean Milne of the Scottish Office for providing me with statistics on ethnic minorities; Nick Troake from the Home Office; Sean Lusk from the Foreign and Commonwealth Office; Stan Crook of the Scottish Refugee Council; and a number of adjudicators and Conservative and Labour MPs (especially Mike Watson). In addition, thanks to individuals from the Indian sub-continent community in Glasgow who made the conduct of the survey and case studies possible, and who entrusted me with much confidential information.

Lastly and most importantly I would like to thank God 'the supreme being' for guiding me through this book, and my family, in particular my mother Maqsooda for her blessing, and my sister Tahira for her confidence in my ability to accomplish my task.

1 Introduction: The Issue at Hand and a Review of Contemporary Literature on Immigration

Introduction: The Issue at Hand

This book will examine the view that the immigration policies of the Conservative party under the Premiership of Margaret Thatcher between the years 1979-1990, enshrined in law were restrictive and discriminatory, and had a severely negative impact on immigrants from the Indian sub-continent. There is considerable evidence from immigrants from the Indian sub-continent and from other actors in the immigration debate such as organisations and MPs that white immigrants have been treated more liberally by the immigration process. They did not face the same procedural problems encountered by those from the Indian sub-continent; nor were so many rejected when they first applied for visas to enter Britain permanently or even temporarily. Officials and MPs admitted that it was easier for white immigrants to satisfy the immigration criteria. Organisations such as the Immigration Advisory Service pointed out that virtually no white persons came to seek their help in immigration matters, which suggests that the process of gaining entry for them was virtually trouble free.

One of the groups of individuals seeking to emigrate to Britain, who suffered from unequal treatment, as a result of the application of immigration policies, were nationals from the Indian sub-continent. This study will draw on a variety of direct evidence and information from the various parties involved in a highly sensitive process which attracted much political debate during the 1980s and early 1990s - documentary evidence and interviews with officials, individuals and organisations will provide proof of the tough and harsh nature of the immigration regime in operation under Thatcher.

The claim that the immigration regime was particularly strict when applied to citizens from the Indian sub-continent will be supported by:

- Analysing the immigration laws passed during the 1980s, which will reveal flaws and unfair regulations;
- comparing the number of immigrants from the Indian sub-continent with relative numbers from other regions, including the White Commonwealth countries;
- looking at the numbers removed as illegal immigrants;
- investigating the actual exercise of authority and powers by the government's agents, e.g. Entry Clearance Officers, in terms of their conduct, interviewing techniques, and wording of questions. The argument will be made that unfairly worded and difficult application forms made entry to Britain difficult to achieve and provided an excuse for refusing entry when many applicants were unable to fill in a form correctly. Deliberately long waiting times, increases in complaints and in the use of organisations indicated that there was a problem with the system of entry in operation;
- establishing which categories of immigrants were adversely affected by the immigration control regime.

The terms 'fair', 'unfair', and 'racial discrimination' will arise at various points in this book in reference to the Conservative immigration regime. The following definition of these terms should be assumed:

Fair/Unfair the immigration regime could be said to be fair if equality of treatment applied to all those seeking entry to the United Kingdom. In the case of the Conservative immigration regime the charge of unfairness arises because many of those affected viewed procedures as not being impartial and unbiased. Evidence in this book will demonstrate that many of the regime's rules and procedures were not applied to all those seeking entry, e.g. the imposition of visas in 1986 singled out specific countries. All the countries of the Indian sub-continent are included in the list of visa countries whereas none of the Old Commonwealth countries such as Australia, Canada, and New Zealand are included. In the case of Indian sub-continent nationals the primary purpose rule is widely considered unfair as it clashes with the culture of that part of the world, and puts extra pressure on those seeking entry by asking them to prove a 'negative'.

Racial discrimination This means unequal treatment solely on the basis of colour and culture. The selective imposition of visas is one example of discrimination. In addition, the Conservative immigration regime did not respect or accommodate the cultural aspects of the Indian sub-continent such as arranged marriages, and the primary purpose rule was perceived as discriminatory. There was also a lot of stereotypical thinking involved which assumed that all black or coloured visitors seeking a temporary stay would end up staying permanently. Some of the procedures and the attitudes of immigration officials were also viewed as discriminatory. This created a sense and perception of racism in the eyes of Indian sub-continent nationals.

Theories of Immigration

Different theories of immigration have emerged over the course of the 50 years or so since the second world war, a period which has seen changes in the degree and direction of international migration. The theories, which have been most accurately highlighted by Parekh,[1] distinguish three attitudes towards immigration and stimulate three types of government policy on immigration:

- Liberal View - According to this theory the policy should be one of unrestricted immigration providing that those who wanted to enter a state committed themselves to obeying the laws and acknowledging the established structure of authority. The liberal view perceives the free movement of people as a basic human right;
- the Centrist View - according to the Centrists, who essentially take the middle ground when it comes to immigration, immigration in principle should be allowed but some element of control has to be exercised in the light of global developments in the 20th Century. If there was totally

unrestricted entry, Centrists argue, this would encourage a huge influx of people merely on economic grounds which would have a detrimental effect on race relations and on the economy. Therefore some restrictions are necessary. Furthermore unrestricted entry would lead to considerable overcrowding, especially in the case of Great Britain which is essentially a small country;

- the Nationalist View - This is perhaps most controversial of the three theories because it advocates a virtual end to immigration and is against the inflow of any 'outsiders' who do not match the common stock of individuals constituting the large majority of citizens.

It is quite clear that the Liberal theory would be unworkable in the modern world given the vast economic disparities between different regions of the world thus attracting economic refugees. It would also be unworkable because of different political situations around the world which would attract many political refugees. In other words most would argue that a line has to be drawn somewhere so that immigration is subject to enlightened control.

The Centrist or middle ground theory is perhaps the most sensible approach to managing the question of immigration for those states like Britain who are concerned by the influx of immigrants. The nationalist view should have no place in today's world because it only serves to perpetuate racial tensions and discrimination, especially in multi-racial societies. States in the modern world are greatly heterogeneous today and many "..are products of considerable ethnic intermingling and cannot pretend to belong to a single ethnic stock".[2] This is no less true of Western states like the USA, Canada, Australia, and Great Britain. However, although it may be the most sensible approach to immigration, the Centrist theory has to be applied equally and justly. It will be argued that the British government did not conform to the principles of the Centrist view in principle (legislative enactments) or practice (implementation) after 1979.

A close look at Conservative Party policy on immigration would suggest that it falls into the category of the centrist view. However, this study will argue that in practice the views of various sections of the party suggest that official Conservative policy belonged somewhere between the Centrist and Nationalist viewpoints. Tory policy makers claimed they were adopting a largely middle ground approach, allowing a measured amount of immigration tempered by various restrictions. In practice however, the emergence of the 'New Right' in the party, who have been advocating a more stringent immigration regime, which largely wishes to end all immigration, has seen the imposition of more pressures on the government to further toughen its already strict policies. A significant point to note is that Conservative policy since 1979 has been discriminatory in the sense that the balanced Centrist approach of keeping immigration to manageable levels has not necessarily been applied equally to potential immigrants from all regions of the world. It has been well documented that the official line has been stricter towards would be immigrants from many coloured and black nations such as India, Pakistan and Bangladesh, while fewer reservations have been voiced about the prospect of immigration from white countries such as the United States, Canada and Australia.

The immigration issue raised considerable controversy during the period of office of the Thatcher administration. The reason for this was the ferocity and vigour with which Thatcher's successive governments tackled the issue of immigration. Certain questions are worth posing. Was Thatcher's fairly hard-line stance on immigration a pre-planned policy waiting to be implemented? Or was it one, which the Conservatives believed would help them sweep to power at a general election? Or was it simply a reaction to public opinion or public disquiet at the flow of immigration into Britain? Also, more importantly was Thatcher's immigration policy discriminatory against those from black and coloured nations?

If we look at the Conservative's party manifesto for 1979 we will find that it laid out a package of measures designed to control immigration once they came to power.[3] In the 1979 manifesto, after initially praising the ethnic minorities for making

> a valuable contribution to the life of our nation…and stressing that the rights of all British citizens legally settled here are equal before the law whatever their race, colour or creed,[4]

there is a comprehensive list of measures[5] aimed at curbing immigration. Such measures can be viewed as discriminatory as they would apply to some while others would be exempt from them. Among some of the more controversial proposals included were:

- Introduction of a Register of those Commonwealth wives and children entitled to entry for settlement under the 1971 Act;
- introduction of a quota system covering everyone outside the European Community to control all entry for settlement;
- the formulation of a new British Nationality Act to define entitlement to British citizenship and to the right of abode in this country. This would not adversely affect the right of anyone already permanently settled here;
- the limitation of the entry of parents, grandparents and children over 18, to a small number of urgent compassionate cases.

The Tory belief since 1979 has been that stricter immigration policies are a solution to easing racial tensions and promoting good community relations. The thrust of Conservative Party policy on immigration did not alter coming up to the 1983 General Election. The manifesto stated that to have good community relations "we have to maintain effective immigration control".[6] This line was maintained in the 1987 manifesto[7] which once again highlighted that "immigration controls are essential for harmonious and improving community relations".[8] Not content with this the manifesto went on to state that "We will tighten the existing law to ensure that control over settlement becomes even more effective".[9] The manifesto even boasted that "Immigration for settlement is now at its lowest level since control of Commonwealth immigration first began in 1962".[10]

An Analysis of Contemporary Literature on Immigration

This section will review the literature on UK immigration policy under Thatcher. Essentially, three perspectives can be isolated from the selected literature.

1. Those authors who unequivocally oppose Tory policy on immigration seeing it as unjustifiably harsh and discriminatory.
2. Those authors who wholly agree with Thatcher's hard-line policies dismissing any accusations of discrimination.

3.   And finally those who take the middle ground, critical of Tory policy but nevertheless acknowledging the need for some sort of controls. They offer their own policy prescriptions to replace some of Thatcher's measures.

The literature on immigration is vast, and this chapter will accordingly make no attempt to refer to all the literature on the subject matter of this study. Instead it will concentrate on arguably some of the most important works like those of Zig Layton-Henry, Ann Dummett, Shamit Saggar and some others.

Zig Layton-Henry in his work, *The Politics of Immigration*,[11] depicts Tory policy on immigration under Thatcher as extremely tough. But rather than classing this tough approach as deliberately discriminatory he saw it as more of a calculated policy on part of the Conservatives to win votes. According to Layton-Henry the Tories clearly believed that the general public was in favour of measures to limit immigration, and by appeasing the public by addressing their concerns

> ...they may well have prevented the rise of the kind of anti-immigrant parties that have been so prominent in other West European countries in the 1980s and early 1990s.[12]

Also, according to Layton-Henry, a series of events such as inner city riots in 1985 in Handsworth, Brixton, and Tottenham, coupled with a rise in political asylum applications from Sri Lanka stimulated the government into taking stricter action on immigration. The introduction of new legislation such as the Immigration Bill (later to become the 1988 Immigration Act) which would repeal the absolute right of men settled in Britain before 1st January 1973 to be joined by their families

> ...appeared to be yet another attempt to reduce New Commonwealth Immigration and to fulfil Mrs Thatcher's promise to bring immigration to an end.[13]

The Tories tried to mask their tough policies by claiming that their actions would serve to improve race relations, and ensure fair immigration policies.

According to Layton-Henry, Thatcher's tough stance on immigration was not all that surprising given that

7

She appeared to have little sympathy with...those who were disadvantaged...including the West Indian and Asian Communities[14]...and in contrast with her predecessor, she lacked sensitivity on race relations matters.[15]

Layton-Henry had no doubt that the Conservatives were out to end immigration, and in order to do this they would introduce legislation to control immigration by strict enforcement procedures. He recognised the fact that tough enforcement of rules would cause misery to individuals - as we shall see in chapter 5, which charts the experience of individuals - but would also hit a substantial number of innocent people (one of the major arguments used in this book). More importantly the execution of immigration rules according to Layton-Henry has 'inevitably' involved some discrimination, as the government has largely focused on reducing the number of immigrants from the New Commonwealth (which includes the Indian sub-continent). This study will examine the nature of such 'inevitable' discrimination. As Layton-Henry points out, and as this study will serve to show, the net impact of immigration policy has been that New Commonwealth Immigration has fallen since the 1970s,[16] and the refusal rates for applications seeking family reunification from the Indian sub-continent rose from 29.8% in 1981 to 44% in 1983.[17] He is critical of the fact that the Conservative government has not been willing to balance its strong control of immigrants with equal measures to "combat racial disadvantage",[18] and that overall since 1979 the race card encompassing immigration has been "cynically exploited" for electoral advantage knowingly full well that doing so stirs up "popular prejudices".[19]

Shamit Saggar[20] also mentions how the race factor played an important part in the 1979 General Election. However, he is less openly critical of the Conservative policy approach to immigration. That does not mean to say that he supports the policies adopted by the Conservatives. Instead he argues that criticism by many academic writers that the Thatcher period "..represented an unparalleled attacks on the rights of black people in Britain.."[21] is not wholly backed by evidence. Instead he prefers to play down or 'neutralise' the debate surrounding immigration arguing that, contrary to popular belief, immigration as an issue was only at the forefront for a short period, and then became less important, and was placed very low on the list of priority issues. He cites internal disagreements and quarrels within the two major parties - Labour and Conservative - as being just as important as the differences between the parties, even though Labour and other opposition parties have accused the Tories of discrimination on the issue of immigration. In fact Saggar even goes as far as to suggest that "The Conservatives' abrupt and risky lurch to the right on immigration during the 1970s was accompanied by a more pragmatic and less hostile approach to black people legitimately settled in Britain".[22] Saggar believes that much of the hostile rhetoric and views within the Conservative party were those of the very far right section and were not reflections of official party policy, and should not be taken as such.

Saggar is overall less critical of Conservative immigration policies, and prefers to adopt the diplomatic approach. He makes no attempt to use statistics or assess the impact of immigration policies on blacks under the Thatcher government. The evidence presented in this book suggests, contrary to Saggar's view, that the issue did not decline in importance after a few years of Thatcher's premiership as he claims. One only needs to look at the legislation and rules passed after the first Thatcher administration[23] to be aware of the continuing significance of immigration issues. Such legislation as the Carriers' Liability Act, the imposition of visas on nationals of selected countries such as India, Pakistan and Ghana, and other measures emphasise this point as chapter two of this book will reveal. A look at the 1983, 1987, and even the 1992 Manifestos will also show that the issue had not declined in prominence within the Conservative agenda.

One natural result of stricter immigration controls has been the development, and in some cases, the enhancement of internal controls. This is the subject of Paul Gordon's work[24] *Policing Immigration*. In this book Gordon provides a clear and concise exposition of internal controls which have been introduced in Britain to police immigration. He defines internal controls as "any aspect of law or administration related in any way to immigration status which operates within the UK".[25]

He uses his study of internal controls as the basis for strong criticism of British government immigration policies. Although his scepticism and suspicion of internal controls goes much further back than 1979, he notes an intensification of controls and the dawning of a new era in immigration legislation from 1979 when Thatcher's Conservative party came to power.

9

He cites two major developments just prior to the Tory victory in 1979 which helped to shape the tough measures adopted by the Conservatives:

> The first was the emergence of a radical new Tory philosophy on racism and immigration which would play a large part in sweeping the party into office....[26]

Secondly, the publication of a Parliamentary Select Committee report on race relations and immigration called "...for a government inquiry into the establishment of a system of internal control".[27] His study represents quite a strong indictment of what he sees as the far reaching impact of Tory immigration laws and rules, noting not only their unwelcome impact on the black and coloured communities in Britain, but also what he saw as the climate of suspicion created by Tory rhetoric and policies on immigration which saw others such as employers, schools and hospitals being encouraged to carry out their own enforcement of immigration laws by checking on black and coloured people.

Having explicitly called the Immigration Act of 1971 "racist in effect and intention",[28] Gordon's continued criticism of immigration legislation in the 1980s is hardly surprising. His justification for labelling the practice of immigration in Britain as discriminatory is based on the strong connection he makes between racism and immigration as two interrelated issues. Gordon reveals how evidence illustrates that black people are treated very differently from white people witnessed by the fact that black people have been subjected to passport raids by police and immigration officers, and required to produce passports and so on by social security officials, hospital clerks, and schools. The overall effect of this has been to create or exacerbate greater divisions between the ethnic minorities and whites with the law institutionalising such divisions. In theory ethnic minorities have the same rights as white people in a democratic nation such as freedom of movement and freedom from state harassment; however there is a perception that in practice they are denied certain rights. Perhaps one of the most fundamental lessons which can be taken in from Gordon's analysis is that a system of control (characterised by state monitoring and at times state harassment through the use of the police and immigration authorities) more sinister in nature has been developing, quietly almost

10

unnoticed, which has been affecting the ethnic minorities for some time. This is a worrying development, especially for those who want to defend civil liberties against the encroachments of the State.

Gordon's work also contradicts the backbone of the Conservative argument since 1979 that strict immigration control is necessary to promote better community and race relations. On the evidence of Gordon's analysis stricter immigration controls incorporating harsh internal controls only serve to damage the division between different races and cultures. Indeed since 1979 we have seen increased racial tensions culminating in racial violence, and an increase in racist murders of black and coloured people, coupled with the enactment of more legislative measures to control immigration. Although many might see Gordon's study as one-sided, concentrating far too much on criticism of immigration policies which have been adopted by British governments over the years, in particular his criticism of the direction of immigration policy since 1979, one cannot dismiss his arguments outright. In short, much of Gordon's findings and claims will be backed up by the evidence from this study, even if at times he puts his findings extremely.

Ann Dummett's views about current British immigration policy set out in various works such as "Towards a Just Immigration Policy"[29] and "Subjects, Citizens and Others"[30] are very thought provoking. She believes that a certain amount of common sense has to be brought into the immigration debate. It is true that the debate on immigration has focused too much on two extreme views: On the one hand there should be no immigration controls because they are not justified; and on the other present controls are necessary, and should even be tightened further. In my view Dummett correctly argues that some middle ground can be found, and that there is an alternative "...between present controls on the one hand and an open door policy on the other".[31] She aims in "Towards a just immigration policy" to offer her own policy prescription on immigration emphasising that "there is a very wide range of possible alternatives to present policy".[32] One of these alternatives would be to have no control at all. Dummett does not favour such an alternative but she does point out some of the positive effects that a policy of no control would have. These positive aspects would include the opportunity for families to be reunited;

refugees to enter freely without anxiety, and the enormous saving of money and bureaucracy.

Dummett does not reject totally out of hand the need for some control. She emphasises that control has to be fairly administered and that the issue should be tackled in British politics from a global perspective rather than by concentrating only on Commonwealth or non-white immigrants. This would be Dummett's preferred policy, and it is one which coincides with the argument presented in this book. Nowhere in this book is it argued that there should be no immigration controls at all. Instead, as Dummett stresses, the need for control is essential but only if it is applied fairly and equally, and the various laws are not characterised by racial discrimination. That current legislation is discriminatory is a finding supported by evidence presented in this book. Indeed we have to start thinking about immigration from European countries as well instead of trying to think of immigration as a clash between black/coloured and the white authorities. Immigration control should encompass control of immigrants from all parts of the world not just those from black and coloured countries; "present controls have aimed at excluding black people rather than white".[33] At times Dummett displays strong opposition to current British immigration policies believing that much of the thinking behind them has been based on outdated feelings of superiority generated by the days of colonialism, a view incidentally shared by Miles and Phizachlea.[34]

Her own policy prescription would be to reform both the laws on nationality and on immigration to replace the current "...irrational, expensive, racially discriminatory structure".[35] She would envisage this to be done by establishing a new British immigration law which is based on British nationality law. Currently she argues we have a system where nationality law, which defines citizenship, is based on immigration law. This is held to be totally unfair because it creates a situation whereby the UK is in effect refusing entry to some of its *own citizens*, e.g. those who fall into the third category of citizenship - British Overseas Citizens who under the 1981 British Nationality Act have no right of abode in the UK because they do not satisfy the entry requirements for immigration, even if they have British nationality. In other words the UK flouts the universally accepted principle that an individual who is a national of a state has the right to enter that state. In practice the system works in such a way that it

12

is the white people who make up around 96% of the population are completely free from immigration control. This is a very fair point which is linked to one of the forms of discrimination noted in this study which is the discrimination inherent in British laws on immigration and nationality. The discriminatory nature of legislation is looked at in some detail in chapter 2. Apart from making the system more fair there would be other advantages of easing controls within reason: Saving of money and bureaucracy through the reduction of immigration officers, and less police time spent on tracing overstayers or illegal entrants.

In their work *White Man's Country*,[36] Miles and Phizacklea essentially attack what they see as racism inherent in British society, not least in British politics. They chart the racist bias of British domestic politics, since the 1950s, and note the particularly extreme right-wing tendencies which had emerged in the Conservative Party just prior to its victory in the 1979 general election. They note how black and coloured people have to suffer from clearly discriminatory government legislation, and have had to suffer crime and abuse. At the same time they have been unfairly blamed for the deteriorating economic situation characterised by a decline in living standards, and rising unemployment, a result, the authors claim, of a growing crisis in capitalism which cannot be blamed on coloured and black immigrants.

Miles and Phizacklea warn of a gradual but definite stride towards a policy of repatriation as a result of developments during the 1980s such as race riots which have seen increased public anxiety and a climate of growing resentment towards immigration. The authors are very direct in their criticism of the British political system which they believe has helped fuel racist attitudes in the country. During the 1980s and to some extent in the 1990s a lot of unnecessary hysteria about immigration has been whipped up by political figures, particularly Tory MPs: witness Norman Tebbit's criticism of Indian sub-continent cricket supporters claiming that although they lived in England they often supported their country of origin when they were playing England. Also Michael Portillo's speech in November 1995,[37] labelled as xenophobic by the press, which attracted strong criticism. Not to mention Thatcher's own pronouncements about the country being swamped by immigrants, and that a threat to British culture was being posed by immigrants. What the Conservatives had effectively done since 1979 was to rekindle memories of "past glories of industrial achievement"[38] and a huge empire during days when Britain ruled the world.

Andrew Geddes, in *The Politics of Immigration and Race*[39] provides a very authoritative account of the connection between immigration and race in British political history, and the role played by the two issues in generating much heated political debate in the late 1970s and 1980s.

In line with most contemporary writers, Geddes in his chapter on the Conservatives and immigration restates the Conservative party's opposition to immigration and the fact that "substantial antipathy towards immigration and immigrants was apparent within the Conservative Party",[40] as far back as the 1960s. The initial instigator of a tough stance on immigration was Enoch Powell who generated much controversy with his infamous rhetoric.[41]

According to Geddes, Thatcher played the race card by appealing to public anxiety about immigration, and her anti-immigration views were highlighted by her speeches leading up to the 1979 general election.[42] Her approach to race relations was peculiar. Rather than adhering to the view that race relations could be improved by re-education and allaying public fears about immigration, she took the view that preventing people from entering Britain was the most positive way of improving race relations. In reality there is no evidence to suggest that restrictive measures of entry have any positive impact on race relations or foster harmonious relations. At the same time there is no evidence to suggest that the entry of immigrants from diverse cultures endanger in any way 'British culture' as Thatcher claimed in a television programme.[43] It appears that the Conservatives antics were an example of relighting an unnecessary fire. If anything the Tory tactics were endangering race relations rather than helping to improve them. This is illustrated by unanimous opposition to Tory policies among ethnic minorities. Could it be that Thatcher was trying to punish the ethnic minorities because they largely voted Labour, and knew that there would be nothing to lose by further alienating them. Simultaneously, the tactic would pay off by attracting some previous National Front voters who found the Conservative 'crusade' against immigration more appealing, perhaps in a milder way and without the racist tag often labelled at the National Front.

Geddes emphasises the Conservatives' wholescale commitment to restricting immigration. This was one election pledge which the Tories did not fail to deliver. They took action to curb secondary immigration, and there was the passage of successive legislation throughout the 1980s[44] including the 1981 British Nationality Act, the imposition of visas on selected countries in 1986, and the Carriers' Liability Act 1987. The impact of such legislation will be analysed in chapter 2.

Geddes quite correctly contends that since Britain's membership of the European Union, there are rumblings once again within the Conservative Party, similar to those during the Thatcher years, about immigration, as particularly Euro-sceptic Conservatives are concerned about provisions for the free movement of people laid out in the 1986 Single European Act. They are concerned that Britain would lose "..its ability to maintain strict entry controls".[45]

This is exactly the point made by Sarah Spencer in *Strangers and Citizens* [46] when she points out that "far from placating the electorate, the form which immigration control has taken and the presentation of policy have served to reinforce prejudice rather than to enhance race relations".[47] In other words Spencer makes a very valid point by arguing that there is a strong correlation between increased immigration controls and an increase in the undesirable image attached to black people which results from such controls. The net effect of this can only be to damage rather than foster race relations. This then is in clear contradiction to the basic Conservative party argument used throughout Thatcher's time in office that stricter immigration was necessary as a way towards improving race relations. Various chapters throughout the book touch on this very point noting that since immigration legislation had provisions which many people regarded as racist, it is not surprising that they induced a deterioration in race relations, as black people felt victimised and hurt by legislation which was discriminatory towards them. Indeed Spencer's work which is a collection of contributions by specialists in various disciplines follows the now familiar trend of lambasting the Conservative government's policy, at the same time exposing the unfairness and discrimination of existing British Immigration Control, controls which have been disproportionately imposed against black and Asian immigrants.   The contributors in *Strangers and Citizens* offer a sensible analysis of the immigration debate and challenge the government to carry out research in order establish "whether, and to what extent some immigrants have a negative impact on..."[48] resources such as housing and welfare "and to what extent they are of positive benefit".[49] The criticisms made by the contributors to this work of current UK immigration policies focus on:

- Flaws in UK government philosophy on which immigration policy is based;
- government policies which have failed to meet international obligations. An example of this is noted in chapter four of this book where the European Commission for Human rights declared that the government was discriminating against males from the Indian sub continent by refusing them entry on the basis that they were seeking to enter for economic reasons;
- the failure to relate immigration policy to any serious study of the economic impact of migrants;
- the discrimination and unfairness inherent in many procedures adopted for immigration and asylum. This is a central theme which forms a major part of this book, and subsequently crops up throughout the study. Indeed, one of the yardsticks for measuring discrimination inherent in Conservative immigration policy is not just the numbers that were allowed entry or denied entry but the way in which the policy was executed and in particular the procedures that were used.

In short the contributors feel that restrictive immigration policies cannot be justified because there is simply no evidence to support the weak bases on which they have been formulated.

Conclusions

The overwhelming amount of literature on immigration in Britain tends to be critical of British government immigration policy in recent years.[50] A number of writers such as Dummett, Layton-Henry and Gordon lambast the Conservative government's notoriously strict immigration policies which they say are characterised by racial discrimination and lack of logic. Without advocating a open door policy, they simply stress the need for a fair and equal application of immigration laws which coincide with respect for human rights and internationally accepted agreements. Chapters four and five of this book clearly demonstrate that individuals interviewed did not see immigration laws and procedures as fair and applied equally. A perfect example of this is illustrated in chapter 4 where over 60% of those interviewed described immigration procedures as unfair or racist. In another example in chapter 5 many respondents labelled immigration laws as discriminatory.

In other words the majority of writers purport to the middle ground or Centrist theory of immigration but clearly believe that the Tory party while also appearing to advocate this policy has not executed it with fairness and equality.

This chapter has revealed that much of the literature on immigration is highly critical of the policies formulated and implemented by British governments, particularly since the late 1970s. The various authors invoke a sense of consensus on many points:

- The Conservative Party in office formulated and implemented a tough immigration policy which aimed at curbing immigration. The policy was aimed clearly at attracting votes by unnecessarily generating public anxiety using the race card;
- Thatcher's immigration regime served to damage race relations rather than foster the greater understanding between different races which she claimed would be the eventual effect of her policies;
- the old argument that immigrants are responsible for growing unemployment among white people, and are a drain on housing and social services is unfounded and flawed. Instead it could easily be argued that it was the Tories right-wing economic and social policies which were to blame for the country's economic and social ills. However, this particular point is not a direct subject of this book;
- a complete overhaul of the present system of immigration controls is necessary in order to ensure justice and equality for all subjected to immigration control procedures.

One immediate and not surprising criticism which springs to mind is that it is easy to be critical of literature on immigration because a majority of it is dominated by writers who are against not only current but previous immigration control policies adopted by British governments. This in itself is not necessarily a weakness of the contemporary literature on immigration. Rather it is an indication that at least in academic circles there is widespread scholarly dissatisfaction with the British immigration control regime.

There is no doubt that the majority of contributors to literature on immigration conclude that Thatcher's immigration measures were discriminatory towards black and coloured immigrants. As this book progresses it will become evident that much of what is said by contemporary literature on the question of Thatcher's immigration policy is in line with the general findings of this book.

It should be noted that there are no specific books or works on Conservative immigration policies relating to Scotland exclusively. This emphasises the fact that the formulation centrally, i.e. in Whitehall and Westminster, of British government policy on such issues applies throughout the United Kingdom. There may appear to be little need for a regional perspective on the formulation of immigration policy and procedures.

Notes

1. Sarah Spencer (ed.), *Strangers and Citizens· A Positive Approach to Migrants and Refugees*, (London: Rivers Oram Press, 1994), pp. 91-110.
2. *Ibid*, p. 99.
3. Conservative Central Office, *Conservative Party Manifesto*, 1979.
4. *Ibid*, p. 20.
5. See *ibid* for a full list of measures outlined.
6. Conservative Central Office, *Conservative Party Manifesto*, 1983.
7. *Ibid*, 1987.
8. *Ibid*, pp. 304-305.
9. *Ibid*
10. *Ibid*.
11. Zig Layton-Henry, *The Politics of Immigration*, (Blackwell Publishers, 1992).
12. *Ibid*, p. 210
13. *Ibid*, p. 207.
14. Zig Layton-Henry and Paul B. Rich, *Race Government and Politics in Britain*, (London: Macmillan, 1986), p. 73.
15. *Ibid*.
16. See *Control of Immigration. Statistics United Kingdom 1990*, p.1, HMSO.

17. See *ibid* various issues.
18. *Ibid*, p. 96.
19. *Ibid*, p. 97.
20. Shamit Saggar, *Race and Politics in Britain*, (Harvester and Wheatsheaf, 1992).
21. *Ibid*, p. 135.
22. *Ibid*.
23. For a review of legislation and rules passed since the second world war, covering the Thatcher period, see chapter 2.
24. Paul Gordon, *Policing Immigration*, (London: Pluto Press, 1985).
25 *Ibid*, p. 2.
26. *Ibid*, p. 37.
27. *Ibid*.
28. *Ibid*, p. 35.
29. Anne Dummett (ed.), *Towards a Just Immigration Policy*, (Cobden Trust, 1986).
30. Anne Dummett and Andrew Nicol, *Subjects, Citizens, and Others*, (Weidenfeld and Nicolson, 1990).
31. Anne Dummett (ed.), *Towards a Just Immigration Policy*, op. cit p. x.
32. *Ibid*.
33. *Ibid*.
34. See Robert Miles and Annie Phizacklea, *White Man's Country*, (London: Pluto Press, 1984).
35. Anne Dummett (ed.), *Towards a Just Immigration Policy*, op. cit p. 237.
36 Robert Miles and Annie Phizacklea, *White Man's Country*, op. cit.
37. *The Times*, November 20, 1995, p. 2.
38. Robert Miles and Annie Phizacklea, *White Man's Country*, op. cit. p. vi.
39. Andrew Geddes, *The Politics of Immigration and Race*, (Baseline Book Company, 1996).
40. *Ibid*, p 55.
41. For more on Enoch Powell and immigration and racism, see *ibid* chapter 5.
42. A classic example is her speech in the World in Action programme broadcast by Granada television on Monday 30 January 1978. In this speech Thatcher makes it clear that she is very much against immigration and appears to be very critical of the presence of different ethnic groups in British society. Her remarks were very controversial and attracted criticism from various circles.
43 *Ibid*
44. See chapter 2 for more details of such legislation.
45. Andrew Geddes, *The Politics of Immigration and Race*, op. cit. p. 66.
46. Sarah Spencer (ed.), *Strangers and Citizens· A positive approach to migrants and refugees*, op. cit.
47. See *ibid*, p. 17.
48. *Ibid*.
49. *Ibid*
50. Although to some extent Saggar is an exception as he refuses to explicitly criticise Conservative immigration policies.

2 The Development of Immigration Legislation and Rules since 1945: An Overview

Introduction

The primary purposes of this chapter are to describe major changes in British law on immigration and to focus attention on particular administrative rules, regulations and procedures comprising the immigration control regime developed between 1979 and 1990. Section one reviews post-1945 immigration legislation. Section two looks at immigration law changes from 1979-86. Section three concentrates on the 1987-90 immigration rules and law changes, with an emphasis on the present immigration rule requirements which have to be satisfied in order to attain a visa. This chapter provides the essential background for the analysis of the impact of the legislative and regulatory regime on individuals and on groups of immigrants which follows in later chapters. It allows us to build a picture of the nature of immigration laws and rules which attracted much criticism from the individuals interviewed Glasgow. The Scottish dimension in respect of the parliamentary establishment of the British immigration regime is very limited. Although Scotland now has its own parliament, this parliament has relatively limited powers, and laws enacted at Westminster on issues such as immigration are applied across the whole of the United Kingdom.

This chapter also analyses the political processes by which the immigration regime reached the statute book, and the debates that were generated during the passage of some of the laws. The views of MPs and interested organisations are analysed with a view to anticipating the impact of the regime on those affected by its implementation.

It is emphasised that this chapter does not set out to provide an in-depth analysis of British immigration legislation. Rather the aim is to provide a brief but adequate picture of the major legal instruments of immigration control in order to evaluate later their impact on the immigration community in Britain, with special reference to Glasgow.

To begin with it is appropriate and necessary to review the most significant pre-1979 legislation in order to provide a contrast to the controversial immigration legislation of the Conservative government in the period after 1979. The legislation covered in this chapter is illustrated in Table 2.1 below.

Table 2.1 Major Legislation on Immigration since 1945

Year	Legislation
1948	British Nationality Act
1962	Commonwealth Immigrants Act
1968	Commonwealth Immigrants Act
1969	Immigration Appeals Act
1971	Immigration Act
1981	British Nationality Act
1987	Carriers' Liability Act
1988	Immigration Act
1993	Asylum and Immigration Appeals Act
1996	Asylum and Immigration Act

This dissertation focuses on immigration from the Indian sub-continent (India, Pakistan and Bangladesh). Therefore the following legislative[1] measures adopted between 1979 and 1990 will not be taken into account because they do not affect immigration from the Indian sub-continent:

The British Nationality (Falkland Islands) Act 1983;
The Hong Kong Act 1985;
The British Nationality (Hong Kong) Act 1990.

Post-1945 Immigration Legislation: A Review

Since 1945 some very important legislation on immigration has been passed by successive governments.[2] The post-war period also witnessed a considerable influx of immigrants particularly from Asian and Africans countries. Immigration legislation was essentially a response to this phenomenon.

The first legislation was the 1948 British Nationality Act,[3] introduced by the Labour Government, which was stimulated partly by a shortage of labour. However, this was an Act which could be regarded as pro - immigrant or being in favour of immigrants as it allowed fairly free entry to Britain for those who wanted to settle in the United Kingdom. It was therefore a liberal piece of legislation which would be unthinkable in Britain today. The Act created a citizenship of the United Kingdom and Colonies common to all who belonged to the United Kingdom and Colonial territories. All such citizens had equal rights in the United Kingdom. Furthermore, they, along with citizens of Commonwealth countries and citizens of the newly independent countries which joined the Commonwealth, all had the common status of British Subject. British subjects had a right to enter and settle in the United Kingdom, and could come and go freely without restriction. So the 1948 British Nationality Act raised no serious questions or controversy.

In 1962 the Commonwealth Immigrants Act 1962[4] was passed and in it one could see the first signs of measures to introduce some form of control on immigration. The liberal element of the 1948 British Nationality Act had given way to more cautious legislation on the entry of people into the United Kingdom. The 1962 Act, introduced by a Conservative Government, made some Commonwealth citizens subject to immigration control. Those immigrants intending to enter the United Kingdom to work had to obtain a voucher[5] issued by the Ministry of Labour before they could enter. However, once a voucher was issued that person had the right to remain in the UK indefinitely if he was a Commonwealth citizen. More importantly, for the first time, Immigration Officers had the power to question and if necessary refuse admission to a Commonwealth citizen.

Under the Act all Commonwealth citizens were subject to immigration control[6] unless: they were born in the UK; or were holders of UK passports issued by the UK and not by the government of a colony; or were persons included in the passport of someone who was excluded from control in either of the above two categories.

Unlike the 1948 British Nationality Act, the 1962 Commonwealth Immigrants Act was controversial and highly contentious. It was widely viewed as an attempt by the then Conservative government to limit black and coloured immigration because it was those groups who were most adversely affected by the 1962 legislation. Since the Act defined British citizenship on the grounds of being either born in the UK or having acquired your passport in the UK it excluded most blacks and Asians. The Government's argument for introducing the Act appeared to be that it would tackle problems such as overcrowding, unemployment and foster racial harmony, not too dissimilar to the type of arguments used later by the Conservatives in the 1980s and 1990s.

Six years later, when Labour was back in power, the Commonwealth Immigrants Act of 1968[7] illustrated the beginning of a period of tough immigration control not previously seen in the United Kingdom. This Act placed controls on those holding United Kingdom passports issued by the United Kingdom government. Citizens of the UK and colonies would come under immigration control unless they could show that they themselves or at least one parent or grandparent had been born in the UK, or had acquired citizenship by adoption, registration or naturalisation in the United Kingdom or by registration in a Commonwealth country. The Act had been targeted largely at East African Asians who had chosen to retain citizenship of the United Kingdom and colonies rather than to take the citizenship of the newly independent countries where they were living.

To facilitate immigration control over the number of East African Asians coming to Britain, a non-statutory special voucher scheme was created. Possession of a voucher would allow heads of households with UK passports to settle in the UK with their dependants. The vouchers would be subject to an annual quota, i.e. a limited number would be issued each year. The government attached a lot of importance to this Act. It had been hurriedly passed in the hope that it would help to stem the flow of immigrants into the UK, particularly the flow of East African Asians who feared for their economic and political status in the newly independent countries. Once again this Act raised controversy as it inevitably proved to be racially discriminatory in the effect it had. As Satvinder Juss correctly points out the aim of the 1962 and 1968 Acts was to "...strike at non-white primary immigration from the new Commonwealth which was undertaken for the purpose of settlement....".[8]

The 1969 Immigration Appeals Act[9] saw an attempt by the Labour government to silence critics who argued that immigrants refused admission or deported by immigration officials had no rights and that government decisions could not be challenged. This Act allowed a right of appeal against decisions of the immigration authorities. A two-tier system was created in which an appeal was heard first by an adjudicator who would on his own make a determination. A further opportunity to appeal against the adjudicator's decision was provided through the immigration appeals tribunal members.

The 1971 Immigration Act[10] provided the Conservative government elected in 1970 with a framework for imposing further stringent controls on immigration into Britain. Under the Act people in the world were divided into two categories:[11] a) patrials, i.e. people with a parent or grandparent born in the UK and b) non-patrials. Patrials were allowed to enter the UK freely to live and work.   Non-patrials had to obtain a 12 month work permit. Only patrials would have the right of abode in the UK and were free from any form of immigration control.

Once again, as with previous and successive immigration legislation, this Act ended up discriminating against black people. This was because non-white Commonwealth immigrants were on the whole in the non-patrial category of what could be termed non-belongers i.e. their parents and grandparents had not been born in Britain. As a result most non-white immigrants from the Commonwealth had no claim of entry, residence and freedom from immigration control. People classified as patrials were mainly of British descent and thus white, while the great majority of black people wishing to emigrate to the UK were non-patrials. This was an obvious negative attribute for black people seeking to enter Britain to live and work. Of course there were some whites who also fell in the category of non-patrials since not all whites had a parent or grandparent born in the UK. However, the number of whites in the category of non-patrials was very few.

Immigration Rules and Law Changes 1979-86

Virginity Tests

We will now move on to the prime purpose of this chapter which is to look at the rules and laws on immigration which came into effect during the 1979-90 period.

The virginity tests controversy was an area that had been in existence since 1968 but documentary evidence of such tests did not come to light until 1979.[12] Such tests were carried out on non-patrial wives who were seeking to enter Britain on a permanent stay basis in order to rejoin their husbands or get married to fiancés who enjoyed British citizenship status. The government's use of virginity tests for women entering Britain was to establish whether they were genuine fiancées. Women found to be virgins were assumed to be genuine fiancées. Not surprisingly such controversial tests were viewed as degrading and insulting by all Asians. Once again it was Asians who would bear the brunt of such a policy since it is Asians from the Indian sub-continent who tend to come to Britain for marriage. The virginity tests were to be used to establish whether Asian women were coming to the UK for marriage as they claimed and not for any other reason.

The storm created by the virginity tests was hardly surprising.[13] They caused great emotional stress for Asian women who had to undergo them. In some extreme cases the tests caused marriages and engagements to break up. Some women were so distraught that they decided to go back home.[14] There was even the case of Mr Bansi Lal Kakha[15] who sued the Home Office after his wife was made to have a virginity test which had affected her so much that she had returned to India and had to be persuaded to come back after two years. The tests also led to anger on the part of the Indian government who protested to the British Home Office.[16] Criticisms

25

of the tests led Home Secretary Merlyn Rees to announce shortly afterwards that they would be stopped.[17] The virginity tests, although not introduced as part of immigration legislation, illustrated the unfair, and in this case, humiliating, procedures used by the British government against Asian immigrants in order to control immigration. Labour had joined the Centrist camp which accepted the need for immigration controls. Clearly the tests were designed with the knowledge that their very nature would dissuade immigrants from wanting to enter Britain because they would not want to undergo such a humiliating procedure. This would of course keep down the number of immigrants seeking to enter Britain.

The British government also resorted to virginity tests because of the common belief that women from the Indian sub-continent are always virgins before marriage, and therefore must be genuine fiancées and unmarried if virginity tests prove they are virgins. However, this kind of thinking was a misconception to some extent. While it is true that most women from the Indian sub-continent are virgins before marriage, it is more likely to be true of Muslim women than of Hindu or Sikh women whose religion does not necessarily outlaw sex before marriage. Furthermore, proving that a woman is a virgin does not necessarily mean that she is planning to enter Britain for the sole purpose of marriage. Thus there is no reason why the tests should wholly answer the doubts the government had over the claims of immigrants.

1981 British Nationality Act

The 1981 British Nationality Act focussed attention on the twin issues of nationality and immigration. It may not be wholly apparent that there is a significant connection between nationality and immigration. The 1981 British Nationality Act[18] provides sound proof that there is a strong tie between the two. Arguably, according to many people, the British Nationality Act of 1981 was "...as much an immigration act as a nationality one".[19] This view claims that the major motive for changing the law on nationality was derived from concerns about immigration. One way to restrict immigration is to define nationality narrowly. In the review of literature in chapter 1 the strong connection between immigration and nationality was forcefully demonstrated by Ann Dummett who argues that the law defining British nationality was written to fulfil the aims of immigration policy. Under the Tories there has always been a very strong co-ordination and correlation between nationality and immigration. Indeed as quite correctly pointed out by the Commission for Racial Equality the Act "brought the law on nationality more closely into line with the realities created by immigration law".[20] The very nature of the 1981 Act and the motives behind it provides yet further evidence of the restrictive nature of Conservative government policy on immigration and its obsession with immigration control.

The 1981 British Nationality Act set out three classes of citizenship.[21] The Act which came into force on January 1st 1983, saw citizenship of the United Kingdom and Colonies abolished and replaced by three new types of citizenship: British citizenship, citizenship of the British dependent territories, and British overseas citizenship. The first category[22] would include those citizens of the UK and Colonies who had a close personal connection with the UK either because their parents or grandparents had been born, adopted, naturalised, or registered as citizens of the UK or through permanent settlement in the UK.

The second category[23] of citizenship of the British Dependent territories would be acquired by those citizens of the UK and Colonies by reason of their own or their parent's or grandparent's birth, naturalisation or registration in an existing dependency.

The third category[24] was British overseas citizens, with no right of abode anywhere. This category was intended for those citizens of the UK and Colonies who did not qualify for either of the first two categories. The great majority of these people were people of Indian, Chinese or Eurasian ethnic origin. They included the British Asians in East Africa, scattered groups of Indian origin in other Commonwealth countries including Malaysia and so on.

The Home Secretary, William Whitelaw made two major changes to the 1981 British Nationality Bill, before it became law. These changes were hailed by the opposition as a climb down by the government.[25] The first change would mean that any child born in the UK who did not acquire British Citizenship at birth might acquire it after ten years continuous residence, regardless of the status of the parents. The second change allowed citizens by naturalisation or registration to transmit citizenship to any of their children born overseas in the same way as British born citizens. This obviously gave some assurance to the ethnic minority communities.

The Bill had originally proposed that citizenship

> ..was acquired automatically at birth only by children born in Britain and one of whose parents was a British citizen or who was settled in this country.[26]

According to the *Herald* the Act's "...most controversial provision ends the automatic right to citizenship of the children of illegal immigrants born in Britain".[27]

Ever since the introduction of the 1981 British Nationality Act, its various provisions have been brandished as blatantly racist and discriminatory by government opponents.[28] Many immigrants felt angry and insulted by the Act. The months and years after the Act was introduced saw continued debate against it. On 2nd March 1984, Mr Dubs (Lab MP) presented a petition on behalf of the Action Group on Immigration and Nationality.[29] He argued that this petition shows that both the Immigration Act 1971 and the British Nationality Act 1981 are unjust. The petition was signed by more than 1,000 people who requested the following:[30] The restoration of the principle of automatic citizenship by virtue of birth in the UK; the granting of British Citizenship to British Overseas Citizens with no other citizenship; the restoration of the rights of Commonwealth citizens settled in the UK before 1973 which, they argued were being drastically reduced or limited by the new legislation; the establishment of a nationality appeal system and a citizen's right to a passport; the reform of British immigration legislation to conform to international standards on human rights respect family life and respect racial and sexual equality.

In Scotland in April 1981[31] one hundred members of immigrant communities and their supporters held a rally in Edinburgh in protest at the Nationality Bill. They demanded that the Bill, which was at this time going through the committee stage in Parliament, be amended to remove its racial elements. They claimed that under the Bill

...many black people with British passports living abroad and some living here would be given a second-class category of citizenship. Some would be left stateless.[32]

Protesters claimed that as many as 4000 non-white people in Scotland would be affected adversely by new legislation.

Long-standing Conservative concern over immigration into Britain and a consequential desire to check this through changes to immigration and nationality were evident in the government's defence of the 1981 British Nationality Act. At the Acts second reading[33] of the Bill on 28 January 1981, Home Secretary Whitelaw argued that it did not discriminate on the grounds of race or sex, and that it allowed a major overhaul of legislation in the area "...that has so long been required and which has long been the duty of the UK government to introduce".[34] Later he went on to say that the

...Act now gives us a clear idea of who belongs here and so remedies a problem which has been the source of difficulties over a long period.[35]

On the government's decision to depart in the Nationality Bill from the principle that every child born in the UK has an automatic right to British Citizenship, Timothy Raison, Minister of State, Home Office, claimed this to be a sound move "based on common sense and the realities of modern times". He went on that

there was a wide range of circumstances in which there was no justification for continuing to allow children citizenship unless one of the parents was accepted for settlement.[36]

Clearly this provision in the Act was aimed at preventing automatic citizenship for a child born to parents who were in Britain for a short visit and people like students who were in the country for a longer period but still temporarily. More importantly it would also cover children of illegal immigrants who had settled in the country in breach of immigration regulations.

Clear anxiety among ethnic minority individuals over the 1981 British Nationality Act provoked a rise in applications for registration and naturalisation as British citizens.[37] The number of applications rose from 38,000 in 1978 to 70,000 in 1981 and to 96,000 in 1982,[38] despite the fact that the government had increased the naturalisation fee from £90 in 1979 to £200 in 1982. The high fee was criticised by many who saw it as an attempt by the government to dissuade or prevent people from applying for citizenship.

The Conservative government's keenness to alter immigration and nationality legislation demonstrated a tough immigration policy which had the effect of further alienating ethnic minorities and their supporters, and increasing uncertainty among many about their future status in 'their' country.

In 1980 the immigration rules were that only a woman who was a British citizen or who had a parent born in the UK could bring in her husband or fiancé. Roy Hattersley, Shadow Home Secretary, quite correctly said that the "the regulations discriminate against women and between sexes".[39] This of course once again affected some Asian women resident in Britain who may have wanted to marry someone and bring him into the country (see chapter 4, section 2).

However, after the British Nationality Act came into force on January 1983, there was a ruling by the European Commission on Human Rights that its provisions were discriminatory and contrary to the European Convention on Human Rights.[40] As a result of this the rules were changed. The new rules gave all British women citizens the same rights. Nevertheless in a way the new rules were even more strict because of the primary purpose rule which made one more important qualification: A couple comprising a British citizen and a fiancée who is not a British citizen and who therefore was applying to enter Britain permanently, had to show that the marriage was not one of convenience, that they did intend to live together and had met before the marriage. In other words the previous rules would apply i.e. the marriage must not be contracted primarily for immigration reasons. So it can be argued that women were still being subjected to strict rules and very little had actually changed.

The bulk of criticism generated by the 1981 Act came from those who argued against its discriminatory nature towards ethnic minorities. Ironically, there was also criticism from some Conservative MPs who argued that the Act did not go far enough in curbing immigration, providing yet more evidence that many members of the governing party did indeed have immigration control as their principal aim and that they were interested mainly in keeping down the number of immigrants rather than in establishing a fair and equitable or non-discriminatory immigration policy. Mr Harvey Proctor (Con) was concerned that despite the passing of the 1981 Nationality Act

> immigration continues from the New Commonwealth and Pakistan at the rate of 30,000 a year....., this year we are claiming credit because the figure might be just under 30,000....This is not a significant achievement..... in view of the manifesto commitments and promises made in 1979.[41]

Introduction of Visas

On 1st September 1986 the Conservative government decided to impose visa requirements on citizens of India, Nigeria, Ghana and Pakistan who sought to enter the UK.[42] The visas came amid the backdrop of a debate which had begun in the autumn of 1985 when members of the Immigration Service Union (ISU) met senior civil servants and ministers to recommend restricting the entry of people from the aforementioned countries, and limiting MPs' rights to intervene when passengers were refused entry. The ISU is a non-TUC union which represents a majority of immigration officers. The union has strong beliefs in the need for strict immigration laws.

The rationale behind the government's visa scheme was the unexplained increase in the number of passengers from India, Nigeria, Pakistan and Ghana who were refused entry on arrival in the UK. Comparing the 1985 and 1986 entry statistics, 681 more passengers from the aforementioned countries were not allowed to enter in the first six months of 1986 than in the same period in 1985.[43] The large number of refusals and the rise in passenger traffic caused delays and inconvenience for all passengers and staff at Heathrow. This led to detention centres being overcrowded with people who had been refused entry. The workload of MPs was increased because they were the only individuals who could stop passengers refused entry from being returned immediately to their country of origin.

It was on 1st September 1986 that the Cabinet announced the decision to impose visas, just 24 hours before the ISU planned to ballot its members on taking industrial action to back its demands.

The visa system came under much criticism from ethnic minorities and the government's political opponents.[44] The visa system was seen as causing much disruption for many people. It would affect thousands of people of those countries who had settled in Britain for many years, since their family and friends would now face complications when hoping to visit the UK. On top of this it would place barriers in the way of visits by families and friends. More annoyingly, although UK residents were exempt from visas, they had to obtain passport stamps from the Home Office in order to prove their exemption in order to be able to return to their homes. Furthermore

> the visa requirement has an indirect but.....damaging effect on race relations in Britain. It is selective and discriminatory, it identifies citizens of some of the largest ethnic minority communities in Britain as potential problems requiring special treatment...[45]

Mr Gerald Kaufman (Labour) argued strongly against the visa system.[46] He basically pointed out that the government had no reason to introduce visas which were causing problems for people from the five visa countries.

> The decision to impose a visa requirement....will impose major hardship on future visitors and their relatives in this country often citizens of this country.[47]

He also went on to claim that it was much more difficult for an Asian or black immigrant to achieve entry into Britain than it was for a white immigrant.

Mr Max Madden (Labour) added his voice to the growing criticism of the visa scheme.[48] He argued that it would damage the promotion of good community relations in Britain as well as having already damaged the relationship between Britain and the black Commonwealth. The government had argued that visas would reduce delays and the inconvenience and difficulties experienced by visitors and their sponsors and relatives here. Mr Madden dismissed this claim by adding that

> The most cost effective way in which to deal with delays, inconvenience and indignities.....is to appoint more immigration officers and more interpreters.[49] ...something which the government should have done long ago.

The whole concept of introducing the visa scheme could have been a clever ploy on the part of the government. Obviously if individuals were to know the government was going to introduce visas then there would be a rush to get into the UK before the visa system was officially up and running. This gave the government an excuse to justify its visa system i.e. the unexplained increase in passengers. Also one cannot be blind to the fact that the visa system targeted only five countries which is discriminatory.

Mr Douglas Hurd continued to justify the imposition of visas. He said "the new system is working smoothly. Hardly any passengers requiring visas have arrived without them on direct flights".[50]

Visas only serve to perpetuate perceptions and feelings of discrimination, through what is seen as unequal rules and regulations. If we were to analyse the list of countries from which a visa is a requirement, the discriminatory aspect is evident:[51] All the Indian sub-continent countries are on this list while none of the White Commonwealth countries are. Even more discriminatory is the fact that all the countries on the list happen to be black or coloured with the exception of communist and post-communist countries on whom visas were imposed for purely political and security reasons, and they can be dismissed as a unique category. Regardless of the reasons why visas have been imposed, it is only fair to ask why not impose visas on all countries or on none? Why single out countries?

Immigration Rules and Law Changes 1987-90

Carriers' Liability Act 1987

The Conservative government took its policy on curbing immigration to a new dimension with the Carriers' Liability Act[52] of 1987. This Act was passed primarily to discourage and prevent bogus refugees from entering Britain. The government was concerned about what it saw as the increasing number of illegal immigrants flowing into the country falsely claiming political asylum. The Carriers' Liability Act made it an offence for shipping companies and airlines to bring people without the proper documents. They would be required to enforce the immigration laws or face fines of £1000....

> for each passenger they bring without a valid passport, identity document or a valid visa (later increased to £2000) where one is required by the immigration laws.[53]

However, under the new law carriers could be exempt from payment of a fine if they could prove that a passenger had the necessary valid documents when he boarded the carrier "or in the case of forged documents, that the forgery was not reasonably apparent...".[54]

No one doubted that this was yet another drive by the government to stem the flow of immigration. As mentioned the Carriers' Liability Act was largely an attempt to discourage asylum seekers. In the past the Home Office had made legislative changes to avoid taking responsibility for asylum-seekers and refugees by the introduction of visas for citizens of certain countries. The visa requirement meant would be immigrants including asylum seekers needed to obtain entry clearance in advance of travelling in order to make it harder for them to reach the UK.

However, since people still managed to board aeroplanes without visas the Home Office made the airlines an important part of the immigration control framework through the Carriers' Liability Act. In addition, as part of the new legislation, immigration officials may be stationed at airports abroad, to advise airlines whether passports and visas are genuine.[55]

Not surprisingly, as was the case with previous Conservative government's immigration legislation, this latest Act attracted widespread criticism from political opponents. One Scottish Labour MP Judith Hart[56] (Clydeside) made the point that if people arriving were genuine refugees, then it was more than likely that they would not have the required documentation. Hence the Carriers' Liability Act was the wrong way of going about trying to limit the level of immigration by trying to target those who were probably genuine refugees. The government surely must have known and appreciated that refugees fleeing their country would hardly have the opportunity to acquire a visa and other essential travel documents. The simple fact is that asylum-seekers are often not able to go to the authorities of their own country to get passports or to the authorities of other countries to get visas without endangering themselves. Opponents of the government therefore, with some justification, viewed the Carriers' Liability Act as a effective means whereby the Conservative government could in effect turn back a particular class of immigrants (refugees) by claiming that they did not have the required travel documents.

It appears as though the Home Office has made legislative changes to avoid taking responsibility for asylum seekers and refugees. The Opposition were clearly enraged by the new restrictions on immigration. Shadow Home Secretary Gerald Kaufman accused the government of "playing the racist card",[57] and of breaching international conventions. The Act meant delegating immigration powers to foreign airlines. Kaufman warned that the new restrictions could send people to their deaths, as had happened to the Jews in Hitler's Germany who failed to get visas to come to Britain.

The fact that the government was indeed breaching international conventions could be seen by the fact that the UN Convention[58] makes it quite clear that asylum seekers/refugees arriving with false documents having fled their country should not have their application jeopardised. The Convention asserts that a country "...shall not impose penalties, on account of their illegal entry or presence, on refugees...".[59]

The impact of the Carriers' Liability Act for those seeking refugee status and asylum was potentially disastrous. To add to their initial

35

problem of trying to leave their country (which was a hard enough job in itself) they now faced a second problem: trying to obtain correct documents for travel or otherwise risk making a journey which could prove to be totally useless as they would be sent back immediately. Since a large number of refugees came from countries which had oppressive regimes the thought of having to go back was not very appealing. Worse still was knowing that new immigration rules would be used against them unless they had the necessary travel documents. The British legislation meant staying at home in their country which could mean a danger to their lives.

Naturally Conservative Party MPs were on the whole pleased with the introduction of the Carriers' Liability Act, and, despite the criticisms levelled at the government, the Home Secretary Douglas Hurd defended the Act vehemently. Speaking in Parliament[60] at the Second Reading of the Carriers' Liability Bill, Mr Hurd said that the aim of the Act would be "....to make sure that our immigration controls remain effective in the face of rapidly changing international pressures...". But at the same time Hurd acknowledged Britain's ".....obligation to help the genuine victims of persecution".[61]

This new legislation was regarded by its opponents as just another method of cutting down immigration into Britain. As such it was consistent with Conservative government policy. As far as the Conservatives were concerned

> Britain could not give asylum to just anyone who came. To do so would lead to a huge, general and open ended commitment inconsistent with immigration control.....[62]

In this respect those coming without the proper travel documents became in effect the scapegoats for tough controls on immigration no matter how grave their situation was. Nothing that Mr Hurd said was comforting to those fleeing from persecution and danger to their lives. Instead he was keen to point out that "...legislation was in line with similar measures taken in Canada, Belgium, and Denmark".[63] According to a report in the *Glasgow Herald* the immediate spur for the new legislation "...has been the arrival of more than 800 people claiming asylum in 3 months up to the end of February (1987)....".[64] As far as the job of carriers was concerned in regard to the Act, Mr Hurd said that the principle of the new legislation was no different from what carriers were expected to do under the 1971 Immigration Act:

> pay for detention, accommodation and maintenance costs when certain passengers are removed the present bill works within the principle.[65]

Mr Hurd went on that

> ....it is intended to ensure that people who cannot show that they have a claim to entry because they do not have the basic travel documents and the necessary visas are not accepted by the carrier for travel.[66]

1988 Immigration Act

On Tuesday 10 May 1988 the Queen signified her Royal Assent to the Immigration Act 1988.[67] This Act introduced a number of very important changes to the immigration regime. To begin with the Act repealed the absolute right of men settled in Britain before 1st January 1983 to be joined by their families[68] (wives or children). The European Court of Human Rights had ruled that this discriminated against women and the government had chosen to comply with the ruling by abolishing the right for men rather than extending it to women. The right now became conditional on showing that dependants seeking entry to the UK would be provided with adequate accommodation and financial support and would not therefore seek resort to public funds.

In addition to the above fundamental change the 1988 Act also placed restrictions on the right of appeal against deportation.[69] There was a restriction on exercise of right of abode for wives in cases of polygamy which stopped second or more wives entering the country. But probably most important of all, as a result of the Act, no British citizen has a right to be joined in the UK by a spouse of either sex.[70] The spouse must apply for a visa to enter the country. Anticipating criticism of the Act the government defended it as another essential immigration statute. Secretary of State for the Home Office Department said concerning the Act "...We need to keep immigration control in good repair".[71] Referring to the possibility of second or more wives entering the country he said that "polygamy in not an acceptable custom in this country".[72] It is fair to say in this last respect that the Conservative government was hardly concerned about the morality of polygamy considering the behaviour of certain Conservative male MPs during the 1990s, but was more concerned about keeping immigration numbers down. This opposition to polygamy would obviously provide one outlet for this. Once again this provision restricting entry for second or more wives would affect black and Asian immigrants who come from countries where polygamy is in many ways an acceptable social custom.

In response to claims that this latest government immigration legislation was separating families Mr Jeremy Hanley (Con) argued that families were separating themselves

> people choose to leave their family home and come here before they have clearance for their family. It is inherent in our immigration rules that people must make sure that their families are entitled to come here before they come here and separate themselves from their families....[73]

Mr Hanley went on to say "if they feel that separation is unacceptable they can always consider returning to their families, thus rejoining family and stopping the separation".[74] Clearly Mr Hanley was laying down the gauntlet here by saying to those immigrants affected by the Act that they had no choice, either they meet the legislative requirements laid down or otherwise risk separation. However, separation could be prevented if they choose to go back and join their families. This of course would mean giving up the desire to stay in Britain.

The Immigration Act of 1988 did cause a lot of anxiety for the ethnic minorities as expected, since they would bear the brunt of the new immigration rules yet again. No political figure epitomised more stronger criticism of the 1988 Immigration Act than Labour MP, Keith Vaz. He was highly critical of comments made by certain Conservative MPs in defence of the government's immigration legislation. He described the 1988 immigration legislation bill as a

...squalid, unnecessary and unwanted bill. It represents all that is rotten and racist about Conservative Immigration Law.[75]

He launched a verbal offensive against Conservative MPs for having what he called an "...obsession with restricting the rights of black and Asian people".[76] Clearly Mr. Vaz believed that the Conservatives had moved decisively from a 'centrist' to a 'nationalist' position.

Certainly the 1988 Immigration Act represented another phase in the toughening of Britain's immigration policy which once again seemed to be discriminatory against black and coloured people. As a result black and other ethnic minority groups expressed their concern about the provisions of the 1988 Act. A Labour MP Mr Jim Cousins presented a petition from over 1000 residents in Tyneside who had voiced their concern about the implication of the Immigration Bill for ethnic minority people.[77] They wanted to press the House of Commons to re-examine the Bill in the light of information submitted by the Council for Racial Equality and the Joint Council for the Welfare of Immigrants. On 1st July 1988, the Scottish Asian Action Committee organised a bus to Edinburgh to lobby the Scottish office about the 1988 Immigration Act.[78] Despite the publicity and opposition generated against the government's Immigration Act 1988 Bill, this had no effect on Conservative immigration policy, which remained harsh in succeeding years.

DNA Testing

The idea of using DNA testing arose in the late 1980s. Briefly, the reasoning behind DNA testing was that such tests could be used to prove the parentage of children who had applied to come to settle in Britain because they claimed that their parents were resident here.

There was much debate surrounding the use of DNA testing in the immigration arena. The use of DNA testing was seen as going some way towards providing a solution in disputed immigration and nationality cases. The tests would provide a boost for applicants who claimed the existence of a relationship with parents and who had in the past been turned away.

How accurate was DNA testing? It was widely accepted that DNA testing was authentic and hence fair. It was said to be about 98% accurate. In a trial conducted at the initiative of the Home Office and Foreign and

39

Commonwealth Office of the use of DNA profiling in immigration casework it was found that

> ...DNA profiling is viable....appears to be the most accurate method now available for determining parentage in immigration cases.[79]

In a boost to applicants, Mr. Hurd Secretary of State, went on and said that

> ....where applicants can show through a validated DNA test a qualifying relationship with both parents....their claims will be accepted and the Home Office will not contest outstanding appeals.[80]

Certainly it appeared that DNA testing was proving relatively satisfactory.[81] Mr Hurd claimed that hundreds of cases had been satisfactorily determined on that basis.[82]

Despite the general talk of positivity about DNA testing in terms of its effectiveness, criticism was levelled at its cost and availability. The introduction of DNA testing by the government had its limitations. For a start the scheme was not available to all on a voluntary basis.[83] It was limited to first time settlement applicants and not for those making repeated applications. On this basis a Scottish MP, Mr Robert Maclennan, (SDP/All) argued that DNA profiling does not meet the test of fairness. According to Mr Maclennan the repeated application cases most require the assistance of DNA testing.

Secretary of State for the Home Office Douglas Hurd touched on this by stressing that DNA testing will not be offered as a matter of routine.[84] He pointed out that such tests will be arranged by entry clearance officers with the applicant's consent only in cases "...where the relevant relationships could not easily be demonstrated by other means".[85] However, Mr Hurd did say that there

> ...is scope for introducing DNA testing into the entry clearance process more generally as a means of resolving relationship disputes.[86]

Probably the most contentious issue regarding DNA testing was the question of funding. The fact was that DNA testing was available only on a commercial basis and was therefore taken only by applicants who could afford it. This was hardly fair as most applicants would tend to be immigrants who were poor. It is true that the government probably would have preferred not to have introduced DNA testing since it was a largely effective means of resolving immigration cases in favour of the immigrants. This is because many immigrant applicants had genuine cases for entry and would therefore have to be admitted.

However, in order to limit the damage, the government, as just seen, placed limitations which proved prohibitive such as the costs of the test and their availability only to certain applicants. This was summed up very accurately by a Scottish MP Alistair Darling (Edinburgh Central, Labour). He said

> The government have reluctantly introduced DNA testing because they know there is no way around it. Applicants...still cannot choose DNA testing at the onset...a barrier both bureaucratic and financial is to be placed in the way of those who wish to prove that they are related to their mothers and fathers.[87]

Also the DNA system seemed to do injustice for those over 18 because while DNA testing was introduced to establish the parentage of children under 18 the government made it difficult for those over 18 to enter even when they had proved they were the children of their parents.

Mr Maclennan (SDP/All) also attacked the DNA testing system because of the financial barriers it placed on applicants. It is clear that "...DNA testing can operate only when rich....applicants seek to employ it. By no standard can that be regarded as fair".[88]

However, the government had made it clear that the taxpayer would not bear the burden of the cost of DNA tests. Even

> ...if we introduced a general scheme for DNA tests as we are proposing to do on a voluntary basis - the schemes cost would in no way fall on the tax payer.[89]

It was quite clear that the DNA testing system was unfair from the financial point of view because many poorer applicants could not afford it even though the government wanted to make sure that not too great a burden should be imposed on the applicant when setting the level of fee to be charged.

DNA testing while effective in terms of its relative accuracy in establishing parentage was seen by the ethnic community as yet another racist and insulting government policy directed against them. It showed once again that the government was singling out black and Asian immigrants for preferential but discriminatory treatment as it did not trust their motives and did not believe their claims for wanting to enter Britain. The financial cost of the DNA system also proved a hindrance i.e. for many applicants who could not afford it and were therefore unable to prove their claim. Some even distrusted the system and were unwilling to fork out financial resources for a scheme which might not even guarantee them securing entry.

Present Immigration Requirements

This sub-section will look at some of the present immigration requirements in operation in the light of the criteria laid out in the rules and laws described in this section. The immigration rules are applied in Scotland in the same way as anywhere else in the UK. The present rules are very similar to those in the 1971 Immigration Act.[90]

To summarise, immigration rules can be divided into two groups, control before entry and control after entry.[91] Figure 2.1 below illustrates the process of entry which nationals from visa countries have to go through if they want to come to Britain. People from the Indian sub-continent come to the UK mainly in the following categories: marriage, dependent relatives and visitor.[92]

Figure 2.1 The Process of Entry to Britain for Individuals from Visa National Countries

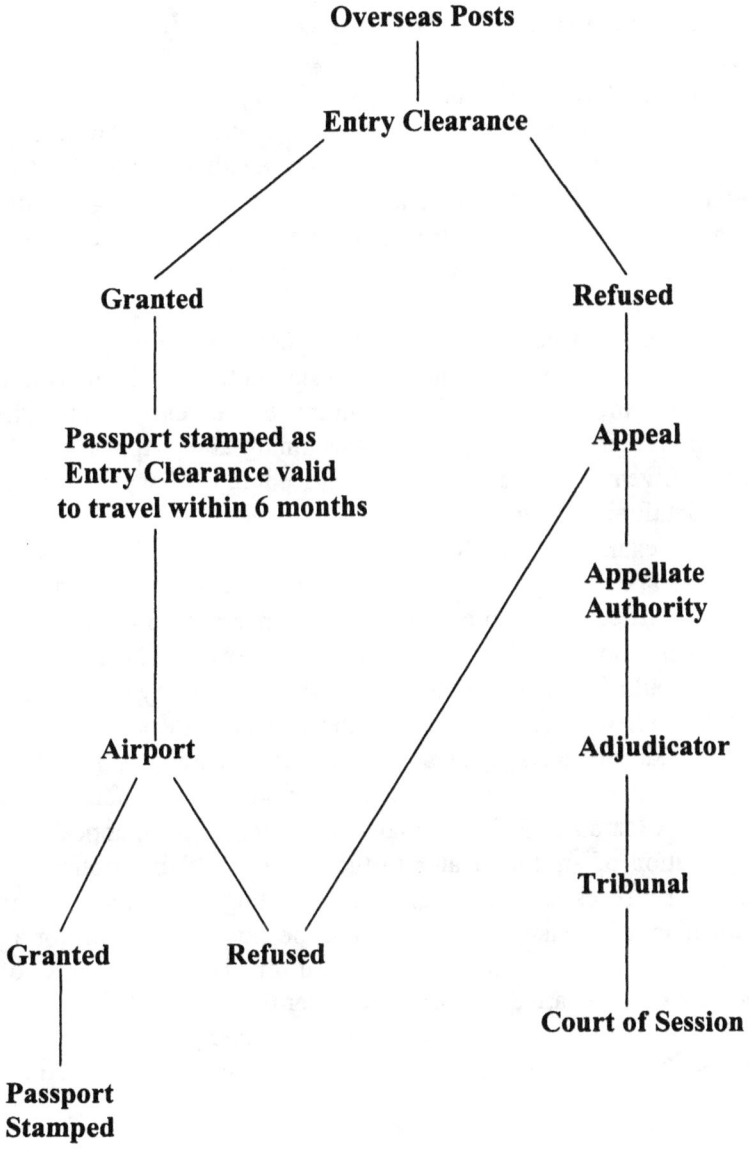

Overseas Posts

Entry Clearance

Granted

Refused

Passport stamped as
Entry Clearance valid
to travel within 6 months

Appeal

Appellate
Authority

Adjudicator

Airport

Granted   Refused

Tribunal

Passport
Stamped

Court of Session

Under 'control before entry' rules, a person coming from a visa country to the UK for any reason must obtain an entry clearance visa at the airport. The visa would be issued by the British Embassies/High Commission abroad. The person would have to satisfy the requirements of the immigration rules (which will be explained below). If an entry clearance is refused, he/she has a right to appeal against the refusal. This appeal is heard in the UK in the absence of the appellant (The Asylum and Immigration Appeals Act 1993 removed the right of visitors to appeal). The Immigration Advisory Service (IAS) or a solicitor would represent the appellant in the UK. The IAS is an organisation which gives the public general advice on immigration matters, presents appeals at the immigration appeals court and makes written representations to the Home Office on behalf of its client.

In the case of control after entry, a person already in the UK applies for a further extension of his/her visa to stay in the UK. If the Home Office refuses, then the IAS or a solicitor can make a representation to the Home Office or present his/her appeal at the Immigration Appeals Court. The IAS's involvement in the immigration procedure in Glasgow can be seen in greater detail in chapter 3.

If, for example a wife, who was a UK citizen, applied for her husband to join her in Britain and the application was refused by the Entry Clearance officer, then an appeal would be heard before an adjudicator at the Immigration Appellate Authority in Glasgow.[93] The Entry Clearance Officer would be represented at the appeal court by the Home Office Presenting Officer (respondent). If the appeal does not succeed then an appellant can appeal against the adjudicator's decisions to a tribunal in London which comprises of a legally qualified chairman and two members. The Entry Clearance Officer can also apply for leave to appeal against the determination of an adjudicator to the tribunal. If the tribunal dismisses the case or refuses leave to enter, and depending on the merits of the case, the appellant can make an application to the Court of Session for a judicial review. The views of adjudicators and of those in charge of Entry Clearance Officers are described in chapter 6.

We will look at the requirements needed to be satisfied for 1) marriage 2) general visiting visas and 3) elderly parents. Applications made abroad to enter the UK for the purpose of marriage or engagement must satisfy the following requirements:

1. The applicant is married or engaged to a person settled in the UK.
2. The couple have met.
3. The reason for the marriage is not to enter the UK (the primary purpose rule).
4. The couple have the intention to live together as man and wife.
5. The couple can prove that they can maintain and accommodate themselves without being a burden on public funds.[94]

To come as a visitor to the UK, the person must prove to the entry clearance officer that:

1. The person is truthfully seeking entry as a visitor for the period stated by him/her and for not more than 6 months.
2. He/she does not plan to take employment in the UK.
3. He/she aims to leave the UK at the end of the time he/she said they would.
4. The person can maintain and accommodate him/herself without recourse to public funds.
5. He/she can afford their return journey.[95]

In the case of a sponsor in the UK making an application for a visitor he must show that he can maintain and accommodate the visitor without recourse to public funds.

Elderly parents wanting to stay or even visit the UK must prove the following:

- That they are 65 or over;
- the parents are mainly and wholly dependent on their sponsors in the UK;
- have no other close relative to whom they can turn to in his/her own country;
- they are living in the most exceptional and compassionate circumstances.[96]

The above are all the requirements of the immigration rules one has to meet to gain an entry visa for the UK. The most critical of these rules, the one most frequently referred to in interviews, is the primary purpose rule. Indeed this is highlighted explicitly in both chapters 4 and 5.

Conservative Party Policy on Immigration in the Post-Thatcher Era

This section will briefly review some developments on the immigration front under John Major who succeeded Margaret Thatcher as Prime Minister at the end of 1990.

When John Major became Prime Minister little changed as far as Conservative policy on immigration was concerned. Further legislation since 1990 continued to demonstrate that the established Conservative philosophy and thinking in place since the first Thatcher administration was still intact even though the issue did not generate quite the large scale debate it did during the 1980s, partly because the Major government had been preoccupied with other issues, and partly because it wanted to prevent further alienation of ethnic minorities.

However, legislation on immigration since 1990 has continued to indicate a strict immigration regime. The Asylum and Immigration Appeals Act 1993 came into force in July 1993 radically altering the system of immigration appeals. Although this Act granted the right of appeal to asylum seekers it was matched by the removal of appeal rights accorded to visitors and short term visitors which had existed since 1971.[97] "Thousands who have successfully appealed refusals of entry will have no remedy against administrative error and abuse".[98] In fact if we look at the 1992 Conservative Party Manifesto we will find that there is nothing in it that suggests a change from the manifestos of the Thatcher governments. The manifesto stated that "We are determined to maintain our present system of immigration controls unless we have evidence that other arrangements would be equally satisfactory and cost effective".[99] This illustrates that the Conservative party was standing by its policy on immigration and did not feel the need to alter the main thrust of the policy.

As recently as 1996 the Conservatives continued to pursue further regulation of immigration with the passage of the 1996 Asylum and Immigration Act. This Act[100] removed benefit and housing entitlements for asylum seekers, and made it an offence to employ someone whose immigration status does not entitle them to work in this country.

In fact there has been a shift of the British immigration debate from the domestic agenda to the European agenda. Indeed what can be termed 'Europeanisation' of the immigration issue has occurred, prompted largely by the move towards closer European integration and by the provisions laid out in the Single Market Act, including calls to make provisions for the free movement of people. This aspect of European integration has exercised recent Conservative governments greatly, providing yet another area of Conservative opposition to full European integration. The British government is particularly concerned about frontier controls in member countries such as Germany, Italy and the Netherlands which it believes are far too lax. In truth the Conservatives do not trust, and have no confidence in, the system of immigration control exercised by many member states. The fear is that subordination to European Union laws, once complete economic and political integration is achieved, will lead to the danger of a mass influx of immigrants. It is likely that in the coming years, as the debate on European integration hots up and British scepticism about borders controls across Europe remain, strict immigration controls are likely to remain. Indeed recent pronouncements by Labour's Robin Cook suggest exactly this. However, under the new government they may be counterbalanced by removing some of the more discriminatory elements of immigration law, and abolishing some of the much-hated rules. Indeed a change introduced regarding immigration is the abolition of the primary purpose rule under Labour Prime Minister Tony Blair.[101] This was one of the Labour Party's pledges in the 1997 Party Manifesto to "...remove the arbitrary and unfair results that can follow from the existing 'primary purpose' rule".[102] Even though Shadow Home Secretary Michael Howard believed that "scrapping a controversial immigration rule would remove a key deterrent to bogus entrants".[103] Nevertheless the recent relaxation in the immigration rules may help to ease the suffering experienced by immigrants. Couples will no longer have to prove that they both married so the husband could gain entry into the UK. Perhaps this could signal the beginning of a fairer and equitable system of immigration, even though controls in general are likely to remain strict. The point is that as long as they are applied fairly to everyone attempting to enter and not selectively as they were under the Conservatives then the feeling of discrimination and injustice will be removed.

Conclusions

This chapter has reviewed and analysed major rule and law changes regarding immigration since 1945. It has not, for reasons of length, covered every rule change which has occurred over the years but has concentrated on arguably the most important legislation and rules and the debate which they generated.

The analysis has revealed that the 1979-90 period was a hectic period in the arena of government activity on immigration. Whereas in the period 1945-79, 5 major Acts affecting immigration were passed in that 34 year period, 3 very significant Acts affecting immigration and nationality were passed in the space of just over ten years in the period 1979-90 (and this is so even when we exclude those acts passed relating to Hong Kong and the Falkland Islands). Furthermore, looking at the nature and content of the Acts, we can see that the Acts passed in the 1945-79 period were relatively more liberal in their treatment of immigrants, particularly the 1948 British Nationality Act and the 1962 Commonwealth Immigrants Act, compared to legislation passed solely under the Conservative government of Thatcher in the 1979-90 period. In addition 1979-90 saw many other rule changes regarding immigrants which were highly controversial.

The crucial point is that the Conservative government's aim from 1979 onwards was to reduce immigration into Britain. This aim is clearly illustrated and represented by government policy in this period. The government attempted to achieve its aim of curbing immigration through various legislative actions such as the 1981 British Nationality Act, the 1987 Immigration (Carriers' Liability Act) and the Immigration Act 1988. These Acts targeted and duly affected various categories of immigrants. In between, there were also other rules implemented such as the visa requirement for citizens from certain Commonwealth countries. It is also worth noting that the Conservatives made no secret that they wished to reduce the number of immigrants in Britain during the Thatcher years, and it is not surprising therefore that their policy reflected those views. This is exactly the point touched on in chapter 1 when analysing the work of Andrew Geddes who stressed that the whole point of Conservative government legislation on immigration under Thatcher was to curb immigration.

Government policy on immigration during the 1980s attracted nothing but criticism from ethnic minority organisations and political opponents and provoked some heated debates in Parliament not only with regard to the legislation itself but also with regard to procedural and administrative rules regarding DNA testing, virginity tests, and visa requirements.

Evidence that the Conservative government's policy from 1979-90 to curb immigration through legislation had been effective can be seen from statistics which show that in 1980 a total of 69,750 people of all nationalities were admitted for settlement. However, this figure had fallen to 52,400 in 1990, representing a fall of almost 25%.[104] The Conservative government was successful in cutting down immigration in the long term. The Tories came to power in 1979 and promised the nation a cut-down in immigration. In 1982 the Conservatives' 1979 Election Manifesto was criticised by Glasgow Hillhead, MP[105] Roy Jenkins (SDP/All) for being discriminatory. Jenkins said

...The right of all British Citizens legally settled here are equal before the law whatever their race, colour or creed. And their opportunity ought to be equal too.

The legislation seemed to get stricter for black immigrants even though the Tories do not admit it. Not even refugees were let off the hook with the Carriers' Liability Act tightening the control on them. Thatcher departed from office in November 1990 leaving behind her a series of immigration laws which were discriminatory in practice and which were to continue to degrade, offend, insult, and separate black and Asian immigrant families.

In short, Conservative government legislation from 1979-90 eroded much of the rights immigrants had enjoyed prior to 1979. It was now becoming increasingly difficult for immigrants to come to Britain whether for temporary or for permanent stay. Apart from the immigration laws the immigration rules an applicant has to meet are very complicated. The marriage rules all tend to be based on probability. The rules require that the person from abroad must not have used marriage as a tool to enter the UK. How can one prove why he/she gets married? The requirement that the couple must show they have met, raises difficulties for couples in arranged marriages where that is not the norm. An elderly parent has to show they have no other relatives in their own country whom they can depend on. The parents may have a daughter but in Asian culture the parents never depend on their daughter, thus showing the complexities people from the Indian sub-continent may face. The cultural difference that British born Asian people experience in the immigration rules are discussed in more detail in chapter 5. The overall impact of Thatcher's immigration policy on people from the Indian sub continent was negative.

The period 1979-90 has also revealed that a number of Scottish MPs were involved in many of the debates generated by the government legislation on immigration, showing that Scotland was not oblivious to what was going on, especially since immigrants in the whole of the country were affected. The nation-wide nature of the immigration issue and the legislation regarding it was summed up by former,[106] Conservative Prime Minister Margaret Thatcher, who when asked by a Scottish Labour MP Ross Ernest (Dundee West), whether she will transfer the responsibility for immigration and nationality in Scotland from the Home Office to the Scottish Office once the British Nationality Bill becomes law, replied

> ...no, the British Nationality Bill does not affect in anyway the view taken by successive governments that responsibility for immigration and nationality matters for the UK as a whole should rest with the Home Secretary.

Immigration laws under John Major like his predecessor were not very lenient towards immigrants either. Although Tony Blair's approach towards immigration and the Indian sub-continent has proved to be a little more laxed than his Conservative predecessors.

Notes

1. See the following on Immigration and Law in Britain: *Immigration, Nationality, and Citizenship* by Satvinder S Juss (Mansell, 1993); Lawrence Grant and Ian Martin *Immigration Law and Practise, First Supplement* (London, 1985); Ian Macdonald, Immigration Law and Practise, 3rd edition (Butterworths, 1991).
2. See Juss, *Immigration, Nationality and Citizenship, op cit.* chapters 2 and 3; See also Macdonald and Blake, *Macdonald's Immigration Law and Practise* (Butterworths, 1995), chapter 1.
3. *British Nationality Act 1948.*
4. *Commonwealth Immigrants Act 1962*
5. *Ibid*
6. *Ibid*
7. *Commonwealth Immigrants Act 1968*
8. Juss, *Immigration, Nationality and Citizenship, op cit.* p. 43.
9. *Immigration Appeals Act 1969*
10. *Immigration Act 1971.*
11 *Ibid*
12. *National Association For Asian Youth, Which Half Decides?, A contribution to the Debate on Sex Discrimination, British Nationality and Immigration Laws,* p. 24, 1979.
13. See *Glasgow Herald*, February 2, 1979, p. 8.
14. See *The Times*, December 17, 1980, p. 3.
15. See *ibid*, p. 3.
16. See *Glasgow Herald*, February 2, 1979, p. 8.
17. *Ibid*, February 3, 1979, p. 6.
18. *British Nationality Act 1981*
19. Juss, *Immigration, Nationality and Citizenship, op. cit.* p. 55.
20. *Immigration Control Procedures Report of a Formal Investigation*, p. 15, Commission for Racial Equality, 1985.
21. See *British Nationality Act 1981.*
22. See *ibid.*
23. See *ibid*
24. See *ibid*
25. See *Glasgow Herald*, February 7, 1981, p. 2.
26. *Ibid*
27. *Ibid*
28. *Parliamentary Debates, Commons (Hansard)*, vol. 973, November 5 to November 16, 1979-80.
29. *Ibid*, vol. 66, col. 55 and 509, 2 March 1984.
30. See *ibid*
31 See *Glasgow Herald*, April 6, 1981, p. 5.
32. *Ibid.*

33. Parliamentary Debates, Commons (Hansard), vol. 997, col. 931-941, 28 January 1981.
34. *Ibid.*
35. *Ibid*
36. *The Times*, February 13, 1981, p 6.
37. House of Commons, *British Nationality Fees,* Third Report, 1982-1993.
38. See *ibid*
39. *Parliamentary Debates, Commons (Hansard)*, vol 31, col. 692, 11 November, 1982-83.
40. *Immigration Control Procedures· report of a formal investigation*, Commission for Racial Equality, 1985.
41. *Parliamentary Debates, Commons (Hansard)*, vol. 34, 15 December 1982.
42. See *Glasgow Herald*, September 1, 1986, p. 1; Glasgow Herald, September 2, 1986, p. 2.
43. *Out of Sight, the new visit visa system overseas*, Joint Council for the Welfare of Immigrants (JCWI), 1987.
44. *Ibid*
45. *Ibid*
46. *Parliamentary Debates, Commons (Hansard)*, vol. 103, col. 78-118, 29 October 1986.
47. *Ibid*
48. *Ibid*
49. *Ibid.*
50. *Ibid.*
51. For a full list of nationals of countries who need a visa for the United Kingdom see appendix in *Statement of Changes in Immigration Rules*, HMSO 1994.
52. *Immigration (Carriers' Liability) Act 1987.*
53. *The Times*, March 4, 1987, p. 1.
54. *Ibid.*
55. *Parliamentary Debates, Commons (Hansard).*
56. *Ibid,* vol. 113, col. 586-590, 26 March 1987.
57. *Glasgow Herald*, 17 March, 1987, p. 5.
58. *United Nations Convention 1951.*
59. *Ibid.*
60. *Parliamentary Debates, Commons (Hansard)*, vol. 112, col. 706, 1986-1987.
61. *Ibid*
62. *Glasgow Herald*, 17 March 1987, p. 11.
63. *Ibid*
64. *Ibid*
65. *Ibid*
66. *Ibid*
67. *Immigration Act 1988*
68. *Ibid*

69.   *Ibid*
70.   *Ibid*
71.   *Parliamentary Debates, Commons (Hansard)*, vol. 122, col. 827, 16 November 1987
72.   *Ibid*
73.   *Ibid*, column 796.
74.   *Ibid*
75.   *Ibid*, column 827.
76   *Ibid*
77.   *Ibid*, vol. 132, col. 855, 3 May 1988.
78.   *Scottish Asian Action Committee Report, 1988.*
79.   *Parliamentary Debates, Commons (Hansard)*, vol. 154, col. 401-462, 14 June 1989.
80.   *Ibid*
81.   See for example *The Times* report on 20 March 1989, p. 5 about the success of DNA testing.
82.   *Parliamentary Debates, Commons (Hansard)*, vol. 154, col. 401-462, 14 June 1989.
83.   See *ibid*, vol. 156, col. 368-410, 5 July 1989.
84.   *Ibid*, vol. 154, col. 401-462, 14 June 1989.
85.   *Ibid.*
86.   *Ibid.*
87.   See *Ibid*, vol. 156, col. 368-410, 5 July 1989.
88.   *Ibid*
89.   *Ibid*
90.   *Immigration into Britain, 1971 Immigration Act, notes on the regulations and procedures*, Central Office of Information, 1981.
91.   See for more detail, Ian Macdonald and Nicholas Blake, *Immigration Law and Practise, op. cit.*
92.   *Interview* with Mr Masood Nabi, Senior Councillor, Immigration Advisory Service.
93.   *Standards of Service for Tribunals*, p. 11, published by Court Service.
94.   *Statement of Changes in the Immigration Rules*, para. P.54, 13 May 1994 HMSO.
95.   *Ibid*, p. 8.
96.   *Ibid*, p. 63.
97.   See *Asylum and Immigration Appeals Act 1993*.
98.   Ian Macdonald and Nicholas Blake, *Macdonald's Immigration Law and Practice*, op cit. p. v.
99.   *Conservative Party Manifesto, 1992*, p. 26.
100.   For more detailed analysis of the Act see: *The Asylum and Immigration Act 1996 Implications for Racial Equality*, Commission for Racial Equality, 1996.
101.   *Guardian*, May 28, 1997, p. 1.
102.   *Labour Party Manifesto 1997*, p. 35.
103.   *Guardian*, May 29, 1997, p 3.
104.   *Control of Immigration. Statistics United Kingdom 1990*, HMSO.

105. *Parliamentary Debates, Commons*, (Hansard), vol. 34, col. 357, 15 December 1982.
106. *Ibid*, vol. 5, col. 188, 1980-81.

3 Channels for Processing Immigration as an Issue in Glasgow: The Organisational Network

Introduction

The legislative enactment of the immigration regime confronting individuals attempting to secure temporary or permanent residence in the United Kingdom and responsibility for that regime's administration are essentially British rather than Scottish in nature. The British Parliament enacts the regime. The Home Office, not the Scottish Office, is responsible for its administration.

The 1997 Labour government White Paper on a Scottish Parliament did not suggest that there would be any major changes in the formulation and implementation of the British immigration regime. Nonetheless a major objective of this study is to analyse the grass roots reaction to the implementation of the immigration regime. The grass roots in question are Asian inhabitants of two Glasgow districts, Hillhead and Pollokshields. A Scottish dimension thus becomes apparent at a local or grassroots level i.e. where the regime impinges on individuals seeking entry and on their sponsors residing in the many ethnic minority communities throughout Britain. The Scottish dimension is clearly visible in a number of organisations in Glasgow helping and advising people experiencing problems with immigration procedures.

This chapter will look at the role played by such organisations in not only providing support and assistance to individuals but also as a source of lobbying the government and representing the interests of these individuals. Some of these organisations play a wider role which is similar to that played by pressure groups. Also in a similar way to pressure groups they allow increased participation and access to the political system thereby enhancing the quality of democracy. They enable the intensity of feeling on issues, in this case immigration, to be considered, and opinions to be expressed.

There are a number of organisations in Glasgow helping and advising people with immigration problems.[1] The most important of these include: The Immigration Advisory Service (IAS - previously known as the United Kingdom Immigration Advisory Service); The Strathclyde Community Relations Council (SCRC); The Scottish Asian Action Committee (SAAC); The Scottish Refugee Council (SRC); and the Strathclyde Interpreting Service (SIS). Other organisations include the Ethnic Minority Advisory Service and Ethnic Minority Law Centre. Some have their origins in government; others are community based.

This chapter will look in some detail at the role played by Glasgow based organisations in dealing with the questions which arise from the issue of immigration. For this purpose the chapter will be divided into three sections. Section one will look in detail at the major organisations, including their structure and make-up, their objectives and functions, their sources of funding, and the degree of autonomy, if they have any. Section two will evaluate the success of the work carried out by the organisations by looking at the contribution made by them towards dealing with the issue of immigration throughout the 1980s. This will be done by analysing annual reports and other sources provided by the organisations themselves. In other words this section will provide an assessment of how adequate the network processing immigration issues has been overall by analysing the effectiveness of the work done by organisations and looking at the problems which the organisations have encountered trying to help immigrants. Section three examines solely the work of the Immigration Advisory Service because it is the only organisation which concentrates on immigration matters entirely. This is done through the use of data and statistics provided by the IAS. The importance of the IAS is highlighted in chapter 4 on a survey that was conducted on people from the Indian sub-continent. This survey showed that out of all the organisations available people preferred making an application for an entry clearance through the IAS. It also demonstrated that when they did have problems with the procedures people again went to the IAS for assistance more than to any other organisation.[2] This is testimony to the key role played by the IAS in the immigration process in Glasgow.

Although the organisations we will look at do not necessarily work together, they nevertheless form an important network for dealing with immigration.

Before going on to look at each of the organisations in turn, it is worth mentioning the point that with the exception of the Immigration Advisory Service (IAS) which specifically deals with immigration, the organisations concerned do not exist primarily for the purpose of immigration but are there to provide general help to ethnic minorities on various issues, with immigration just happening to be one of them i.e. they deal with immigration as one issue along with a number of other connected issues.

Organisations and Immigration

Immigration and Advisory Service

The Immigration Advisory Service (IAS - formerly known as the UKIAS) was initially formed in 1972 under the name of the United Kingdom Immigration Advisory Service (UKIAS) on the recommendation of the Wilson Committee according to Section 23 of the Immigration Act 1971.[3] Section 23 required the government to form an independent organisation which would help people facing immigration problems and represent appeals at the Immigration Appeals Court. According to Section 23 this service will be free to the people and the government should fund the organisation.

The IAS is a voluntary independent and charitable organisation funded by the Home Office. The organisation's Head Office is situated in

London. It has regional offices throughout the United Kingdom in Manchester, Birmingham, Cardiff, Gatwick, Hounslow and in Glasgow. The Glasgow office has been open since 1972. The present structure of the Immigration Advisory Service in Glasgow is illustrated in Figure 3.1 below:

Figure 3.1 Structure of the Immigration and Advisory Service in Glasgow

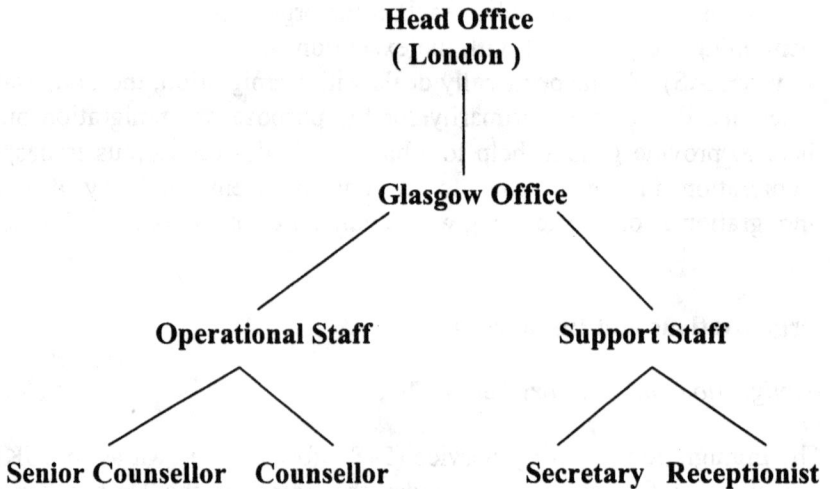

```
                        Head Office
                        ( London )
                             |
                             |
                       Glasgow Office
                      /               \
                     /                 \
          Operational Staff          Support Staff
              /    \                     /    \
             /      \                   /      \
Senior Counsellor   Counsellor    Secretary  Receptionist
```

Figure 3.1, which shows the present structure of the IAS, reveals 3 operational staff consisting of two Counsellors and one Senior Counsellor. The Operational Staff are backed up by support staff composed of a secretary and a receptionist.

The main functions of the office are:

- to represent those appealing against decisions in immigration cases or to present the appeals at the Immigration Appeals Court before the Adjudicator (this is dealt with mainly by the Counsellors);
- to make written representations to the Home Office on behalf of the clients (this is dealt with by the counsellor who is always present in the office);
- to give general advice on Immigration matters (this is also taken care of by the Advisor);
- to make visits to the prisons where illegal immigrants are detained.[4] Confidentiality is observed at the highest level in these matters.

The Strathclyde Interpreting Service (SIS)

The foundation of the Interpreting Service was important for the ethnic minorities. As the spokesperson Mr Singh[5] said in the late 1970s, many immigrants could not speak English and there was no help available from the social, health and judicial services. The Strathclyde Regional Council set up a research team and formed a language unit (oral interpreting). This Unit, the Interpreting Service, is made up of a Senior Interpreting Officer who deals with Urdu and other languages such as Chinese and Arabic, while various Interpreting Officers for Chinese and Indian languages along with the Administrative Officer make up the rest of the unit. This structure of SIS is illustrated below in Figure 3.2.

Figure 3.2 Structure of the Strathclyde Interpreting Service

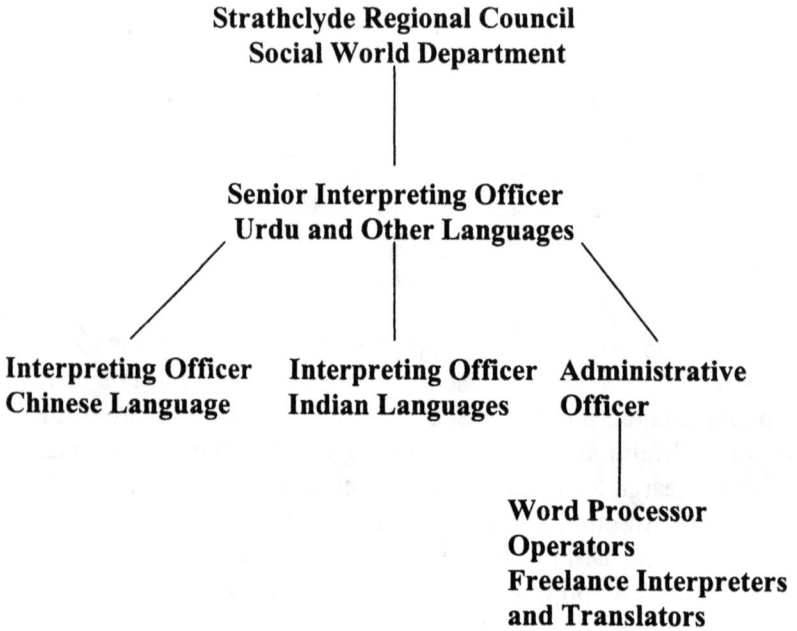

Strathclyde Regional Council
Social World Department

Senior Interpreting Officer
Urdu and Other Languages

Interpreting Officer   **Interpreting Officer**   **Administrative**
Chinese Language   **Indian Languages**   **Officer**

Word Processor
Operators
Freelance Interpreters
and Translators

In 1981 SIS was funded by Urban Aid. In 1988 Urban Aid funding stopped. The Strathclyde Regional Council decided the project should be taken on mainstream funding and since 1988 the interpreting service became a part of the Social Work Department. When asked what the interpreting service does,[6] Mr Singh replied that it does oral interpreting in 35 languages; translations from English to community languages; and helps word processing in different community languages.

The interpreting service is free for voluntary organisations and for the unemployed, pensioners, and students. However, private firms and companies have to pay for the service.

The interpreting service is used in a variety of different situations regarding immigration. In this respect it provides an important service for individuals seeking to stay in Britain. People applying for political asylum may need interpreters; illegal immigrants interviewed by immigration officers at Glasgow Airport need interpreters. Also interpreters are used when the immigrant is in prison, for general requirements, (for example food). Even at the appeal stage an interpreter may be needed.

Strathclyde Community Relations Council (SCRC)

This body was set up in 1971 (then as Glasgow Community Relations Council) under the Race Relations Act 1968.[7] The organisation dealt with immigration only up until 1983.[8] It highlighted the problems experienced by immigrants with the immigration regime by acting as a kind of pressure group. Now it has a broader race relations agenda. The present function of the SCRC is: To promote within Strathclyde Region, equality of opportunity in all areas of life between all people of different race and colour, and to work towards the elimination of racial discrimination and disadvantage within the multi-racial, multi-cultural society; to enhance the education of all inhabitants concerning equality in a multi-racial society, and the intellectual, artistic, economic and cultural backgrounds of all inhabitants of Strathclyde.[9]

The organisation was funded by the Commission for Racial Equality, and the local authority - Glasgow District Council (now called City of Glasgow Council) and the Strathclyde Regional Council (now defunct).[10]

Scottish Refugee Council (SRC)

The SRC office opened in 1985 in Edinburgh and in 1990 in Glasgow. The Council basically exists to provide advice, support and practical help to refugees and their families in Scotland, and to campaign on issues which affect them. On this basis the SRC's objectives are: to provide a range of services matched to the needs of refugees and asylum seekers and specifically, counselling and support; advice and information on seeking asylum, welfare benefits, family reunion; help in finding accommodation and work; help in gaining recognition for training/professional qualifications acquired elsewhere than in Scotland; in the future a legal advice service; and to improve understanding among the community at large of the problems facing refugees.[11]

In carrying out its work the SRC aims to: develop specialist services for refugees only when there is an insurmountable reason which impedes access to services used by the community at large; co-operate with voluntary and statutory agencies and to initiate such co-operation; develop and maintain a commitment to high standards of management to ensure that refugees receive the best service that the organisation can provide. Funding comes from both Central and Local Government, including the Home Office, Scottish Office, and Strathclyde Regional Council.[12] The flow diagram 3.3 below illustrates the make up of the SRC.

Figure 3.3 Structure of the Scottish Refugee Council

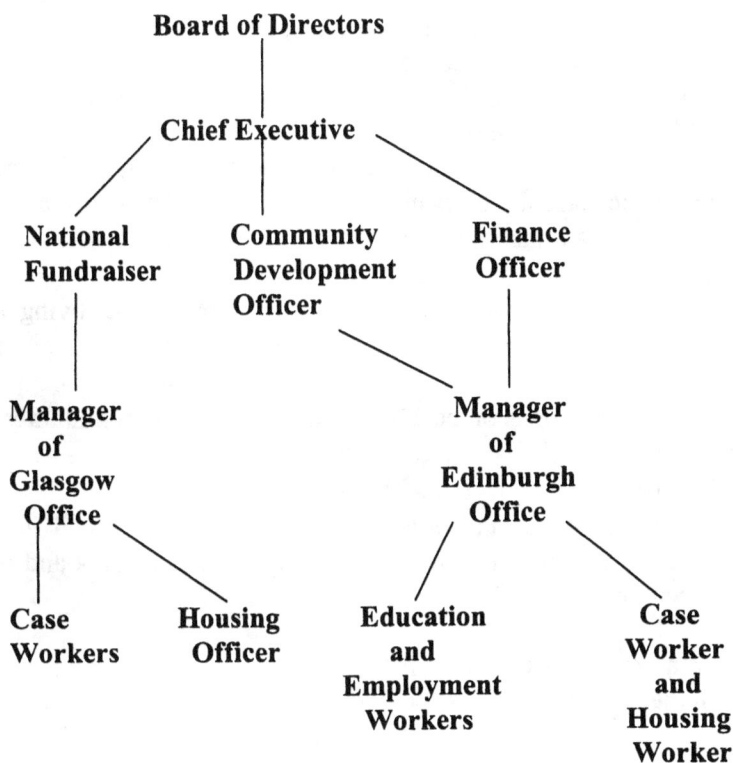

Board of Directors

Chief Executive

National Fundraiser   Community Development Officer   Finance Officer

Manager of Glasgow Office

Manager of Edinburgh Office

Case Workers   Housing Officer   Education and Employment Workers   Case Worker and Housing Worker

As can be seen in Figure 3.3 the Board of Directors form the core of the SRC with the most important individual person being the Chief Executive. As the caseworker for Glasgow office Stan Crook said "The Board of Directors are a legally responsible body and they make the policy decisions".[13] At the next level of the organisational pyramid we have the National Fund Raiser, Finance Officer and the Community Development Officer. Then at the lower level there are the managers of both the Glasgow and Edinburgh offices where Case Workers are employed, along with Housing Workers.

Scottish Asian Action Committee (SAAC)

The Scottish Asian Action Committee (SAAC) was set up in 1984 as a community based initiative. The committee was an Urban Aid project. When that was discontinued, the Strathclyde Regional Council continued to fund SAAC. The committee deals with race problems in general.

At its General Meeting on 5th June 1994 SAAC adopted an Amended Constitution[14] which stated the organisations objectives. The major aims of SAAC as stated in its Constitution are:

- to work to safeguard the interests of and improve the living and working conditions of Scotland's Asian and ethnic minority communities;
- to make representations on behalf of Scotland's Asian communities;
- to promote, through special committees or sponsored organisations, activities beneficial to people of Asian origin;
- to support the people and organisations in this country and in any other country in the world who are fighting for equal rights and self-determination.

As far as the structure of SAAC is concerned, according to the constitution the

Annual General meeting is the supreme body of the organisation and has the right.....to take final decisions on behalf of the organisation.[15]

In addition to General Annual meetings a special general meeting can also be called by the Executive Committee or by a request from a third of the affiliated organisations and by a third of individual members. The make-up of the Executive Committee itself is illustrated in Figure 3.4 below:

Figure 3.4 Structure of the Scottish Asian Action Committee

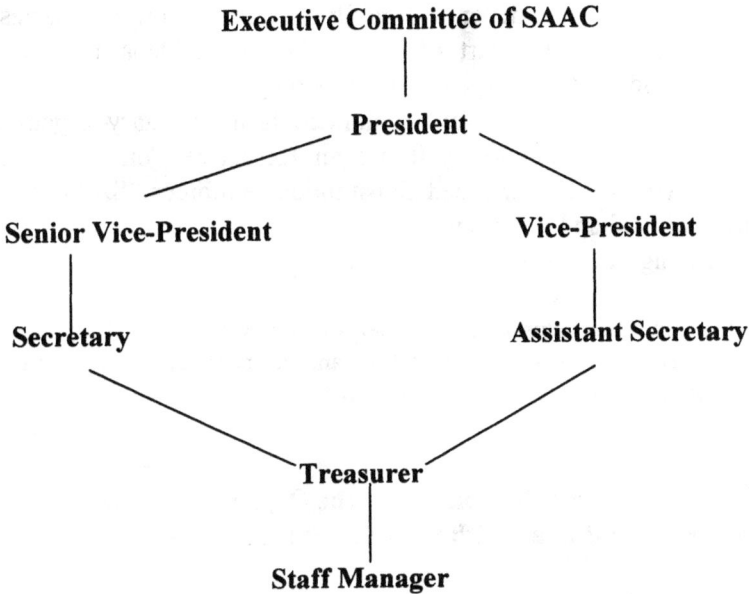

Executive Committee of SAAC
|
President

Senior Vice-President   Vice-President
| |
Secretary   Assistant Secretary

Treasurer
|
Staff Manager

The functions of each of the office bearers in the above diagram are described in section 5.0 of SAAC's Constitution.

The Autonomy Question

As far as the question of autonomy regarding the organisations listed above is concerned, the Scottish Refugee Council is a voluntary organisation completely independent of the government. It is self-governing but it is funded by governmental institutions. The Council's autonomous status is assured by the fact that it is not allowed to do political campaigning. It is funded by the Home Office, Scottish Office (Education Department, Industry Department) and Strathclyde Regional Council.[16]

The Strathclyde Interpreting Service is not independent of government. In fact it is dependent on Strathclyde Region for salaries and supervision. It is totally part of the Social Work Department and is mainstream funded. It therefore has no autonomy.[17]

The Scottish Asian Action Committee is a voluntary organisation which has complete autonomy. It has an Executive Committee, which decides everything. Its Amended Constitution reinforces "SAAC shall be non-party political and non-sectarian".[18]

The Immigration Advisory Service is

> an independent organisation which helps with advice and legal representation an all matters affecting immigration and in particular with immigration appeals before adjudicators and tribunals.[19]

The Work of the Organisations: How the Organisations have Contributed to and Dealt with the Issue of Immigration

This section will look at the work carried out by each of the organisations described in the previous section and assess if and how their work has contributed effectively with dealing with processing immigration issues. In other words the emphasis is on the efficiency of the organisational network in dealing with problems of immigration. In order to do this detailed analysis will be presented of the work of the organisations based on information provided by the organisations themselves, e.g. in their annual reports and other sources. Comments from individuals within the organisations themselves will also provide an insight into whether the organisations themselves believe that they have achieved their aims regarding immigration. Views of individuals who have sought the help of the organisations will be left to a later chapter. As well as assessing the achievements of the organisations, attention in this section will also be paid to problems, which the organisations said that they encountered because of the government's policies, which may have jeopardised some of their work.

It has to be remembered that the different organisations play a key role in the area of immigration, and constitute collectively a vital resource for many individuals seeking a fair deal on immigration matters. It is not only the actual practical work that these organisations do which is of utmost importance. Their usefulness can also be seen in their adoption of strong verbal stances on behalf of immigrants. The organisations criticise what they see as unfair government policies and legislation. By doing this they therefore bring to the forefront or draw attention to matters affecting those they are helping. In this respect they act as pressure groups in the political process by lobbying the government and by bringing to public attention particular grievances and issues/problems.

Strathclyde Community Relations Council (SCRC)

The Strathclyde Community Relations Council set up in 1971 as the Glasgow Community Relations Council under the Race Relations Act 1968[20] dealt with immigration up to 1983.

As can be seen from the Community Relations Council's annual reports,[21] the organisation did a lot of work in the early 1980s on behalf of immigrant interests by constant criticisms of government policies and legislation on immigration. In 1981 the Chairman of the CRC, Rev A.J. Langdon, was highly critical of the Nationality Bill calling it "....unjust and morally indefensible...".[22] His major criticism of the bill centred on the following points among others: the Nationality Bill divides citizenship into categories which is seen as morally objectionable; it lacks any clear statements of the rights of citizenship; it seriously increases the sense of insecurity amongst the ethnic minorities; and it gives uncontrolled discretionary powers to the Home Secretary without right of appeal, a development contrary to British Justice.

Mr Walter Fyfe, the senior Community Relations Officer, was pleased that at least in the struggle against the Nationality Bill, the ethnic minority organisations looked at in this chapter had got together to fight against it, "in contrast to the situation a decade ago when organisations seldom joined the struggle".[23] This opposition to the Nationality Bill on the part of minority organisations meant that the Glasgow Community Relations Council's first objective which

> was to encourage the growth of the ethnic minority organisations so that their voices would be heard on matters of public concern and in particular on the legislation that successive governments passed against them [24]

had largely been achieved.

However, despite this, Mr Fyfe went on that no matter how much effort was made by organisations it would never be wholly productive due to the government's harsh policies.

In its annual report for 1983[25] the CRC criticised the government's virginity tests which had caused families great embarrassment. The Senior Community Relations Officer (SCRO) Walter Fyfe recalled occasions[26] when he was present at interviews where young married women "were being asked very personal questions about the sexual aspects..." of their marriage. He went on that

> ..it is quite appalling that the UK government have sunk so low that virginity testing and prurient questioning are used as means to establish rights of UK citizens.

Overall the Community Relations Officer felt that discrimination in immigration had been rife throughout the life of the Council.

After 1983 the CRC did not deal with immigration problems. Instead all cases were referred to the United Kingdom Immigration Advisory Service. However, in the 1988 report[27] the controversial subject of immigration was mentioned by the Parliamentary Advisory Committee[28] (Set up by the CRC in 1987). The formation of this committee allowed the CRC to keep in touch with the immigration issue (even although it did not deal directly with the issue any longer), since the Parliamentary Advisory Committee decided to raise immigration as one of its issues. More encouraging for the Committee was the support promised to it by a number of Strathclyde MPs including Euro-MPs.[29] At the SCRC's half-yearly meeting on 20th November 1987 the following resolution was passed urging

> ...Strathclyde MPs to develop a campaigning lobby for fair, non-racist, non-sexist immigration laws. In the short term there is a need to challenge the current issues of visitor's visas, the primary purpose rule and the separation of families.[30]

> In the long term, preparations must be made to arrange legislation which could replace the racist 1968 and 1971 Immigration laws when they are repealed by a future government .[31]

In its bid to prepare a non-racist, non-sexist immigration bill, a number of MPs responded to the SCRC's calls[32] including the following: George Foulkes; the then Shadow Scottish Secretary, Donald Dewar; Dr Jeremy Bray; George Robertson; Maria Fyfe; and George Galloway. The MPs who responded believed that there was indeed a need for such a just immigration bill, and expressed their greatest sympathy with the suffering endured by minority individuals at the hands of Conservative immigration policies.

From the evidence before us - we can see that the CRC was heavily involved in the immigration arena particularly up until 1983 after which this duty was essentially passed on to the UKIAS. Its Parliamentary Advisory Committee set up in 1987 continued to promote issues such as immigration as we have just seen and believed there could be "Some light at the end of the tunnel where some of the Scottish MP's were concerned". In fact the CRC was so committed to its work and put in so much effort that case studies show immigrants writing or asking the Community Relations Officer (CRO) for help and advice and thanking him for his efforts.[33]

Scottish Asian Action Committee (SAAC)

The Scottish Asian Action Committee (SAAC) set up in 1984 has in the past ten years carried out a lot of work which has aided the cause of ethnic minorities in Scotland. One of the issues affecting the minorities has of course been immigration, and on this matter SAAC has provided a lot of help to individuals encountering difficulties. In the period 1988-89 the Scottish Asian Action Committee dealt with more cases relating to immigration (sponsorship/deportations) and connected issues (such as Registration, Nationality and Passport Renewals) than any other.[34] In fact these issues together accounted for 28% of all cases dealt with by SAAC, highlighting the importance of the issue of immigration in Scotland.

To begin with, SAAC has provided useful and relevant information to individuals on immigration. In its 1994 annual report[35] SAAC stressed that issues of immigration and nationality took up much of its time, and that situation was likely to continue in the future particularly as these issues had become more and more controversial due to stricter government legislation in recent years. "Indeed SAAC has consistently raised the immigration issue, pointing out the injustices inherent in both legislation and rules".[36]

Darnley Street Family Centre in conjunction with SAAC produced a leaflet providing information beforehand to individuals who wished to visit the UK.[37] In the 1986-87 annual report SAAC announced that it was

> ...providing publicity material giving details of the advantages and disadvantages of becoming a British Citizen and intended to distribute this material throughout all the ethnic minority communities in Scotland...[38]

On top of this SAAC gave "...sound advice.." and help in making sure that application forms were properly completed by persons who had decided to register for British Citizenship.[39]

SAAC even hosted a surgery for people with immigration problems in March of 1989.[40] At this surgery two lawyers - specialists in immigration - from London were present. This was an innovative idea which allowed a number of people to talk to these lawyers.

Vigorous campaigning has been a hallmark of SAAC's work in the area of immigration. This was highlighted by SAAC in 1989[41] when it said that it would "...continue to campaign for the rights to family unity and for a just immigration policy". In the late 1980s SAAC launched its campaign in unison with other groups and organisations in highlighting its concerns about the possible impact of the Single European Market which was due to take effect from 1992.[42] SAAC's main worry on this front was that the removal of the internal barriers to the movement of European Community Nationals within the Common market "....could mean a deterioration in the quality of life for black people..." and the "creation of a fortress Europe primarily for white people". Such a Europe could entail

> ...greater reliance on immigration controls and visas for nationals of many non-EC countries wanting to enter EC countries.[43]

As part of its campaign against the 1988 Immigration Act,[44] SAAC organised a visit to Edinburgh to lobby the Scottish Office about the Act.[45] The organisation did feel it received good media attention i.e. television regarding their disapproval of the Act.

1987 was another example of a year which saw active SAAC involvement in issues of Immigration and Nationality.[46] SAAC focussed strongly during these years on giving help to those involved in the process of registration for British Citizenship. The SAAC noticed an alarming number of problems which faced individuals seeking registration.

For a start the government made no effort to publicize the fact that registration before the 31st December 1987 was required.[47] Instead it was left to organisations like SAAC "...to publicise the facts..."[48] In addition to this other conditions had to be satisfied such as filling in the correct type of form and paying the appropriate fee.

SAAC had also written to all prospective MPs in Scotland[49] regarding changes to immigration legislation which were due to come into effect on 31st December 1987. While campaigning on a number of immigration cases SAAC noticed a disturbing trend which saw families having to wait years before the Home Office reached a decision and blamed the slow Home Office administration for this.

SAAC's efforts in opposing the immigration bill attracted much praise from the Labour party and the only Asian MP, Keith Vaz, praised the organisation for its work.[50]

The SAAC felt that the government was generally being unfair and was discriminating against blacks. This is in line with a view shared by Miles and Phizacklea, in their work reviewed in chapter 1, in which they argue that black people have suffered from discriminatory government legislation. The term 'black' as used by SAAC is a political word for non-white, thus also referring to people from the Indian sub-continent.

> All the evidence supports the view that current immigration legislation is aimed at keeping black people out of the country. SAAC's experience of immigration cases show that entry clearance officers (ECO) are using the 'catch all' primary purpose rule to exclude Asian fiancés and husbands from those countries. White people do not suffer from the same delays although in principle the rules apply to all.[51]

Support for this claim is to be found in the IAS report for 1988-89 which showed that very few Old Commonwealth nationals had the need to take their case to the appeals stage: Only one Canadian and 4 Australians took their case to the appeals stage. In comparison the figures for the Indian sub-continent revealed that 356 Indians, 415 Pakistanis and 257 Bangladeshis had to take their case to the appeals stage. This illustrates that Old Commonwealth nationals had fewer problems first time round in gaining entry, while Indian sub-continent nationals often had to take their case to an appeal after being initially rejected. This in turn meant delays for Indian sub-continent nationals. A further reason for longer delays experienced by Indian sub-continent nationals is the fact that they have to obtain a visa, and quite often have to go through the process of satisfying the requirements for one, while Old Commonwealth nationals are exempt from visas.

Another important point to remember is that the primary purpose rule does not affect white immigrants, most of whom come from countries which are relatively prosperous, and their desire to enter Britain is not viewed with suspicion. SAAC's argument is supported by the survey results in chapter four which confirmed that the second most important reason for refusal of visa was thought to be the primary purpose rule.[52]

Strathclyde Interpreting Service

Unfortunately, there are no annual reports or similar documents available from the Strathclyde Interpreting Service (SIS) which has made it impossible to look at and assess the work done by the organisation in great detail. However, the organisation did carry out a survey to establish how effective its service was. The results of this survey illustrate that the SIS has also done a very effective job. Seventy-five per cent of respondents felt that the speed of translation was excellent, while around 90% said that regarding availability of the oral interpreting service it was good.

Scottish Refugee Council (SRC)

Moving on to the Scottish Refugee Council (SRC), this organisation has a lot of liaison with other organisations. This point was emphasised by Stan Crook, case worker for the Glasgow office,[53] who said that the SRC was in touch with the Immigration Advisory Service and the Ethnic Minority Law Centre, as well as having links with the Social Work Department of Strathclyde Regional Council.

During the period 1989-1994, the SRC has done a lot of significant work which has gone some way towards meeting the council's established objectives. Many achievements as a result of the SRC's activities have been noted. In its 1990-91 report,[54] the Chairperson Lynne Barty said that fund-raising had been increasingly successful due to the great dedication shown by the councils part-time fund-raiser, the Treasurer and the finance sub-committee, "working to rationalise priorities and to provide on going support and practical help". Two significant achievements have been firstly: a grant approved by the Unemployed Voluntary Action Fund to employ a volunteer co-ordinator in Strathclyde; secondly, there was an acceptance of SRC's applications for funds to employ a housing worker in Strathclyde. This was vital since according to Lynne Barty it would ease the burden on SRC's case work to some extent, although it will not solve the problem of initial temporary housing. Chairperson Barty explained

> The long term aim of the Scottish Refugee Council is to establish a refugee flat, a safe haven for incoming asylum seekers, based in Glasgow, where new arrivals would be accommodated in the short term until more suitable permanent housing could be arranged.[55]

The SRC has put a lot of energy and effort in providing help in a variety of cases and situation. The Refugee Support Worker Danusia Zaremba[56] said the case worker load consisted of: asylum applications and subsequent Home Office questionnaire completion; extension of exceptional leave to remain; immigration; immigration and nationality enquiries; travel documents and passport enquiries; UKIAS referrals; and temporary/ permanent housing and other type of cases.

The need for a recognised housing policy has been of the utmost importance to SRC, and this has been recognised with partial funding being granted for a specialist housing worker.

"Long term development depends on practical and financial support," and if one looks at the number of cases dealt with by SRC (e.g. over the past year) it cannot be granted high enough praise. The SRC, in the past year dealt with an average of 3 new clients per week who required ongoing support.[57]

One disturbing aspect outlined by the SRC's 1990-91 report[58] was the lack of knowledge other organisations and law firms have of the refugee situation. This point was touched on by Danusia Zaremba,[59] refugee support worker, who made the point that people should be trained to help asylum seekers as there is a lack of knowledge i.e. it has been recognised that a deficiency exists within the legal service to cater for refugee representation. To work towards this Danusia Zaremba points out that there will soon be the first specialist seminar in Scotland, aimed towards training and advising those participants interested in representation work for refugees. In this respect the Refugee Council at least has shown that there may be light at the end of the tunnel by giving hope to refugees.

Overall the SRC deserves much commendation for the great support and aid it has provided to refugees and the direct way it has gone about in attempting to fulfil its objectives. It has to be remembered that the SRC is involved in a difficult and sensitive area since the refugee question is always a controversial one in the overall immigration debate and political refugees need a fair hearing or fair treatment especially since in the case of genuine refugees a negative decision in their case can mean a threat to their life if deported. Effective campaigning on their behalf by the SRC is crucial.

The UKIAS and Developments in Immigration 1982-1991

Now we come to the single most important organisation for helping those seeking help and advice on immigration matters - The Immigration Advisory Service (IAS).

The work of the IAS is carried out by the head office in London and by various regional offices throughout the country. The Immigration Appeals Tribunal of the IAS is located in Central London (in addition the IAS did have a Refugee Unit located in Central London (but this was abolished). Although this study is concerned with the issue of immigration in Scotland (more precisely Glasgow) we will be looking at developments regarding the IAS in general as well as the work of the IAS Scottish Office.

Throughout the 1980s the IAS constantly voiced its concern over various developments on the immigration front. One of these concerns was the fall in the number of individuals accepted for settlement in the UK from the Indian sub-continent,[60] which was linked in many ways to the generally restrictive immigration policy of the British government.

The entry certificate system was at the centre of IAS concerns throughout the 1980s.[61] The effective working of the system according to the IAS was deliberately hampered by the government with those applying for such certificates being "....subjected to long delays at almost every point in the system...".[62]

The operation of the entry clearance system in a negative fashion by British Missions in the Indian sub-continent was a major worry to the IAS

75

and it contributed greatly to the fall in the number of persons admitted from the Indian sub-continent.

Overall, according to the IAS, government immigration policy was discriminatory and unjust to those entitled to enter Britain. The government was preoccupied with preventing those not entitled to enter even if this led to genuine cases being turned away. In other words

> ... controls which are designed to exclude those not entitled to come in are being administered in such a way as to exclude a number of people who are entitled to enter the United Kingdom..[63]

In March 1983 the IAS submitted to the Race Relations and Immigration Sub-Committee of the Home Affairs Committee of the House of Commons (SCORRI) its memorandum of evidence into an inquiry carried out by the Sub - Committee of the Home Affairs Committee of the Home Office.[64] This inquiry was prompted by the IAS belief that some aspects of established British Immigration legislation required modification in order to ensure, in particular, that individuals did not suffer any discrimination in the implementation of government policies by the Immigration and Nationality Department (IND). At the heart of UKIAS evidence was its argument that Britain's immigration policies were essentially restrictive not only in the 1980's but also in the past and that

> ..a fair balance has not in fact been struck by the IND in the way it implements government policy, and that there is too much emphasis on controlling evasion and not enough on the rights of genuine applicants......[65]

In addition

> ...at the present time official attitudes within the service towards the implementation of government policy appear in some respects to have gone beyond what is required by the Acts and the Rules, so that quite a significant additional brake is being applied to legitimate immigration flows ....[66]

Naturally, the IAS as an organisation established for the purpose of lending advice and a sympathetic ear to individuals seeking immigration and to represent the interests of individuals, was keen to put forward the most effective case on behalf of its present and future clients. The IAS in effect was therefore representing those who had to go through the immigration procedures. It was therefore keen to ensure that such procedures were as fair as possible.

It is hardly surprising therefore that the IAS submitted in 1983 a rather comprehensive report containing its evidence on the work of the IND.[67] This report covered every aspect of the major mechanisms or procedures deployed under the immigration system. Among some of the major concerns the IAS pin-pointed in its evidence were the following:

- Unfair and insensitive application of the so called 'primary purpose' rules which state that the man must satisfy the Entry Clearance Officer that the primary purpose of the marriage is not to obtain admission to the UK;
- the Immigration System is more concerned with catching bogus applicants at the expense of processing quickly and fairly people who have a genuine case of entry;
- the employment in the immigration department of 'insensitive' personnel who lacked sensitivity in their approach with clients;
- the need for interviews to be more of an 'informal friendly meeting' rather than an interrogation;
- the need for more funding for an important organisation like the IAS so that it can provide an adequate service.

These are just some of the many concerns expressed by the IAS. Although the organisation argued that it was not attempting to subject government policies to examination, its evidence nevertheless represents a thorough criticism of the work of the IND and offers many recommendations for improvement.

In June 1985 the IAS submitted evidence to SCORRI as part of its the inquiry into Immigration from the Indian sub-continent.[68] In connection with this inquiry the IAS's major concern centred chiefly on

...increasing evidence that the entry clearance system is being operated in a negative fashion by British Missions in the ISC (Indian Sub-continent).[69]

The IAS claimed that the negative attitude adopted by Entry Clearance Officers suggests an assumption that each application is necessarily a bogus one.

The IAS also showed its value as an advisory organisation for immigrants by its thorough scrutiny of yet another aspect of the British Immigration System, the entry clearance system. The IAS was offering again its own conclusions and recommendations.

The Entry Clearance System was once at the centre of controversy in 1986.[70] In response to the report published by the House of Commons Home Affairs Committee on Immigration from the Indian sub-continent, an IAS press statement[71] welcomed the Committee's recommendation regarding

... delays and waiting times, and the need for an effective procedure for investigating complaints against Entry Clearance Officers (ECO).

The report also mentioned that the

... ECO's interview notes should be attached...to the explanatory statements prepared by the Home Office for appeal hearings ...[72]

The IAS felt that the House of Commons Home Affairs Committee did not follow through in its recommendations and the criticisms it makes of the manner in which ECO's conduct interviews. The survey results on people from the Indian sub-continent in chapter 4 show the length of time waited for a visa, and the attitude of entry clearance officers was disliked.[73] The response of the Home Office to the complaints regarding the waiting time to attain a visa is looked at in chapter six.

Analysis of IAS Work

A look at any IAS annual report will reveal that in keeping with its functions, the organisation carries out work such as: giving advice; making written representations on behalf of clients to the Home Office; and most importantly presenting appeals on behalf of those turned down at the immigration appeals court.

As Table 3.1 shows the IAS offered advice to a total of over 60,000 individuals in 1982-1983. This figure had risen to over 70,000 by 1987-1988. The number of individuals receiving IAS advice has increased annually since 1983-1984. According to the IAS

> ...there seems little doubt that the increasingly complex nature of immigration law and rules...has been responsible for this upsurge in advice requests.[74]

Table 3.1 Annual IAS Advice to Individuals

Year	Advice
1981-1982	47,361
1982-1983	61,721
1983-1984	49,141
1984-1985	51,146
1985-1986	61,179
1986-1987	63,433
1987-1988	72,404

Source: *IAS annual reports* 1981 through to 1988

It is the function of the IAS to make written representations to the Home Office on behalf of the clients. When we look at total representations made to the Home Office by the IAS we can see that the success rate in terms of immigration being allowed has been high as well as markedly consistent throughout the 1980s. Table 3.2 shows that the number of cases in which immigration was allowed, as a result of written representation to the Home Office, was over 70% (except for 1985-86). Throughout the early and mid 1980s, unlike the case of the Scottish Office where the number of cases pending rose dramatically during the mid 1980s,[75] the number of cases pending in the area of representations for the IAS in general fluctuated,[76] and when they rose they increased by a much lower amount than was the case with the Scottish Office. Only in 1986-87 did the number of cases pending rise by a substantial 37%.

Table 3.2 Total Representations to the Home Office: Immigration Allowed or Rejected on the Basis of these Representations

	Total Representation	Immigration Allowed	Immigration Rejected	Success Rate
1981-1982	1563	1116	447	71
1982-1983	1979	1449	530	73
1983-1984	2357	1764	593	74
1984-1985	1762	1240	522	70
1985-1986	2460	1672	788	67
1986-1987	2655	2037	628	76

Source: IAS annual reports various years
* Success rate has been derived from figures in the other columns.

Presentation of Appeals against rejection forms a second important part of the work carried out by the IAS and in this respect the success rate for the organisation has been rather poor (see Table 3.3). From the early 1980s up to the end of the eighties the success rate was less than 40%. Although the figure of 39% for 1988-89 was much higher in comparison to 1981-82, it was still below 50%.

Table 3.3 IAS Appeals before Adjudicators 1981 - 1990*

	Total Appeals[a]	Total Allowed	Total Dismissed	Success Rate (%)[b]
1981-1982	3118	788	2330	25
1982-1983	2670	772	1898	29
1983-1984	2624	914	1710	34
1984-1985	1360	519	841	38
1985-1986	2041	726	1315	35
1986-1987	2062	725	1337	35
1987-1988	1897	646	1251	34
1988-1989	1983	784	1199	39
1989-1990	3009	1166	1843	39

Source: *IAS annual reports*, various years

[a] The total appeals made does not include appeals withdrawn, transferred, or still pending. This therefore allows a more accurate analysis of the success rate by taking into account only the total number of appeals on which a decision was made.
[b] Success rate has been derived from figures in the other columns.

While the workload of the IAS has greatly increased over the years the government grant which the organisation receives - and which forms the core of the source of income for the IAS - has actually decreased during the 1980s (see Table 3.4). Indeed in 1982-83 and 1983-84 the grant from the government accounted for 90% of the total income of IAS. However, by 1987-88 the government grant made up only 80% of IAS income (see Table 3.4).

Table 3.4   % of Total UKIAS Income Accounted for by Government Grant 1982 - 1991

Year	%
1982-83	90
1983-84	90
1984-85	88
1985-86	89
1986-87	87
1987-88	80
1988-89	81
1989-90	81
1990-91	82

Source: Derived from figures in various *UKIAS annual reports*

In view of the government's tough stance on immigration it would have been reasonable to expect the government to provide a much larger share of IAS income over the years in order to help more people or compensate those who had suffered as a result of its harsh policies. Unfortunately this was not so and the government grant continued to make up less than 90% of IAS income even well into the 1990s.

The IAS Scottish Office

The Glasgow Office of the Immigration Advisory Service (although just one of various regional offices in Britain) is an important one not least because it is the only IAS office in Scotland. Throughout the 1980s it has carried out a large volume of work, and in 1983-84 it was reported that it "represents in most appeal cases heard in Scotland".[77] In 1984-85, the IAS Scottish Office complained that the workload was too high considering the level of staff they had at their disposable. This in fact had led to "queries from the Chief Adjudicator regarding the unusual delays in the hearing of appeals in Scotland..."[78] In 1986 the IAS Scottish Office was reported to have handled 90% of the appeals caseload in Scotland and had a very high success rate.[79] However delays in the hearing of appeals was still causing concern and the IAS Scottish Office attributed this to the "pressure of work on the single counsellor ...".

1986 and 1987 were eventful years to say the least for the IAS Scottish Office. For a start it had no senior counsellor in place from February 1987 to June 1987.[80] The situation regarding delays in appeals waiting to be heard had not improved from previous years and the overall situation did not look optimistic for the future.[81] This pessimistic outlook was justified in the 1987-88 IAS Annual Report which reported a further increase in the volume of work.[82] However, the post of senior counsellor was filled on June 3rd 1987.[83]

The late 1980s confronted the Scottish Office of the IAS with severe problems because the demand for its services had continued to increase. The office was said to be seriously understaffed in 1989,[84] and the office had received numerous requests to provide 'surgeries' in other parts of Scotland. However, a major plus for the office was that the IAS Refugee Unit sent a counsellor to Scotland roughly every two months.[85] This was of great help to asylum seekers who did not therefore have to travel to London to seek advice. This arrangement of a counsellor being sent to Scotland to help asylum seekers continued into the start of the 1990s but pressure to provide surgeries outside Glasgow still remained unrealised because of the shortage of staff.

Nevertheless, it was reported in 1991 that "there will be a surgery once a week in Edinburgh on a six month trial basis.."[86] to satisfy requests. Along with an increase in the number of hearings, in 1991 three new part-time adjudicators were appointed,[87] raising hopes that such developments will help to improve the situation regarding the backlog of appeals.

It has been seen that the IAS Scottish Office has had to deal with a considerable amount of work despite the fact that it has encountered many problems, such as the pressure of work on its staff, and inadequate staffing levels at times throughout the 1980s. It has to be emphasised that the problems associated with the Scottish branch of IAS have been made through no fault of the IAS itself.

If we were to evaluate the success of the IAS Scottish Office in the period beginning from the 1980s through to the end of the 1980s we can see from the evidence that in terms of total representations made by the IAS Scottish Office to the Home Office success was very high (see Table 3.5). The success rate was over 70% throughout this period (in terms of immigration being allowed).

Table 3.5 IAS Scottish Office - Total Representations to the Home Office - Immigration Allowed or Rejected on the Basis of these Representations, 1981 - 1987

	Total Representation	Immigration Allowed	Immigration Rejected	Success Rate (%)
1981-1982	81	65	16	80
1982-1983	136	108	28	79
1983-1984	93	80	13	86
1984-1985	58	46	12	79
1985-1986	70	54	16	77
1986-1987	78	56	12	71

Source: *Annual reports*, various years
* Success rate has been derived from figures in the other columns.

Despite this high success rate regarding representations, one worrying aspect for the IAS was the dramatic increase in the mid-1980s in the number of cases pending.[88] In 1982-83 there were only 20 cases where immigration was still pending as a result of representation made to the Home Office. However by 1984-85 this number had risen to 96.

If we look at the area of appeals, the Scottish Office of the organisation had relatively little success. From 1981 through to 1989 the success rate for total appeals made was below 40% (see Table 3.6). Indeed with the exception of 1985-86 and 1987-88 the success rate was only 30% or less. However, the adjudicators at appellate authorities believe that each case is dealt with fairly and within the immigration rules. Their views on immigration rules and procedures are examined later.[89]

Table 3.6 IAS Scottish Office: Appeals before Adjudicators, 1981 - 1989

	Total Appeals	Total Allowed	Total Dismissed	Success Rate (%)*
1981-1982	47	10	37	21
1982-1983	65	11	54	16
1983-1984	57	17	40	30
1984-1985	31	7	24	22
1985-1986	67	24	43	36
1986-1987	54	12	42	22
1987-1988	51	19	32	37
1988-1989	55	16	39	29

Source IAS Annual reports, various years
* Success rate has been derived from figures in the other columns.

Conclusions

The work of the organisations that we have looked at in Glasgow indicates that people from the Indian sub-continent, and immigrants from other parts of the world, still experience difficulties with the immigration process. It can be said that the organisations together form an important channel for processing the immigration issue in Scotland. Through their active work the organisations have in fact provided a means by which the issue of immigration in Scotland has been allowed to filter through to Westminster and Whitehall. In other words the organisations have made immigration in Scotland part of the political debate by giving it much publicity. Interestingly enough as we shall see in chapter 7 Scottish Conservative

MPs said they were very rarely contacted by organisations such as the IAS and believed the immigration laws and procedures were fair,[90] while the Labour MPs such as Maria Fyfe and George Galloway were frequently in contact with the IAS and strongly criticised aspects of the immigration regime, in particular the primary purpose rule.[91] Obviously the organisations would contact MPs that were sympathetic to their pleas and critical of immigration practice.

The evidence in this chapter has also revealed how many of the organisations viewed the harsh immigration legislation adopted by the British government such as the 1981 British Nationality Act and 1988 Immigration Act, and virginity tests, as seen in detail in the previous chapter,[92] and the action that they took to demonstrate their opposition to such legislation. In view of this, the importance of organisations such as the IAS and the SRC to help immigrants increased. This increase in the workload of the organisations put added pressure on their ability to reach successful outcomes.

The IAS (formerly known as UKIAS) provides a cheap but very effective service. It meets an important need because there is no legal aid available for immigrants. Not only does it provide advice to thousands of individuals each year, it also makes written representations to the Home Office, as well as carrying out the important task of presenting appeals. Therefore a lot of individuals put their faith in the IAS to solve their difficulties. Statistics have shown that the Scottish Office branch of the IAS has had mixed success. It has been very successful in the area of representations made to the Home Office but enjoyed less success in the field of appeals. Nevertheless, the organisations importance to the cause of immigration cannot be underestimated.

The Strathclyde Community Relations Council up to 1985 did important work in the area of criticising and campaigning against harsh government policies on immigration. The help provided by SCRC was acknowledged during the 1980s by individuals who wrote to the organisation thanking it for its support. The SCRC did well in bringing out immigration related issues.

The Scottish Asian Action Committee,[93] provided useful general help on ethnic minority issues, one of those being immigration. Their framework showed that they were eager to combat what they viewed as racist legislation in any form introduced by the Government.

The Scottish Refugee Council for its part provided major support to refugees and asylum seekers, even helping in accommodation and housing and providing advice to the legal profession on the area. The Strathclyde Interpreting Service took on the responsibility of helping individuals in the ethnic minority community whose lack of English was posing problems.

Has there been a need for such organisations in Scotland? The answer is overwhelmingly yes, simply because there is a demand for their services. In addition to the general racism suffered by ethnic minorities in Scotland, the lives of ethnic minorities have been adversely affected by government policies throughout the 1970s as well as 1980s and 1990s.[94] Studies[95] show that ethnic minorities suffered from immigration problems which made the need for sympathetic organisations imperative. The Strathclyde Community Relations Council (SCRC) was very active in immigration during the 1970s. At that time the Community Relations Officer, Mr Akram found in a study *Firm but Unfair? Immigration Control in the Indian sub-continent*, that the attitude and practice of immigration officials was discriminatory.[96] The SCRC reports provided case studies of how families in Scotland were treated. The 1979 report gave an idea of how deplorable some of the questions were that were asked by Entry Clearance Officers during the immigration procedure. This view was also supported by the Scottish Labour MPs such as Michael Martin in regard to the type of questions asked.[97]

Further proof that immigration has been a problem for Asians in Scotland is provided by the fact that many opposition MPs have been sympathetic to organisations such as IAS and SAAC in Scotland.[98] They have taken part in the campaigns against various aspects of government immigration legislation and have taken up the cause of immigrants in Parliament. The support of MPs has been vital to the organisations in their quest to promote their cause at the highest political channels, since the organisations themselves have no effective political power or leverage despite the fact that many of them enjoy relative independence or autonomy.

It is fair to end by saying that on the whole the five major organisations examined represented quite effectively immigrant interests during a period of controversial Conservative immigration policies which were generally perceived to have discriminated against individuals seeking immigration. As indicated in the previous chapter the passage of Conservative immigration laws and rules led to claims of discrimination. It is hardly surprising therefore that the organisations looked at in this chapter were more active and more in demand during the period concerned. This chapter has demonstrated the way in which the organisations had to take more action on behalf of their users. Remarks made by the organisations as reported in this chapter bear unequivocal testimony to the fact that Conservative immigration policies were discriminatory and unfair, and the fact that a majority of the organisations clients tended to be from the Indian sub-continent is further evidence that the impact on this group was particularly severe.

Notes

1. For a full list of such organisations see: *A Directory of Black and Ethnic Minority Organisations in Glasgow and Strathclyde*, Town Clerks Office, Glasgow City Council, 1994; See also *Ethnic Minorities Directory* (Hasib Publications 1993), pp. 297-289.
2. See *chapter 4*.
3. See *Immigration Act 1971*.
4. *Interview* with Mr Nabi, Senior Counsellor, Immigration Advisory Service, Glasgow office, May 1994.
5. *Ibid*, Dr. Singh, Interpreter, Strathclyde Interpreting Service, July 1994.
6. *Ibid*
7. *Race Relations Act 1968*
8. After 1983 the Community Relations Council no longer dealt with immigration matters. Any immigration cases arising after 1983 were passed on to the Immigration Advisory Service.
9. See *Annual Report, Strathclyde Community Relations Council*, 1981, p. 20.
10. *Interview* with officer, Strathclyde Community Relations Council, November 1994.
11 *Ibid* with Stan Crook, Case worker, Scottish Refugee Council, Glasgow office, June 1994.

12.   *Ibid.*
13.   *Ibid*
14.   Amended Constitution, Scottish Asian Action Committee, section 3.0.
15.   See *ibid* section 4.6.
16.   *Interview* with Stan Crook, Case worker, Scottish Refugee Council, June 1994.
17.   *Ibid* with Dr Singh, July 1994.
18.   Amended Constitution, Scottish Asian Action Committee, section 1 3.
19.   *Interview* with Mr Nabi, Senior Councillor, Immigration Advisory Service, Glasgow Office, May 1994.
20.   See *Race Relations Act 1968.*
21.   See for example *Strathclyde Community Relations Council Annual Reports* for 1981 and 1983.
22.   *Ibid*, Annual Report 1981, p. 3.
23.   *Ibid*, p. 6.
24.   *Ibid.*
25.   *Ibid*, 1983, p. 3.
26.   *Ibid*
27.   *Ibid*, 1988.
28.   *Ibid*, pp. 22-24.
29.   *Ibid*, pp. 22-24.
30.   *Ibid*, p. 22.
31.   *Ibid.*
32.   *Ibid*, pp. 22-24.
33.   See for example *ibid* 1983, p 4.
34.   See *SAAC Annual Report, 1988-1989*, p. 10.
35.   See *ibid*, 1984, p. 10.
36.   *Ibid*, 1987-88, p. 8.
37.   *Ibid*, 1994, p. 11.
38.   *Ibid*, 1986-1987, p. 10.
39.   *Ibid.*
40   *Ibid*, 1988-1989, p. 14.
41.   *Ibid*, p. 3.
42.   See *ibid*, pp. 3-4.
43.   *Ibid*, p 4.
44.   *Immigration Act 1988.*
45.   *Scottish Asian Action Committee, Annual Report, 1988-1989*, p. 15.
46.   See *ibid*, 1987-1988.
47.   See *ibid*, p. 4.
48.   See *ibid*, p. 5.
49.   See *ibid*, p. 5.
50.   See *ibid*, p. 6.
51.   See *ibid*, p. 8.
52.   See *chapter 4.*

53   *Interview* with Stan Crook, Caseworker, Scottish Refugee Council, June 1994.

54.   *Scottish Refugee Council, Annual Report 1990-91*

55.   Chairperson, Lynne Barty, Scottish Refugee Council.

56.   *Interview* with Danusia Zaremba, Refugee Support Worker, Scottish Refugee Council, Glasgow Office, August 1994.

57.   *Ibid.*

58.   See *Scottish Refugee Council, Annual Report 1990-1991*, p. 7.

59.   *Interview* with Danusia Zaremba, Refugee Support Worker, Scottish Refugee Council, August 1994.

60.   This concern was expressed by the Immigration Advisory Service in its *annual reports* throughout the 1980s. See for example the following reports: 1983-1984, p.3; 1984-1985, p. 3 and 1985-86, p. 5.

61.   See *IAS Annual Reports 1983-1984, 1984-1985, 1985-1986*; See also: *Memorandum of Evidence*. Submitted to the Race Relations and Immigration Sub - Committee of the Home Affairs Committee by UKIAS in connection with their inquiry into immigration from the Indian Sub-continent, June 1985; and memorandum on the work of the Immigration and Nationality Department to SCORRI by UKIAS, March 1985.

62.   *IAS Annual Report 1982-1983*, p. 5.

63.   *Ibid*, p. 7.

64.   *Memorandum of Evidence on the work of the Immigration and Nationality Department.* Submitted to the Race Relations and Immigration Sub-Committee of the Home Affairs Committee of the House of Commons by UKIAS, March 1985.

65.   *Ibid*, p. 1.

66.   *Ibid*, p. 2.

67.   *Ibid.*

68.   *Memorandum of Evidence submitted to the Race Relations and Immigration Sub-Committee of the Home Affairs Committee* by UKIAS in connection with their inquiry into immigration from the Indian sub-continent, June 1985.

69.   *Ibid*, p. 1.

70.   See *IAS Annual Report 1985-1986*, p. 5.

71.   UKIAS, *Press Statement*, 22 May 1986.

72.   *Ibid*

73.   See *chapter 4*

74.   *UKIAS Annual Report, 1982-1983*, p. 12.

75.   See *IAS Annual Reports, 1980-1988*

76.   See *Ibid*

77   *Ibid*, 1983-1984, p. 9.

78.   *Ibid*, 1984-1985, p. 13.

79.   *Ibid*,1983-1984, p. 13.

80.   See *ibid*, 1986-87, p. 18.

81   See *ibid*

82.   See *ibid*, 1987-1988, p 18.

83.   See *ibid.*
84.   See *ibid*, 1988-1989, p. 4.
85.   See *ibid.*
86.   *Ibid*, 1990-91, p. 23.
87.   *Ibid.*
88.   See *IAS Annual Reports*, 1981 through to 1988.
89.   See *chapter 6*
90.   See *chapter 7.*
91.   Interview with MP George Galloway (Hillhead), 19 April 1996 and communication with Labour MP Maria Fyfe (Maryhill), 1 April 1996. Also see *chapter 7.*
92.   See *chapter 2*
93.   When any form of contact was made with SAAC, they showed very little interest and were arrogant.
94.   See *chapter 2.*
95.   See for example: *Firm but Unfair? Immigration Control in the Indian sub-continent*, a preliminary report by Mohammed Akram and Jan Elliot, The Runnymede Trust, August 1976; *Summary of Appeal Dismissed· The Final Report of the Investigation into Immigration Control Procedures in the Indian Sub-continent*, Research by Mohammed Akram and Jan Elliot, Runnymede Trust; See also: The Runnymede Trust Submission to the Parliamentary Select Committee on Race Relations and Immigration: Immigration Inquiry regarding the assumptions by the government about potential immigration and matters related. The Runnymede Trust, 27 June 1977.
96.   See *ibid.*
97.   *Interview* with Labour MP Michael Martin (Springburn), April 1996 and see also *chapter 5.*
98.   See for example various *Annual Reports* of the Scottish Asian Action Committee from 1985 to 1990.

4 Survey Analysis: Impact of Immigration Laws and Rules on Indian Sub-Continent Nationals in Glasgow

Introduction

This chapter focuses on two central themes of this book: 1. How the particular laws and rules analysed in chapter two and immigration policies in general were perceived by the very people who were likely to be affected by the immigration control regime, and on whose behalf the organisational network examined in the previous chapter lobbied and criticised the government; 2. How the rules and procedures of the immigration regime influenced the pattern of immigration into Glasgow. The objectives of this chapter are to show how immigration procedures are perceived by people from the Indian sub-continent, to illustrate how they assess the immigration control regime, and to assess the impact of particular rules and procedures. The findings are essentially the perceptions and reflections that immigrants have of the immigration process.

In order to achieve these objectives a survey was conducted in the Pollokshields and Hillhead areas of Glasgow.[1] I chose the areas of Pollokshields and Hillhead because people from the Indian sub-continent tend to be more concentrated in these areas of Glasgow. For interest, Pollokshields has 673 residents from the Indian sub-continent. Of these 66 are of Indian origin, 595 of Pakistani origin and 12 Bangladeshi. One can see that the largest ethnic concentration is overwhelmingly Pakistani.[2] The Hillhead area has 645 residents from the Indian sub-continent. The largest ethnic group in the Hillhead area is Indian (385) followed by 239 who are of Pakistani origin and 21 of Bangladeshi origin.[3] Thus Pakistanis and Indians are predominant while there are very few from Bangladesh.

To conduct the survey, Indian sub-continent names were selected from the electoral register[4] covering Hillhead and Pollokshields. These areas have the highest concentration of immigrants from the Indian sub-continent within the city of Glasgow. The relevant names were then checked against the telephone directory so that contact could be made. Hence the survey conducted was a telephone survey.[5] Prior to interviewing, respondents were sent a letter informing them about the research. This letter was sent in four different languages: English and the three most common languages of the Indian sub-continent - Urdu, Punjabi, and Hindi. The letter received by respondents outlined briefly the objectives of the research, asking for their co-operation. The actual questionnaire compiled for the survey can be found in the Appendix to this chapter.

The response rate was high, helped by the fact that I am tri-lingual. I managed to persuade a lot of people about the benefits of taking part in the survey. If contact could not be made during the day I phoned them in the evening. The advantages of using the telephone method were that it was more productive than carrying out a door to door survey. People can get very nervous over a sensitive area such as immigration and it was therefore safer to make contact over the phone.

The final sample comprised 137 people from Pollokshields and 88 from Hillhead making a total of 225. All the Pollokshields respondents had direct experience of immigration procedures, or knew a family member who had had such experience. Of the 88 people who were interviewed from Hillhead 64 claimed some experience of or awareness of immigration procedures. That gave a sample of 201 people with actual experience, directly or indirectly, of immigration procedures. I proceeded to ask them questions from my questionnaire.

In section A of the questionnaire the questions asked: provide knowledge of the age group of the interviewees and from which country of the Indian sub-continent they came from; the period in which immigrants entered Britain, which does show the possible relaxation or tightening of the immigration laws at the time; and whether the person or a relative had been subjected to immigration procedures.

Section B looks at which country of the Indian sub-continent the sponsors mainly originated from, the occupation of the sponsor and the immigrant seeking entry (person from abroad). It became clear that professional people experienced fewer problems when applying for an entry visa. The ages of the people coming from abroad showed which age groups tended to come to the UK for marriage or holiday. The age profile of the sample will show whether younger men or women were more keen to enter the UK than older people. The analysis will uncover whether an application was made for a temporary stay such as a holiday or for permanent stay leading to British citizenship. The question of when the visa was applied for and when it was granted reveals the length of time people had to wait for a decision. The survey also reveals if an application was made through a solicitor or another organisation, since the intense involvement of the Immigration Advisory Service (IAS) in the immigration arena has already been discussed.[6] The questionnaire also asked whether the applicants understood the application form since English was for many, a secondary language, and in many cases applicants were unaware that the application form was available in an ethnic language. The questionnaire also reveals whether the entry clearance officer was seen to be fair in his or her conduct. It also shows what people thought the main reasons were for refusal of a visa and from which organisation help was sought; the number of people appealing; and the reasons of those who did not bother to appeal.

Section C of the questionnaire looks at how all those interviewed, including those with no form of immigration experience at all, viewed immigration procedures whether they saw it as fair or racist. It also reveals the range of views interviewees developed about immigration procedures. The survey shows whether those sampled knew of the legislation which was determining the fate of their application. The final question showed which newspaper was most commonly read and if it covered immigration issues.

For the purpose of convenience the chapter is divided into sections. Section one provides detailed analysis of responses to the survey questions. Section two of this chapter investigates in more detail one of the central findings, i.e. the general impression that males from the Indian sub-continent experience greater problems gaining entry into the UK compared to females. Section 3 of this chapter looks in more depth at the nature of the link between an applicant having a good occupation abroad and the degree of difficulty experienced when applying for a visa. In other words sections two and three tackle issues which have proved particularly controversial in the whole debate surrounding immigration.

Survey Analysis

Question 5 in section A of the questionnaire, asked whether "you or anyone in your family have had experience of immigration procedures?" The total number of people interviewed were 225 i.e. 137 from Pollokshields and 88 from Hillhead. Every individual approached in Pollokshields acknowledged experience, direct or indirect, of the immigration regime. In Hillhead 73% of those approached claimed some experience of immigration procedures. Taking both areas together, 201 interviewees (89 percent of the combined sample) had some experience of immigration procedures. The 201 interviews generated information about both sponsors and those sponsored; the sample generated information about 201 individuals seeking to enter Britain and about 201 sponsors.

What is your Country of Birth?

Table 4.1 Country of Birth of Interviewees

Country of Birth	Number	Per Cent (%)	
Scotland	57	United Kingdom	28
England	6	Indian Sub-Continent	70
Pakistan	109	Africa	2
India	43		
Bangladesh	5		
Kenya	4		
South Africa	1		
Total	225		

In this survey a high proportion (70%) of those interviewed were born in the Indian sub-continent (see Table 4.1), i.e. they are themselves immigrants. This is particularly appropriate because this study is interested in the experience of immigration procedures of Asians from the Indian sub-continent. Those born in the United Kingdom are also useful for analysis because many have had an indirect experience of immigration procedures as sponsors when trying to bring over a partner or family member.

How Long Resident in the UK?

Those interviewed entered Britain over almost half a century from the 1950s to the 1990s. As shown in Table 4.2 more immigrants entered Britain in the 1960s and 1970s than during the 1950s or the 1980s onwards. The increase in the 1960s and 1970s may be accounted for by economic reasons.[7] It was encouraged by the post war reconstruction of the British economy which stimulated a need for cheap labour which the New Commonwealth immigrants provided[8] under the terms of the 1948 British Nationality Act. The decline in the 1980s followed the establishment of the immigration regime described in chapter 2.

Table 4.2 Entry into Britain by Decade*

Number of People Entering Britain	Decade of Entry	%
11	1950s	7
49	1960s	30
59	1970s	36
29	1980s	18
14	1990s	9
Total 162		

*This table excludes those interviewees born in the UK.

Have you or your Family been Subjected to Immigration Procedures?

Overall 100% of people interviewed from the Pollokshields area acknowledged an immigration experience, i.e. either they had entered Britain as immigrants or they had tried to sponsor a person wanting to enter Britain; 73% of the people interviewed in Hillhead had an immigration experience.

Who was the Sponsor?

Of the people interviewed 81 had sponsored or were sponsoring spouses or spouses-to-be i.e. women seeking to join husbands or fiancés and men seeking to join wives or fiancées. 118 individuals interviewed had been sponsored by other family members, e.g. by father, mother, cousins and so on. The remaining two were political asylum seekers.

In other words over half the interviewees had themselves sponsored a spouse or spouse-to-be rather than relying on others for sponsorship. Many of those to whom I spoke indicated that they felt the process would be quicker and more successful if no third party was involved. The survey findings suggest that this is not in fact the case. Whether you sponsor yourself or are sponsored by someone else has no bearing on the outcome. If anything, sponsoring yourself may make entry more difficult unless you can convince the authorities that you have the required financial means to support your stay in Britain.[9]

What is your Country of Birth?

All those who sponsored someone seeking entry either for temporary stay or for permanent settlement with a view to achieving citizenship were British Nationals (British Citizens either by birth or naturalisation), although their country of origin or birth varied along the following lines, as illustrated in Table 4.3.

Table 4.3 Country of Birth of Sponsor

Country of Birth	Number of People	% Born in:	
Pakistan	90	UK	34
Scotland	61	Indian Sub-Continent	64
India	36	Africa	1
England	7		
Bangladesh	3		
Kenya	1		
South Africa	1		
Political Asylum Seekers*	2		
Total	201		

*The two political asylum seekers were from Pakistan.

According to these figures a considerable number, 64%, of those who acted as sponsors for individuals in the Indian sub-continent had themselves been born in that part of the world.

What was the Occupation of the Sponsor and the Person from Abroad?

The purpose of this question is to investigate whether there is a link between occupation and therefore status of either the sponsor or the would be immigrant and the outcome of the application to come to Britain (there is more detailed analysis of this in section 3). The occupation of those who had acted as sponsors varied considerably, although most could be classified according to the model of the class structure developed by Heath, Jowell, and Curtice, as illustrated in Table 4.4 below.[10]

Table 4.4 Occupation of Sponsor at the Time of Application[a]

Occupation of the Sponsor at the Time of Application	Number of People	%
Petty Bourgeoisie	112	56
Salariat/Intelligentsia	26	13
Routine Office Worker	25	12
Routine Manual Worker	14	7
Middle Class Employee	12	6
Student	5	2
Retired	3	1
Managerialism	1	0
Unemployed	1	0
TOTAL	201[b]	-

[a]See glossary and section 3 for examples of jobs which fall into the above occupational categories. [b] This includes two asylum seekers.

Sponsors are effectively individuals living in Britain many of whom had themselves successfully come through the immigration process. They are British citizens either by birth or naturalisation. The striking feature of the sponsors in class terms was the large proportion of individuals from the 'petty bourgeoisie'. The 'petty bourgeoisie' consists of self-employed business people. In sharp contrast only about 8% of the British electorate in the 1980s belonged to the 'petty bourgeoisie'. Another quarter of the sponsors can be located in two middle class categories - salariat and routine office worker.

The occupation of individuals seeking entry to Britain was extremely wide ranging (see Table 4.5). Students topped the list at 42 (over 20% of the applicants), a significant finding because it is particularly difficult for students to satisfy the immigration requirements. Students are unlikely to have a bank balance or an occupation, and consequently might be considered to be coming to Britain to find a job. This would in turn strongly suggest to immigration officers that they should pay special attention to verifying if the person is entering Britain primarily for economic reasons.

Another quarter of applicants represent rural occupations and communities - farmers and farm labourers. Another 20% can be classified as middle class, i.e. mainly salariat and 'petty bourgeoisie'.

Table 4.5 Occupation of Immigrants from Abroad at the Time of Application

Occupation of Immigrants From Abroad at the Time of Application	Number of People Entering	%
Student	42	21
Housewife	24	12
Farmer	18	9
Farm Labourer	32	16
Routine Manual Worker	4	2
Routine Office Worker	3	1
Managerialism	4	2
Salariat/Intelligentsia	20	10
Petty Bourgeoisie	20	10
Retired	16	8
Unemployed	16	8
Political Asylum Seekers	2	1
TOTAL	201	

The 201 people interviewed were asked to tell of only *one* case that came to mind in order to keep the sample simple, therefore in Tables 4.5 and 4.6 the sample is out of 201.

What was the Age of the Person Coming from Abroad?

There is a clear age profile characterising applicants for entry visas. Table 4.6 shows that more than half of those who wished to enter Britain, 56%, were under 30 at the time of application. This was true for both males and females for whom the figures were 54% and 53% respectively. Only 20% of applicants fell into the 30-50 age group. Another 20% were over 50 at the time of application.

More males than females applied to come to Britain. Again this characteristic would probably suggest to British immigration officials that young men were coming to the UK for economic reasons.[11]

Table 4.6 Age and Gender of Immigrants at the Time of Application

Age Group of Immigrant at the Time of Application	Females	%	Male	%	Both	%
20 or Younger	22	28	7	6	29	14
21-24	11	14	26	21	37	18
25-29	11	14	36	30	47	23
30-34	2	3	14	11	16	8
35-39	3	4	7	6	10	5
40-44	1	1	6	5	7	3
45-49	5	6	3	2	8	4
50 or Over	20	25	19	16	39	19
50 or Over Couples	4	5	4	3	8	4
Total	79	(39.3)	122	(60.6)	201	

What was/is the Relationship between the Applicant and you, the Sponsor?

There are basically two different types of applications: those seeking a short stay and those seeking permanent residence in the UK. A large proportion (49%) came as 'visitors' as shown in Appendix, Table 4.21, which indicates a diverse range of applicants. A visitor can be defined as someone who has come to Britain solely for a holiday or to "transact business" such as attend meetings, and is not intending to stay beyond the maximum 6 months granted. The gender breakdown of the visitor category was: 65 males and 34 females i.e. a total percentage of 49. As well as illustrating that visiting is one of the prime reasons why application for entry visas are made, Table 4.21, also shows the diverse categories of entrants such as husbands, parents, wives, and asylum seekers.

Did you Apply for the Person to: a) Stay Permanently b) Visit on Holiday

The difference between those who had applied for someone to stay or come for a holiday was very low. Out of a total of 199 (excluding 2 political asylum seekers) 81 applied to stay (husbands, wives, male fiancé, female fiancées) and 118 (male and female visitors, parents) applied for a holiday. On a holiday visa a person can stay in the UK for up to 6 months.[12] (see Appendix, Table 4.21).

Who did you Apply through?

Most applications (47%) were made through a solicitor (see Appendix, Table 4.22). Most people viewed the solicitor as the most effective and business like channel through which to conduct an application. Almost one-third (29%) preferred to go it alone, processing their application independently. Generally, apart from contacting the IAS (which is an organisation which deals specifically with immigration), individuals did not seek assistance for application from other organisations which could have helped such as the Scottish Asian Action Committee, the Scottish Refugee Council or the Joint Council for the Welfare of Immigrants. The reason why people made an application through a solicitor was because they did not know about the IAS which like the other organisations listed help free of charge, unlike a solicitor who charges money.

What Year (Month) did you Apply for the Visa and when did he/she get it?

One hundred and forty two people out of 201 applications (81 applied for permanent stay; 118 applied for a holiday; and 2 were political asylum seekers) provided by our respondents were allowed to enter i.e. were granted a visa, therefore a success rate of 72%. This is excluding 4 husbands who were still waiting for their appeal date, which would determine whether they will be able to enter the UK. Of the 142 permitted to enter, 107 were granted a visa within less than 2 years of application, 15 were granted a visa within 2 or more years, and 20 were granted a visa after 5 or more years. This excludes 4 husbands waiting on their appeal and 2 political asylum seekers (see Appendix, Table 4.23).

Although 72% is in a sense a high success rate, it does not show the length of time it had taken people to attain the visa or the number of appeals they had to make. Waiting times and the initial rejection before a successful appeal are common grievances noted by sponsors and applicants. The length of waiting time may have a very significant impact on peoples' lives as seen in individual cases[13] and is a common complaint heard by Scottish MPs, and even admitted by the civil servants working in the Immigration and Nationality Department of the Home Office.[14]

When Applying for him/her did you Understand the Rules?

Out of the 201 people interviewed, 141 (70%) said they understood the rules and 60 (30%) did not understand the rules. The 30% who did not understand the rules is more significant than the 70% who did, given that the former figure represents almost a third of all applicants, and that a lack of understanding of the rules can only add to the difficulties of achieving a successful result.

When Applying for him/her did you Understand the Application Forms?

Application forms themselves were clear enough: 190 (95%) people out of 201 understood the form and 11 (5%) did not understand the form. The figures show that a large majority were fully aware of the rules and regulations regarding entry into Britain for their respective applicant. Even more were quite clear about what the application form was asking. Unfortunately, what was not clear from those interviewed or surveyed was whether someone explained the form to them or they discovered and interpreted the rules themselves. Similarly, it is not possible to wholly establish whether the interviewee received help from another person or source when filling the application form. Many were not willing to admit, or were embarrassed to admit whether they indeed had received assistance (especially since many of them had a low standard of English). Nevertheless, the evidence appears to suggest that the relevant regulations were fairly well understood, and the relevant form was reasonably straightforward. The fact that the application form was generally well understood should not be surprising given that application forms are printed in different ethnic languages. However, the fact that some people still could not understand the form is explained by the fact that there are people from the Indian sub-continent who are illiterate and cannot even read Urdu or any other ethnic language.

Do you Feel the Entry Clearance Officer Treated you or your Family Fairly?

Much criticism has been levelled over the years at Entry Clearance Officers (ECOs) and this question analyses the views of the people interviewed who come into contact with such officers. This question might help to establish whether accusations about intimidatory treatment, insulting and embarrassing questions, and subjection to strict questioning by ECOs were widely supported. Complaints on questions about consummating the marriage, trick questions and the attitudes of ECOs were amongst the reasons for discontent.

One hundred and twelve people out of 201 (55.7%) acknowledged that the Entry Clearance Officer treated them well. Eighty-seven (43%) out of 201, asserted that the ECO did not treat them well. Two made no comment as they were political asylum seekers. The result shows that over half were satisfied with their treatment by the ECO; i.e. satisfied in the sense that they believed the ECO treated them fairly. A figure of 44% indicates that there must be some aspect of the ECO's questioning or behaviour which does not please all potential immigrants.

Why do you Think he/she was Refused?

Out of the 97 people denied an entry visa at some stage (i.e. some were at first refused and subsequently granted entry on appeal or re-application) twenty said that the rejection of individuals they had sponsored was due to racism. Thirty-one said it was due to the primary purpose rule. Thirty-nine said it was because officials believed that they might stay permanently. Seven said it was because officials believed the sponsor did not satisfy the requirements, i.e. not having accommodation and occupation in the UK (see Appendix, Table 4.24). Basically 21% claimed racism on the part of the authorities, 32% said primary purpose (marriage to a UK citizen solely to gain entry into Britain), 40% said "might stay permanently" and 7% said a failure to satisfy such requirements as stable finances back home, having accommodation in the UK, and not being a financial drain on British social services such as housing benefit, income support and family credit. As many as 40% claimed that the ECO's belief that the would-be temporary immigrant might stay permanently instead of just visiting was the major cause for refusing entry.

A significant proportion asserted that the most likely reason for refusal was that the immigration officials believed that marriage was being used as an excuse to gain entry into Britain. The 'primary purpose rule' was being implemented. The intense controversy over whether to admit male fiancés and female fiancées centred on the primary purpose rule. This rule has had a massive impact on nationals from the Indian sub-continent because it is part of the culture of that part of the world to have arranged marriages which involves parents who arrange a marriage with a relative. Problems arise when one of the partners is British and wants to bring over their fiancé or fiancée from the sub-continent to Britain.

The fact is that Immigration Officials, in Britain and in overseas posts, frequently believe that due to the arranged nature of the marriage there cannot be any love involved and that the marriage must therefore be one of convenience and a ploy to settle in this country. However this belief will often amount to a misconception and illustrates a lack of understanding of Indian sub-continent cultural practices. It is common nowadays for parents in Asian culture to ask both the male and female if they like each other before marrying them, and they are given an opportunity to meet and get aquainted. Unfortunately the British immigration regime does not make any special allowances in such cases, and immigration officials often believe that if the male and female do not know each other then there is no strong basis for a credible marriage. This often leads to problems and protracted immigration cases (see chapter 5).

Only 21% felt that they had been racially discriminated by being barred entry.

Who did you go to for Help?

Table 4.7 Sources of Help

Sources of Help	No. of People	%
IAS	32	32
No-one	53	54
MP	6	6
SRC	2	2
Other (Solicitor)	6	6
Total	99	

Out of the 99 people experiencing an immigration problem, over half did not bother seeking help because they were basically pessimistic about the immigration procedures (interviewees said all that hassle for a short break in the UK was not worth it). Of those seeking help 32% went to the only organisation which deals solely with immigration - the Immigration and Advisory Service (see Table 4.7). Only 6% bothered going to an MP.

Did you find the Above Sources Helpful?

Forty-two people (i.e. of those who made use of such sources of help) out of 99 found that they did get help from the IAS and MPs. No person said they did not find them helpful. Four people out of 99 were not sure yet (were waiting for the outcome of their case) i.e. 4%. Overall the various channels for help were by and large perceived as effective.

Did you Appeal?

Out of all those refused, i.e. 99 out of 201, only 46% bothered to appeal. Over half i.e. 54% decided against an appeal. It was therefore interesting to find out why they did not bother to appeal.

Why did you not Appeal?

The reasons they gave for not appealing on behalf of someone else varied. Almost a quarter (24%) felt it would be a waste of time because the appeal would be unsuccessful anyway. Another 30% could not be bothered to wait for the outcome, as many had heard about the long delays and the waiting times involved.

If you Appealed, did it Succeed?

Out of those who did appeal 87% were successful. This is a very high success rate until one considers the length of waiting time (four people did not know the outcome of their appeal i.e. were still waiting on a decision). But the interesting point to note here is that many felt that they should not have had to appeal because their application was launched on a sound basis in the first place. In other words they viewed the appeal process as a unnecessary delaying tactic.

General Perceptions

This section involves everyone who was interviewed irrespective of whether they had themselves any first or even second hand experience of immigration procedures.

How Would you Describe Immigration Procedures?

Table 4.8 How Immigration Procedures are Viewed

Views	No. of People*	% of People
Fair	57	25
Unfair (but not racist)	69	31
Racist	73	32
Honest People Suffer Due to Increase in Illegal Attempts to Enter	13	6
Don't Know	13	6
Total	225	

*Out of 225 people interviewed, including 2 political asylum cases.

The answers to this question were pretty evenly spread out between those who felt procedures were fair, unfair or racist (see Table 4.8). However, taken together 63% viewed immigration procedures as either racist or unfair which is significant given that this is precisely one of the central arguments of this study. Interestingly only 6% believed that the government's desire to crack-down on illegal immigrants and those entering under false documents had led to honest people suffering. The actual number of illegal immigrants found by Strathclyde Police in Scotland was 90-100 cases.[15] The number of illegal immigrants detected in the UK from the Indian sub-continent will be examined in chapter 6.[16]

What have you Heard from others About Immigration Procedures?

Only 5% felt they were fair, 36% said unfair, 44% said racism and 13% said they did not know. 1% thought that the increase in frauds meant honest people suffered. While only 1% said that there were too many Asians here already (see Appendix, Table 4.25).

Do you Know Anything About: a) The 1971 Immigration Act b) The 1981 British Nationality Act c) The 1988 Immigration Act?

This question was asked to see if anyone knew about the existence of important immigration legislation passed during the 1970s and 1980s. Only 22 people out of the 225 (10%) surveyed knew about the 1971 Immigration Act. Another 18 (8%) people knew about the 1981 British Nationality Act. While only 10 people (4%) knew about the 1988 Immigration Act. These figures indicate that many knew either nothing about the existence of immigration legislation, or knew nothing about it by name. Earlier evidence suggested they may have known a lot about the various rules which affected them as a result of experience of the application of the rules.

What Newspaper do you Read and does it Cover Immigration?

Table 4.9 below shows the response to the above question.

Table 4.9 Coverage of Immigration by Newspaper

Newspaper	No. of People Who Read the Paper	Cover Immigration: Yes	Cover Immigration %	Cover Immigration: No	Cover Immigration %
Herald	66	53	24	13	6
Jang	49	38	17	11	5
Evening Times	25	1	0	24	11
Daily Record	23	2	1	21	9
Guardian	8	6	3	2	1
London Times	6	5	2	1	0
Sun	6	5	2	1	0
Asian Voice	5	5	2	0	0
Independent	4	4	2	0	0
Daily Telegraph	3	2	1	0	0
Observer	1	1	1	0	0
Cannot Read	4				
Do not Read	25				
Total	225				

Topping the list of English language newspapers were those that were Scottish based: The Herald, Daily Record and Evening Times. Out of all those who read English language papers, 58% read Scottish based ones. The most widely read Asian paper was the Jang, read by 82% of all those who read Asian newspapers (only 60 did so). The Asian Voice which tends to cover immigration related stories quite frequently was read by only 5 out of the 225 interviewed, largely because it has no mass circulation, and is not regarded by many as a newspaper but more a community bulletin, whose publication can sometimes be erratic and unreliable. Not surprisingly the five who did read it said it covered immigration.

The analysis also reveals that perceived coverage of immigration by various newspapers varied considerably depending on whether they were tabloids or part of the quality newspapers. Quality newspapers such as the Herald, Times, Independent, Guardian, and Daily Telegraph all had high rates of immigration coverage according to those who read them. In comparison tabloids such as the Record, Sun, and Evening Times had very low rates of immigration coverage. And not surprisingly Asian newspapers had a significantly high rate of covering immigration issues according to interviewees.

Sex Discrimination: The Case of Males Entering from the Indian Sub-Continent

One of the most noticeable areas of strict government control in the area of immigration concerns males coming from the Indian sub-continent seeking to settle permanently in Britain. This is because it is widely believed in British government circles that the prime aim of males seeking to enter Britain was to gain permanent settlement for economic reasons, and that they attempted to achieve this aim by getting married to females in Britain.[17] Against this background males since the late 1970s have had considerable difficulty in gaining entry, and the results from my survey reflect experiences of such difficulties.

The claim of discrimination against males has been taken to the European level. In 1985 some Asian women complained to the European Commission of Human Rights that although they were settled in the UK they could not bring their husbands into the country, while the men settled here had no problem bringing their wives over. The government argued that "...allowing them to be so joined would pave the way for 5700 new entrants who would harm the employment situation at home".[18] The Commission did not accept the government's argument on the basis "..that the proposed figure (revised from the government's initial 2500 figure of prospective entrants) constituted only 0.02 per cent of the working population" that it had no great affect on Britain's employment.[19] The main point the Commission made was that the likely economic consequences of permitting entry could not justify sex discrimination and the disruption of family life.

Analysis of the responses generated by survey question 10 found that women were much more successful than men irrespective of whether they were applying for a temporary stay or permanent settlement. The charge of *de facto* discrimination against males is supported by the data presented in Table 4.10 which compares the outcomes of applications for entry visas by men and women.

Table 4.10   Comparison of Males and Females Seeking to Enter Britain by Category

Category	No. Seeking Visas	No. Successful in First Instance	No. Unsuccessful	No. Appealing	No. Successful on Appeal
Husbands	31	9	22	20	10
Wives	17	13	4	4	4
Male Fiancés	18	4	14	8	8
Female Fiancées	15	12	3	3	3
Male Visitors	65	27	38	4	4
Female Visitors	34	27	7	-	-
Totals	180	92	88	39	29

Table 4.10 summarises the attempt of different categories of males and females to enter Britain.

Analysing from survey question 10 "What year/month did you apply for the visa and when was it granted?", found that 31 males applied as husbands to enter Britain between 1981-1995 in the Pollokshields/Hillhead area. Out of the 31 males (29%) who applied only 9 were successful in the first instance and attained their visa in 18 months or less. Only 2 out of the 22 (10%) refused decided not to appeal and that was because they decided to stay abroad. Of the 20 out of the 22 who appealed, 10 eventually got a visa but it took them 2 or more years to obtain one. The maximum waiting time for the 6 who appealed and got a visa was 5 years. Another 4 were waiting to have their appeal heard. This whole process of being refused entry, and subsequently appealing illustrates the lengthy nature of the whole process. Some who applied as far back as 1987 got their visa in 1992.

Not surprisingly, the majority of those males (63%) refused entry at first believed it was because of the application of the primary purpose rule, i.e. they were believed to be using marriage as an excuse to gain entry into Britain. The reason for refusal is normally communicated to the applicant.

The majority of the male applicants were generally unhappy about the whole procedure involved regarding their application; 74% felt that the entry clearance officer did not treat them well. About 40% felt that immigration procedures were unfair and the same percentage of people felt that immigration procedures were racist. Unfair could also mean sexual discrimination against the applicants: the perception of discrimination towards males seeking entry from the Indian sub-continent.

In the case of male fiancés, 18 applied between 1977-1995. Out of these only 4 were successful (22%) the first time in that they got their visa within 18 months; 14 men were at first refused of whom only 8 appealed. Out of the 6 who did not bother to appeal, 4 got married elsewhere (to a person from their own country) and 2 got married to the same person but decided not to live in Britain. The 8 who did appeal eventually got the visa but again the maximum length of waiting time was 5 or more years. Again the ECO was unpopular; 78% were not at all pleased with the ECO. In describing immigration procedures 38% said they were unfair, another 22% said they were racist and 22% said fair. The common knowledge of public criticism of ECOs or immigration officers is acknowledged by officials from the Home Office and Foreign and Commonwealth Office.[20]

The same could be seen when male visitors applied between 1960-1995 to enter Britain on a temporary visa. Out of the 65 who applied only 27 were successful. The great majority (74%) of those turned down believed that they were refused in case they attempted to stay permanently. Once again applicants criticised the treatment they had received from entry clearance officers - with 57% saying that they were not treated well. Fifty per cent also argued that the immigration procedures were racist. What was also noticeable was the low inclination on the part of those refused to launch an appeal. Out of 38 would-be male visitors refused entry only 4 decided to appeal and they got their visas after 5 years. The main reason for not appealing was that they only wanted to come for a holiday to the UK and were therefore not desperate to get involved in the appeal system. Under the 1993 Asylum and Immigration Appeals Act the right for visitors to appeal has been abolished. So even that right has been taken away.

Comparison with Females wanting to Enter Britain as Wives, Fiancées, and Visitors

The survey revealed clearly that females who applied to enter had much greater success than their male counterparts. This difference could be explained either by an element of discrimination against males from the Indian sub-continent inherent in the immigration control regime or by different implications for British public expenditure of male and female entry. Wives and female fiancées are joining a British male citizen who is likely to enjoy employment and accommodation and who is able to support his spouse. Husbands and male fiancés joining their British wives will be seeking employment. An interesting explanation was suggested by an official from the Migration and Visa Unit, of the Foreign and Commonwealth Office, who told me that females have fewer problems than males when applying for a visa because they are more direct at interviews e.g. "I am getting married there because my father arranged it".[21]

Out of the 17 females who had applied as wives, 13 (76%) were successful. The other 4 were successful on appeal; two who got their visas in two years and two had to wait 5 or more years. In sharp contrast, in the case of husbands 6 men had to wait 5 or more years for their visa. A large majority of the wives applying felt that they received fair treatment from entry clearance officers i.e. 86% (fair treatment in one's own perceptions could also mean gaining a visa after a long time, but still feeling successful at the end of the day). One can compare this with the husbands: 74% felt they were not treated fairly. So fairness is perceived in terms of success and failure of the visa application. Although 65% of wives described immigration procedures as unfair, this is a general view, maybe due to the fact that it seems to be well known that immigration officers and immigration policy seems to be more lenient towards females who want to come to Britain to join their husbands but more strict when females from Britain want to bring a husband from the Indian sub-continent to join them.

A similar pattern can be seen in applications on behalf of female fiancées. Fifteen women applied from 1978-1995 and 12 got a visa without any problems. Even on appeal the longest waiting length for the three refused at first was 2 years. While the longest waiting length for male fiancés was more than 5 years.

The great majority of female fiancées felt that the ECO treated them well, i.e. 87%. The attitude of the ECOs was fine but that does not mean the female fiancées believed that the actual procedures were fair as Table 4.11 shows.

Table 4.11 Description of Immigration Procedures by
Female Fiancées

Female Fiancées Describing Immigration Procedures	%
Fair	33
Unfair	33
Racism	33

These widespread opinions on describing immigration procedures reflect a general view of the immigration regime. It is commonly known that many people have had complicated immigration experiences. The Asian community is a close knit community.

Consequently a 'community view' of the immigration issue is developed. An interesting finding emerged when women were asked why their application as fiancées had been refused; the only reason given was racism. In this context racism means refusal on the basis of the individual's colour. This is similar to the case of the wives who were refused of whom 50% said racism and 50% said they did not satisfy the requirements. While in the case of husbands the majority gave the reason as the primary purpose rule as shown in Table 4.12 below.

Table 4.12 Reason for Husbands' Refusal

Reason for Husbands' Refusal	%
Primary Purpose	63
Racism	30
Did Not Satisfy Requirements	7

Women believed that the main reason for the refusal of an application by a male fiancé was the primary purpose rule only. This suggests that the women did not feel they were being tested on the basis of primary purpose, unlike the men who were refused on these grounds.

Out of the 34 females who applied as visitors, 27 were granted entry while 7 were refused. The women refused felt they were denied the visa in case they stayed in Britain permanently. This seemed to be a common factor shared by male visitors as well. Out of the 65 who applied 38 were refused, 28 of whom gave the exact same reason for refusal, 7 said racism and 3 said did not satisfy the requirements. Once again 79% of would-be female visitors said they had been treated fairly by the ECOs. Whilst 57% of men applying as visitors had disagreed with this.

To give an idea of the length of waiting time involved to attain a visa, Table 4.13 below shows the waiting time for husbands and fiancé and for wives and fiancées in this sample.

Table 4.13 Length of Waiting Time for a Visa for Husband/Fiancé and Wife/Fiancée

Husband and Fiancé		Wife and Fiancée	
Length of Time (Years)	No. of Males	Length of Time (Years)	No. of Females
1	-	1	25
2	13	2	5
2 or more	10	2 or more	-
5 or more	14	5 or more	2

116

Table 4.13 above shows that males had to wait longer than females, thus indicating the tougher measures placed on male applicants to join their spouse in UK. According to a senior IAS counsellor, males who succeeded in attaining the visa first time normally wait 18 months or less, while women applicants for settlement usually attain the visa within 0-6 months.

Table 4.14 Length of Waiting Time for Male Visitors

Male Visitor: Length of Waiting Time	No. of Males
1 Year	-
2 Years	1
3 Years	1
4 Years	1
More than 5 Years	1

Table 4.14 above shows only a small number of men appealing. Many male visitors decided not to appeal because it was too much effort for a holiday. None of the female visitors in the survey appealed. Male or female visitors when successful can normally acquire their visa within one week. Therefore the waiting time indicated above is surprising. Since 1993, visitors have no right of appeal and thus have to make a fresh application if their application is refused first time.

Lastly in the case of visitor parents there were 8 couples, 9 females and 2 males who applied to come here from 1980-1995. The couples represent one entity, considering application was made for them as one and they were refused as one. Two females were refused a visa and two couples, the reason given by the four groups of parents was the fear of the immigration officials that the parents might not return to their mother country. Most parents (79%) felt the ECOs were fine with them.

Occupation and Immigration

This section seeks to examine further the reasons for the pattern of gender discrimination noted in the previous section. In particular the survey questions provide information on the occupations of both sponsors and applicants. Such data allows us to consider whether having a high status occupation enhances the chances of gaining an holiday visa or a settlement visa for the United Kingdom. When looking at the occupation of the sponsor when wives residing in Britain applied for settlement visas on behalf of their husbands, the biggest category comprised routine office workers which included occupations such as bank clerk and secretary. The second largest group can be described as 'Petty Bourgeoisie' who were self-employed or employers; in this group shopkeepers dominated. Another 19% can be described as lower middle class employees i.e. sales assistants. Only a small minority were students (see Table 4.15 below).

Table 4.15 Occupation of Wife as Sponsor

Occupation of Wife (sponsor) (N= 31)	%
Routine Office Worker	39
Petty Bourgeoisie	32
Middle Class Employee	19
Salariat/Intelligence	6
Students	3

Taking into account that all the British wives except the students were employed and earning some money it is surprising that no fewer than 27 men out of 31 were refused a visa and had to appeal. Maybe if the female sponsors and the would-be immigrants occupied more middle-class occupations in the salariat/intelligence category, there would have been a different result. Of the 27 husbands refused 17 were farm labourers; 2 were students; 3 were routine manual workers; 3 were petty bourgeoisie; and 2 were salariat/intelligence.

The 4 husbands who were *not* refused a visa had occupations which fell in the category of salariat/intelligence (3) and petty bourgeoisie (1). Similarly the sponsors (wives) of the 4 husbands who were *not* refused visas had jobs which fell in the category of salariat/intelligence (2) and petty bourgeoisie (2).

This suggests the argument that having a high status occupation increases the likelihood and a low status occupation decreases the likelihood of obtaining a visa. Only 6% of the sponsors (wives) had post school qualifications as such i.e. doctor, chemist, lecturer. This is perhaps not surprising given that the traditional culture of the Indian sub-continent has always put less stress on females having a job or on educating themselves to higher levels. It is the need to demonstrate financial independence to satisfy the immigration requirements when applying for husbands which has forced Asian females living in Britain to seek employment today. Even so, refusal of a visa granting permanent settlement in the first instance is the norm when women seek to bring husbands and fiancés into Britain.

Not surprisingly, given that farming is the source of income of the great majority of people in the Indian sub-continent, out of the 31 males who applied as husbands, 17 (55%) were farm labourers, which could possibly be linked by the immigration officials to the primary purpose rule. The fact that farm labourers earn low wages at home contributes to a perception that they therefore are probably coming to Britain for economic reasons using marriage as an instrument to secure entry. Nevertheless, the second highest figure was 6 (19%) and that was for salariat/intelligence i.e. post-school qualification.

Fiancés were just as likely as husbands to be rejected a visa on first application. The females sponsoring their fiancés were mainly factory or office workers (see Table 4.16). A third were routine manual workers, and 28% were routine office workers such as secretaries and bank clerks. Almost a fifth (17%) were students. Only 11% were petty bourgeois, meaning self-employed, and there was no-one with post-school qualification. The pattern of refusal was close to that of the refusals of husbands application. Out of the 18 male fiancés sponsored, 14 were refused. The occupations of those who were refused a visa was: 8 were farm labourers; 4 were students; 1 was unemployed; and 1 was a routine office worker. The occupations of the 4 who were *not* refused fell in the category of salariat/intelligence (2) and petty bourgeoisie (2). The occupations of the sponsors of the 4 who were *not* refused fell in the category of petty bourgeoisie (2) and routine office worker (2).

There is a strong correlation between having a high status occupation (for the sponsor and the would-be immigrant) and the chances of gaining an entry visa. It has to be emphasised that the occupation of the would-be immigrant is just as important as the occupation of the sponsor when influencing the decision of the entry clearance officer. This is because a would-be immigrant who has a low paid occupation might be less reluctant to return to his/her country of origin, and in the case of husbands/wives or fiancée/fiancé is more likely to use marriage as a means of gaining entry into Britain, irrespective of the occupation of the sponsor.

Table 4.16 Occupation of Fiancée as Sponsor

Occupation of Fiancée (sponsor) (N=18)	%
Routine Manual Worker	33
Routine Office Worker	28
Students	17
Petty Bourgeoisie	11

Two of the many requirements a sponsor has to satisfy are "there will be adequate accommodation for the parties... in accommodation which they own or occupy exclusively" and "the parties will be able to maintain themselves and any dependants adequately without recourse to public funds".[22]

Even the occupations of the male fiancés seeking entry tended to be dominated by farm labourers e.g. 44%. Another 22% were students and 11% were salariat/intelligence i.e. post-school qualifications, while 11% were self-employed (salariat) and 6% were actually unemployed. Therefore 27 husbands and 14 male fiancés being refused was linked to their occupations as has been illustrated (see Table 4.17).

Table 4.17 Occupation of Male Fiancés from Abroad

Occupation of Male Fiancé Abroad, N=18   %

Farm Labourers	44
Students	22
Salariat/Intelligence	11
Salariat	11
Unemployed	6

In the situation of British Asians applying for male visitors (65), 48 (74%) of the sponsors were petty bourgeois i.e. self-employed. Eleven percent (7) had post-school qualifications, yet 38 out of 65 males were still refused a visa when they first applied to enter as visitors. Of these 25 were farm labourers or farmers, 8 were students, 3 were unemployed and 2 were routine office workers. Of the 27 who succeeded in obtaining a visa, 10 were petty bourgeois, 8 were salariat, 4 were in the category of managerialism, 1 was a routine manual worker, 2 were retired and 2 were unemployed. Hence the connection between low status occupations and refusal of a entry visa is evident yet again. In the survey it was thought that the main reason for refusal was in case the visitor ended up staying permanently. The immigration officials may have felt justified in believing this, as 11% of the visitors were farm labourers. The other categories were the following, 28% were farmers, 12% were students and 2% were routine office workers i.e. bank clerk. A mere 2% were routine manual workers such as bus drivers, taxi driver and 8% were unemployed. Last but not least 3% were retired (see Table 4.18 below).

The fact that 33 (86%) of the sponsors of the 38 male visitors who were rejected a visa were petty bourgeois is a reflection of the fact that very often it is the occupation of the would-be immigrant which is regarded as more important than the occupation of the sponsor in the decision of whether to grant a visa or not. In other words even if the sponsor has a high status job that in itself is unlikely to help the would-be immigrant to gain a visa if he has a low status occupation in his country of origin.

121

Table 4.18 Occupation of Male Visitors from Abroad

Occupation of Visitors From Abroad, N=65	%
Farm Labourers	11
Farmers	28
Students	12
Petty Bourgeoisie	15
Salariat	12
Managerialism	6
Routine Office Workers	3
Routine Manual Workers	2
Unemployed	8
Retired	3

Immigration officials are inclined to believe that if a person given a visitor's visa has a low paid occupation in his/her own country then they are less likely to return to their own country.   However, if that person has a well paid job in his/her own country then the chances are he/she will return to their own country. Which does seem like an unfair predisposition for every individual applying from India, Pakistan and Bangladesh. In the case of 27 male visitors attaining a visa first time, this could be connected to 15% visitors being petty bourgeois such as self-employed. While 12% had post-school qualifications i.e. salariat/intelligence. Six per cent were in the managerialism category i.e. bank manager.

The male sponsors living in the UK who applied for their wives from abroad enjoyed much more success than female sponsors. This is explained partly by the impact of the primary purpose rule already discussed. It is also the case that male sponsors in the UK had better occupations than their female counterparts (see Table 4.19); 35% had post-school qualification i.e. salariat; 24% were self-employed business people; and 18% were routine office workers including those working in insurance companies and bank clerks.

Table 4.19 Occupation of Husband as Sponsor

Occupation of Husband (sponsor), N= 17	%
Salariat/Intelligence	35
Petty Bourgeoisie	24
Routine Office Workers	18

The wives coming from abroad seemed to experience fewer difficulties i.e. 4 wives out of 17 refused. No fewer than 59% of wives seeking to enter Britain were students; another 35% were housewives; and 6% were unemployed. There is a popular belief in British society that women entering as wives, in comparison to husbands entering, will be housewives and thus not a threat to the British job market. In addition it is assumed their husbands can support them without recourse to public funds.

The pattern of male sponsors applying for their fiancées was very similar to wives applications, with 73% of male sponsors being petty bourgeois. Similarly out of the 15 females who applied as fiancée only 3 were refused, which again is very low in comparison to men. The woman fiancée refused visas could be associated with the 7% of the male sponsors being students. It is therefore probable that they lack accommodation and occupation which is an immigration requirement that needs to be satisfied.

In the category of female visitors (see Table 4.20), 74% of the sponsors were petty bourgeoisie, 15% had post-school qualifications thus quite educated. Nonetheless 34 females applied as visitors and only 7 were refused a visa. The success rate in attaining visas is very high when considering the fact that 32% of females visiting were students, 38% were housewives, 15% were petty bourgeoisie, 12% salariat and 3% unemployed. The 7 female visitors refused believed that it was in case they stayed in the UK and never returned.

Table 4.20 Occupation of Females as Applying Visitors

Occupation of Female Visitor N = 34	%
Students	32
Housewives	38
Petty Bourgeoisie	15
Salariat	12
Unemployed	3

The visitor parents were all retired, but 63% of the sponsors were petty bourgeoisie and 26% were salariat. However 2 couples and 2 females were still refused a visa. The reason for refusal was in case they stayed permanently in the UK. Now for a parent to enter the UK for a holiday or indefinite leave to remain, they have to be aged 65 or over. Also the person entering "is financially wholly or mainly dependent on the relative present and settled in the UK".[23] These are just two of the many requirements that need to be satisfied. Parents wanting to holiday are subjected to the same criteria as those wanting stay in the UK. Another difficult requirement to satisfy is the parent "has no other close relatives in his/her own country to whom he could turn for financial support".[24] This requirement mentioned is very complex in that a person from his/her homeland is bound to have close relatives. It can therefore be a very difficult task to visit his/her son living in the UK.

There is no doubt that having a good occupation abroad may take away the suspicion that a person is getting married primarily to enter the UK i.e. for economic reasons. The same could be said for a person just visiting the UK as the chances are that he/she will want to return to their good position. Evidence seems to show that immigration officers are more lenient towards female applications to enter the UK in comparison to males. As long as the female's spouse in the UK has an occupation and accommodation, then the female tended to have no problem at all, even if she herself was unemployed. The husband or male fiancé applying from abroad should have an occupation in the country he is coming from to prove that he is not using marriage as an excuse to enter the UK for economic reasons and his sponsor must be able to support and accommodate him. Again the link between occupation and immigration, could be noted when Mr Lusk from the Foreign and Commonwealth Office, Migration and Visa Unit agreed that being an educated person means he/she gives a better interview and makes a better impression on the Entry Clearance Officer.[25]

Conclusions

The results of this survey serve as a useful indicator of the effects of Conservative policies. It has to be remembered that the survey throughout is based on respondents' perceptions which may, or may not, be accurate. Nevertheless, their perceptions are interesting in themselves, whether accurate or inaccurate. The reason why there has been no analysis of any differences between the two areas selected Pollokshields and Hillhead, is because this book is not interested in inter-city comparisons but simply in assessing the impact of immigration policies on the two areas of Glasgow taken together, i.e. the interest is on the overall picture of the impact of immigration policies in general on people from the Indian sub-continent.

The survey has helped to both confirm and deny certain held views about the issue of immigration in Britain. A number of expected and unexpected points were evident from the survey. Some of the less surprising findings were:

- Concern that individuals might stay permanently through marriage etc. or were getting married in order to achieve stay were the chief reasons why individuals were refused entry (the primary purpose rule);
- There is an element of discrimination towards males whose entry has been strictly controlled under government legislation since the 1980s. Males find it more difficult to gain entry visas than females, largely because of the implementation of the primary purpose rule by British administrators of immigration rules and procedures;
- Having a good occupation abroad such as a doctor or academic (salariat intelligence) or even a wealthy businessman, may make all the difference to the application, since most men in the sample tended to be farmers or farm labourers;

- Majority of interviewees described immigration procedures as unfair and racist.

Some of the more unexpected findings included:

- A considerable number of those who had entered Britain from the Indian Sub-continent were between the ages of 20-30, some even under 20;
- More males than females had applied to come to Britain;
- The main reason for wanting to come to Britain was to visit;
- The need to demonstrate financial independence to satisfy the immigration requirements when applying for husbands has forced Asian females living in Britain to seek employment today;
- Apart from the Immigration Advisory Service, other Scottish organisations dealing with immigration were not used for processing an application. This maybe viewed as a matter of concern. It could mean that either individuals do not know about other organisations or are not confident about using them;
- Even though some immigrants may have got an entry clearance without too much trouble, they were still pessimistic about the immigration procedures overall, as was seen in the case of female fiancées. This again can be linked to people's perceptions;
- The most common occupation for wives in the Indian sub-continent tended to be students and their husbands (sponsors) in the UK were mainly salariat/intelligence. The success rate in gaining a visa was very high in such cases. The wives in the UK who were sponsors were mainly routine officer workers and their husbands were mainly farm labourers; a majority of such men had to appeal for an entry visa. The occupation of men sponsoring female visitors was mainly petty bourgeoisie and the success rate was high considering the female visitors were mainly students. The main occupation of those sponsoring male visitors were petty bourgeois and the male visitors tended to be mainly agricultural workers and their success rate for a visa was very poor.

In other words the connection between occupation and immigration revealed some very interesting findings: when wives sponsored husbands the success rate in obtaining a visa was low especially if the husband had a low status occupation such as farm labourer or routine manual worker. This was the case even when the wives who were sponsoring husbands had high status jobs. Though the few who did succeed first time round did have higher status jobs. The story was similar in the case of female fiancées who sponsored male fiancés: the success rate for obtaining a visa was low if the male fiancé had a low status occupation.

However, an entirely different picture emerges when we look at males sponsoring wives or female fiancées. In the case of husbands sponsoring wives the success rate for obtaining a visa was high if the husband had a high status job even if the wife had a poor occupation. The story is similar in the case of male fiancés sponsoring female fiancées. This is in line with another finding of this survey which is that males had much more difficulty obtaining entry into Britain than females.

- The two most commonly read papers are firstly the Herald and then an Asian tabloid, the Daily Jang. Both papers cover the most immigration issues according to the interviewees.

By and large this survey give credence to the basic argument developed throughout this book, and established at the outset, that the Conservative government's immigration regime was discriminatory in its impact. It may be considered to be unfair towards people from the Indian sub-continent. The regime took no account of the special cultural characteristics of the sub-continent. The evidence is seen in the wide ranging implications that policies and procedures have had for Indian sub-continent nationals.

Due to the sensitive nature of this issue, and the controversy which it has raised in British politics over the years, many Asians (Indians, Pakistanis and Bangladeshis) still feel very cautious about wanting to express their true viewpoint on immigration matters. In fact many people were not too keen to communicate with me. Some thought I might be an immigration official who was trying to extract personal information from them, which could be passed to the government, allowing it to take measures if any discrepancies stand up about the legitimacy of their stay here. This is the kind of fear factor which has been generated by the strict control which successive governments have instilled since the late 1970s.

I managed to persuade most people that I was neutral, and was conducting my survey in complete confidence. This survey simply demonstrates the view point and experiences of people from the Indian sub-continent living in Glasgow on immigration.

Notes

1   D.A. de Vaus, *Surveys in Social Research*, (George Allen & Unwin, 1986).
2.   Statistics provided by General Register Office for Scotland, Population Statistics Branch.
3.   *Ibid*
4.   This is a technique used by Dr Le Lohe, *University Ward Survey Bradford. A confidential report to the CRE*, July/August, 1981, Department of Social and Economic Studies, University of Bradford.
5.   See also for more extensive details on telephone surveys: Groves R M and Kahn R L, *Surveys by Telephone*, (Academic Press, 1979).
6.   See *chapter 3*.
7.   Walvin J, *Passage to Britain*, (Penguin Books, 1984), p. 109
8.   Zig Layton-Henry, *The Politics of Immigration*, (Blackwell, 1992).
9.   This was one of the conditions laid out in the *1988 Immigration Act*
10.   This is a technique used by Heath, Jowell and Curtice, *How Britain Votes*, (Pergamon Press, 1985).
11.   *Interview* with Sean Lusk, Head of Policy Making, Migration and Visa Unit, Foreign and Commomwealth Office, London, 20 September 1996.
12.   *Statement of Changes in Immigration Rules*, para. 41, p. 8, 23 May 1994, (London: HMSO).
13.   See *chapter 5*
14.   *Interview* with Nick Troake, Policy Directorate, Immigration and Nationality Department, Home Office, London, 19 September 1996 and see also *chapter 7*.
15.   *Ibid*, Detective Sergeant, Police Nationality Department, 19 April 1996.
16.   See *chapter 6* for statistics on illegal immigrants.
17.   The 'primary purpose rule' itself gives the government's views on the issues. Also *interview* with Nick Troake, 19 September 1996.
18.   Satvinder S. Juss, *Immigration and Nationality and Citizenship*, (Mansell 1993), p. 11.
19.   *Ibid.*
20.   *Interview* with Nick Troake, 19 September 1996.
21.   *Ibid* with Sean Lusk, 20 September 1996.
22.   *Statement of Changes in Immigration Rules*, op. cit. para 284, p. 54.
23.   *Ibid*, para. 317, p. 63.
24.   *Interview* with Sean Lusk, 20 September 1996.
25.   *Ibid*

Appendix

Survey Questionnaire

Section A

1 Are you male or female?
2 What is your age-group?
   20 or younger
   21-24
   25-29
   30-34
   35-39
   40-44
   45-49
   50 or Older
3 What is your country of birth?
4 How long have you been resident in the UK?
5 Have you or your family been subjected to immigration procedures?

Section B

6a If yes, who was the sponsor?
6b What is your country of birth?
6c What is you nationality?
7a What was the occupation of the sponsor and the person from abroad?
7b What was the age of the person coming from abroad?
8a What was /is the relationship between the applicant and you the
    sponsor?
    • Husband
    • Wife
    • Fiancé
    • Fiancée
    • Mother
    • Father

- Children
- Other

8b Did you apply for the person to: stay permanently or visit on holiday?

9 Who did you apply through?
- Solicitor
- Immigration Advisory Service (IAS)
- Independently
- Other

10 What year (Month) did you apply for the visa and when was it granted?

11 When applying for him/her did you:
   a. Understand the rules?
   b. Understand the application form?

12 Did you feel the Entry Clearance Officer treated you or your family fairly?

13 Why do you think he/she was refused?

14a Who did you go to for help?
- IAS
- Scottish Asian Action Committee
- Community Relations Council
- Councillor
- MP
- Place of worship
- Other

14b Did you find the above sources helpful?

14c Did you appeal?

14d If not, why did you not appeal?

14e If yes, did the appeal
- Succeed
- Fail
- Don't Know?

Section C

15 How would you describe immigration procedures?

- Fair
- Unfair (but not racist)
- Racist
- Honest people suffer due to an increase in illegal attempts to enter
- Don't know

16 What have you heard from others about Immigration Procedures?

17a Do you know anything about the 1971 Immigration Act?

17b Do you know anything about the 1981 Immigration Act?

17c Do you know anything about the 1988 Immigration Act?

18a What newspaper do you read?

18b Does it cover immigration?

Table 4.21 Classification of Visa Applicant by Number

Applicant by Type	Number of Applicants
Husband	31
Wife	17
Male Fiancé	18
Female Fiancée	15
Male Visitor	65
Female Visitor	34
Parents	19
Asylum Seekers	2

Table 4.22 Channel for Processing a Visa Application

Channel for Processing Application	Use of Channel by % of Applicants
Independently	29
Solicitor	47
Immigration Advisory Service	22
Scottish Refugee Council	1
Don't know	1

Table 4.23 Duration of Time before Visa Granted and Number of Applicants

Duration of Time before Visa Granted	Number Granted Visa
5 or more years	20
2 or more years	15
Less than 2 years	107

Table 4.24 Reasons for Visa Refusal

Reasons for Refusal	Number Refused
Racism	21
Primary Purpose Rule	32
Stay Permanently	40
Did not Satisfy Requirements	7

Table 4.25 Description of Immigration Procedures*

Description of Immigration Procedures	% Assigning Description
Fair	5
Unfair	36
Racist	44
Don't	13

* 1% said that the increase in frauds meant honest people suffered, while 1% said that there were too many Asians in Britain.

5 Case Studies: Real Life Immigration Cases and Experiences of Individuals

Introduction

Chapter 4 has described the overall perceptions of Indian sub-continent nationals on the immigration issue in general. This chapter analyses the specific immigration experiences of 8 different people. It examines in closer detail the personal experiences of and the range of problems encountered by potential immigrants. Since immigration problems are varied in character some involving permanent stay, others temporary visiting, the chapter will allow us to build a picture of how each type of case is handled and to decide whether there are significant differences between how different types of applications are dealt with. The aim is to analyse what happens when the cultures and practices of people from various parts of the world such as the Indian sub-continent come into contact with British immigration rules and with the attitudes of the Entry Clearance Officers (ECOs).

The case studies illustrate the difficulties encountered by individuals as they go through the immigration process. Every single case involves a unique category of individuals e.g. husband, wife, fiancé, visitor and even an individual suffering from an illness seeking entry for an operation. The case studies show how the rules impinge on individuals acting as a sponsor or as an appellant. It will be shown how the culture of the Indian sub-continent is at odds with the attitudes of ECOs and adjudicators, and with the basic principles of the British immigration regime. The chapter will show how cultural divisions between Britain and the Indian sub-continent dominate the processes and outcomes of immigration control in Britain.

I myself attended many of the appeals heard at the Immigration Appellate Authority. Most of these appeals tended to be for individuals trying to prove the purpose of their marriage. The appeal stage dominates the case studies which are going to be looked at in this chapter. Each case is controversial because it involves refusals and rejections, which subsequently require the appeal stage.

When an entry visa for settlement is refused one can appeal against the Home Office decision as described in chapter 2. In the cases discussed in this chapter the appeal at the first instance is heard by the adjudicator at the Immigration Appellate Authority. In such cases the appellant subjected to the process of immigration control is represented by a lawyer or by the Immigration Advisory Service. The appellant's opposition is the respondent, e.g. Home Office, who is making the case against the appellant. If the appeal is dismissed by the adjudicator the appellant can apply for leave to appeal to the tribunal. If that appeal is allowed the respondent (Home Office) can apply to the tribunal for leave to appeal against the adjudicator's decision. In this chapter, cases 4 and 5 reached the tribunal stage and emphasised the difficulty of attaining an entry visa for a spouse. Case 1 simply concerned an emergency situation as a family tried to obtain short-term visas to visit a dying relative in Scotland. Cases 2 and 3 demonstrate that there is no right of appeal for visitors under the 1993 Immigration and Asylum Act. Cases 6 and 7 did not involve the appeal process.

It has to be pointed out that although this book looks at Conservative immigration policies implemented between 1979 and 1990, some of the cases in this chapter refer to the post-Thatcher period. However, this does not pose any problems for our analysis because the immigration regime established during Thatcher's reign was not reversed under John Major, and the rules and laws established during Thatcher's term in office were still in operation and determined the nature of the specific decisions reached in the cases analysed. In some cases the cases overlapped from the pre-1990 period to the post-Thatcher period. The names of individuals in the cases have been changed for confidential reasons except for those cases which were covered by the press. Due to the nature of this chapter the format will be such that there will be no sections. There will simply be a detailed analysis of each case one by one, followed by some concluding remarks. Table 5.1 below illustrates the cases dealt with in this chapter, and the length of time it took for them to be resolved.

Table 5.1 Selected Visa Cases and Length of Time to Attain a Visa

Case Number	Type of Visa and Reason for Admission into Britain	Length of Time to Attain a Visa (approx.)
Case 1	Visiting visa for a family to visit a dying relative	1 month
Case 2	Visiting visa for grandparents to attend a family wedding	refused
Case 3	Visiting visa for grandparents to attend a family wedding	refused
Case 4	Visiting visa for Glasgow politician's sister to attend a family wedding	3-6 months
Case 5	Settlement visa for husband	9 years
Case 6	Settlement visa for husband	2 years
Case 7	Settlement visa for wife	4 years
Case 8	Visiting visa for treatment	refused

Source: Interviews with individuals

Case 1: Visiting Visa - Family from Pakistan Trying to Visit a Sick Relative

Case 1 focuses attention on an application for a visa by a Pakistani citizen to enter the UK temporarily in order to visit an elderly relative, a Glasgow resident and British citizen who was likely to die in the near future. This case study involved Labour MP Mike Watson.[1] The MP tried to help the British citizen, an 82 year old constituent, Mrs A,[2] from Pollokshields who was very ill and wanted her granddaughter Mrs B and her family to visit

135

her from Pakistan. Consultant Neurosurgeon Mr Johnston from the Southern General Hospital sent a fax on the 25th of October 1994 to the British High Commission so that Mrs B and her family could obtain an Entry Visa to see her grandmother. The surgeon wrote "Mrs A is a patient.........with a serious condition and it would be advisable that Mrs B and her children are allowed to leave Pakistan to be with her at this time".[3] A letter dated 11th November 1994 was sent from the Western Infirmary to the High Commission in Pakistan referring to Mrs A: "Her condition remains stable but serious...".[4] Mrs B, her husband and their five children during an interview at the British High Commission in Islamabad with the ECO were asked to provide proof of her mother's illness and were asked to provide evidence of the family being able to support themselves while visiting Scotland temporarily. Mike Watson wrote to the ECO in the British High Commission in Pakistan on the 11th of November 1994 in which he emphasised that "A letter was subsequently faxed to you by a Consultant Neuro Surgeon, confirming the seriousness of Mrs A's illness". Also regarding stay in Scotland he wrote "A sponsor's letter was dispatched to your office 2 days ago...". Mr Watson again stressed the time factor: "I would ask that you treat Mrs B and her family's case with compassion and grant an entry visa as quickly as possible".[5] The Foreign and Commonwealth Office in London informed Mike Watson by letter four days later that they could not even find Mrs B's application. "If you are able to supply further information including the reference number of her visa application in Islamabad, they will make further checks".[6] Then another letter written on the 18th of November and sent to the MP from the Foreign and Commonwealth Office, apologised about the confusion over the applications. Mrs B and the two youngest children were given their visa at that point and the other members of the family were to be interviewed on the 22nd of November.[7]

Unfortunately Mrs A died and her grand-daughter was not able to arrive in time to see her mother. The Labour MP wrote to Douglas Hurd, the Secretary of State about how badly the family were treated. "Mrs B's grandmother was clearly seriously ill as outlined in the attached letters from the two consultants....". He goes on to say "...it seems to me to have been excessively harsh for the family's request for entry clearance to have been delayed. As a result of the delay, Mrs B was not able to see her grandmother before she died". The MP asked the Secretary of State to investigate the case to allow a short term visa for the whole family so they could participate in the funeral ceremony which lasts 40 days.[8] The Foreign and Commonwealth Office wrote back that Douglas Hurd had acknowledged the situation and that "the matter is receiving attention....".[9]

On 2nd December the Foreign and Commonwealth Office (FCO) wrote to Mike Watson to justify their actions. Their justification was that Mrs B applied on the 31st of October (ignoring the fax sent by the hospital on the 25th of October) and was interviewed soon after on the 8th November. But she did not bring any evidence to support her application, thus she was refused a visa. The fax detailing Mrs A's medical condition was not deemed sufficient evidence. Mrs B again applied on the 14th of November and this time the immigration official spoke by phone to the doctor in charge of Mrs A and thus on compassionate grounds gave the visa to her and her two youngest children. Mrs B's husband was interviewed on the 22nd of November but was refused a visa when the entry clearance officer found out that he did not own a prosperous business.

What the FCO was basically saying was they were correct in the way they handled the case. Significantly the FCO pointed out that "....although the entry clearance officer must consider the compassionate circumstances of an application he must primarily adhere to the immigration rules".[10] Nevertheless the MP then informed the sponsor on the 12th of December that he had been contacted by the FCO that the entire family could collect their visas for the funeral.[11]

The case suggests that the immigration regime is inflexible and that rules are applied rigorously whatever the circumstances of particular cases. The authorities attracted bad publicity because even when there were compassionate grounds, a person still had to satisfy all immigration criteria. One of the many criteria a visitor has to satisfy is that the visitor "will maintain and accommodate himself and any dependants adequately out of resources available to him without recourse to public funds...." and "can meet the cost of the return or onward journey".[12] One can question whether, although Mrs B's husband may not have had as much finance in the bank as he stated, it is fair to refuse a visa in a life and death situation. Under normal circumstances, as the above rules state, his refusal of a visa could be seen as fair in immigration policy terms, but this was a totally different situation. The critical issue arising concerns the degree of discretion, if any, permitted in balancing the consideration given to the "compassionate circumstances" and the primary "adherence" paid to specific rules which should be satisfied before a visiting visa is granted.

This case hit the headlines and was covered by Scottish Television. This case highlighted what many Indian sub-continent people saw as the unfairness and discrimination involved in the application of immigration rules. It also emphasises that the time taken to process applications is a major source of perceptions that the system is unfair.

Case 2: Visiting Visa for the Elderly - Grandparents from Pakistan Trying to Attend their Grandson's Wedding in Glasgow

The second case also involves the Labour MP Mike Watson whose Glasgow Central constituency had a considerable Asian community. This case referred to an application for a holiday visa for grandparents from Pakistan to visit relatives in Glasgow.[13] Where grandparents or parents are invited on a holiday, the immigration officers are inclined to believe that the parents will remain in Britain and will not return. In this case a grandson is getting married. He is a commercial manager in a well-known company, and his father is a contracts manager in another company. Their granddaughter, a British citizen, is a social worker with Strathclyde Regional Council, and she sponsored the grandparents. In spite of these individuals possessing sound economic standing her grandparents were refused an entry visa. An example of the reasons for the refusal are "You state that the trip will be paid for by your granddaughter in the UK but you have not provided any evidence that she can do so". The entry clearance officer said "..you have a large family in the UK and a son abroad in Dubai, leaving only one son in Pakistan". Finally he said "I am not satisfied that the cost of this trip and your support and accommodation in the UK can be met without recourse to public funds".[14] So the reasons for refusal were:

1) inadequate funds;
2) the probability in the eyes of immigration officials that the grandparents would seek to stay permanently and;

3) the probability therefore that the British public purse would finance the visit.

MP Mike Watson wrote to the FCO in London on behalf of the family, to refute the explicit and implicit reasons for the refusal of a visa. Watson emphasised to the FCO that the sponsor had a reasonable occupation with Strathclyde Regional Council, that the bride groom was a manager holding secure employment and that even the future father-in-law was well established and was willing to help if any problems arose regarding their stay in Scotland; "...the future father-in-law is a consultant psychiatrist...and...offering to provide food and lodging in the unlikely event that that should be necessary". The MP mentioned that the refusal letter also stated that the grandparents only had one close relative, a son living in Pakistan. This was not the case because the grandparents also had two daughters, and their own brothers, sisters and numerous grand-children lived in Pakistan. He also wrote "They also own some property there and have every intention of returning to Pakistan". Mike Watson told the FCO that he had seen the wedding invitation and requested they inform the British High Commission in Pakistan that the family were going to make a fresh application.[15] The spokesperson from the FCO wrote back "I have copied this correspondence to the entry clearance section at Islamabad so that they will be aware of your interest when they re-apply".[16] An interesting comment which suggests MPs have some influence on the decisions made in Pakistan.

The above is a typical case of the type of grounds on which elderly parents are refused visas to visit children domiciled in Britain. In this case one of the criteria applied to grandparents visiting temporarily which the entry clearance officer again felt was not fulfilled was:

Applicants can, and will be maintained and accommodated adequately, together with any dependants, without recourse to public funds in accommodation which the sponsor owns or occupies exclusively.[17]

The immigration authorities, as also seen in case 1, tend to assume that people allowed into the UK on a temporary visit will stay permanently, instead of returning to their country of origin after their short visit to the UK is over.

The attitude of immigration officials on immigration cases is analysed in greater detail in chapter 6. But case 2 highlights the severity of the immigration regime, and how the lives of individuals and families can be adversely affected when they are prevented from being reunited, even on a temporary basis. It appears that, as seen in this case, even when clear evidence of adequate funding and accommodation is provided, entry is still not granted. So even when the criteria laid out are met it seems that immigration officials appear to be making discretionary judgements which are essentially unfair because they fly in the face of the evidence. Such cases attract the perceptions of discrimination discussed in chapter 4.

Case 3: Visiting Visa - Grandparents Refused a Visit to Attend their Granddaughters Wedding

This case is another example of grandparents being refused visitors' temporary visas to attend a wedding in the UK. The interviewee, Mr Raja,[18] informed me that he wished to bring his parents and a niece over to attend his daughter's wedding. His parents were refused a visa for what amounted to a holiday visit. Mr Raja was a well respected citizen in Glasgow. He has been a member of the Strathclyde Community Relations Council for ten years. He was a chairman of the Labour Party Shawlands Branch, a member of the Glasgow District Executive and a District Council candidate for Shawlands. He applied for his parents to visit in July/August 1994. Their interview date arrived and the parents had to travel 100 miles to Islamabad. Once they were there they had to wait in a queue until their turn came. Some inefficient interpreter according to Mr Raja was there to help with the language difficulties. The parents were refused the visa because the British immigration officials considered that the probability of their staying permanently in the UK was high.

Mr Raja has two married sisters in England. Thus the visit was also a good opportunity for his parents to see their children and grandchildren. The interviewee told me his parents had been here before in 1987 and had no immigration problems then. In fact the parents wanted to go back because they did not like the British climate. Mr Raja told me that his parents were comfortable in Pakistan and had no financial reason to stay in Britain. Indeed his father had two pensions: one from the British army and one from the police. He tried to get help from Alan Stewart, Conservative MP for Eastwood, one of the wealthiest constituencies in Scotland. Mr Stewart wrote to the British High Commission on 14/10/94 guaranteeing that Mr Raja would keep to his terms and the parents would return after the wedding.[19] Mr Raja received a letter from Mr Stewart's private secretary Jeanette Muir informing him that the MP had been in contact with the Migration and Visa Correspondence Unit "...and they have promised to investigate your case immediately and they will report back to Mr Stewart at the beginning of the week".[20] *The Herald* reported that the parents were to be interviewed again and the MP said "I am hopeful that any misunderstandings can be cleared up and the grandparents allowed to travel for what is clearly a very important family occasion".[21]

According to Mr Raja the immigration officials believed that the elderly couple and Mr Raja's niece would visit the UK but would not return. The niece would remain there by getting married to a British citizen. With such thoughts "His niece had withdrawn her application in disgust after the original refusal three months ago....".[22] The Foreign Office spokesperson in London said the immigration officer would be looking at how the cost of air tickets would be covered, proof that a wedding was being attended, and at whether the parents had enough finance without having recourse to public funds. Also important would be proof of return air tickets to Pakistan.[23] After the second interview the parents were again refused "...the immigration officer and the consul in Islamabad did not believe that they would return to Pakistan at the expiry of their visa".[24] Alan Stewart wrote to the Foreign Office in London numerous times to change the decision and even wrote to Mr Douglas Hurd the Foreign Secretary about the case. The reply received by "Mr Hurd's officials had simply said it was a matter for the consul in Islamabad".[25]

The Herald reported the Conservative MP, Mr Stewart saying "Had these been some elderly white colonial visitors they would have been strolling through Heathrow without a second glance". Mr Raja also said "My parents are bitterly disappointed and so is my daughter. My parents were here before and returned to Pakistan. We all feel a deep sense of injustice and outrage".[26] When I interviewed Mr Raja I asked him if he would ever apply again. He said "They don't have a criminal record not to visit, I will try again next year".[27]

This particular case is interesting, in that it shows a Conservative MP articulating views commonly held by Labour MPs about the impact of immigration procedures on individuals from the Indian sub-continent. Mr Stewart's charge of racial discrimination implicit in the administration of the immigration regime constitutes evidence which is more powerful than a single case study would normally provide. The attitudes of Labour and Conservative MPs on immigration are compared in chapter 7.

Case 4: Visiting Visa - A Future Politician Succeeds in Getting a Visa for his Sister to Attend a Wedding

The fourth case focuses on a refusal to grant a temporary visa for the purpose of attending a wedding. Councillor Sarwar (now Labour MP for Govan) tried to bring one of his sisters over from Pakistan to attend another sister's wedding in Scotland.[28] The Councillor applied in 1995 for his sister to visit for two reasons. Firstly, he had just lost a brother here. Secondly his youngest sister was getting married in Glasgow. Mr Sarwar's parents are also resident in Scotland but his sister for whom he applied lives in Pakistan. It was a very sentimental time for the family and the sister's presence was deemed necessary. Mr Sarwar sent the application forms to the embassy and to his sister. He did not foresee any problems as the sister is happily married, has four children and her husband is wealthy.

The family was shocked when the visa was refused, so Councillor Sarwar sought help from MP George Galloway. The MP wrote and faxed the British High Commission in Pakistan about the sponsor's political and business credibility. On this occasion the British High Commission took an MP's involvement seriously. They wrote to Sarwar's sister in Pakistan to come to the embassy and collect the visa.

An interesting comment made by Mr Sarwar was "It does not make me happy that I got the visa ...Suppose I did not have the business and suppose I did not have political connections then my sister would have been unable to join us".[29] George Galloway MP for Hillhead said to me

142

"even if somebody like him can be treated in that way, then what about all the people with no voice, who don't have any political profile or any political friends"? [30]

Mr Sarwar's sister was initially refused in case she stayed permanently and did not return to Pakistan. One of the requirements a person has to prove to the ECO to attain a visitors visa to the UK is that he/she "is genuinely seeking entry as a visitor for a limited period as stated by him, not exceeding 6 months and intends to leave the UK at the end of the period of the visit as stated by him".[31] This refusal appears to be an over zealous application of rules because her husband and children were remaining in Pakistan.

As in case 3, there was a fear that visitors would stay permanently in the United Kingdom. In case 3 evidence to the contrary was not accepted in spite of the 'political' support forthcoming from an MP (Stewart) and a significant local Labour politician (Raja). In case 4, the combination of 'political' support (an MP, Galloway, and an elected ethnic minority Councillor, Sarwar) was sufficient to 'legitimise' other evidence about the intention to return to Pakistan and the availability of sufficient funds to support the applicants during their stay in the United Kingdom.

Case 5: Settlement Visa - Marriage

To illustrate the most common type of immigration problem facing people from the Indian sub-continent, I interviewed a young woman of Pakistani origin, a British citizen born here, trying to bring her husband, a Pakistani citizen, to Britain on a permanent basis.[32]

Miss C went to Pakistan for a holiday at the age of 17 with her father. She said to me the reason for going to Pakistan was nothing to do with finding a future husband. She stayed there for eight weeks. However three weeks later during her visit she met 23 year old Mr D, who was a student. They got on exceedingly well with each other and Mr D asked her if she would like to get engaged. Miss C said 'yes' because this young man was a friend of the family and she found him very charming. Thus they both informed their parents and held a small informal engagement. Miss C then came back to Britain.

When Miss C got back in August 1987 she applied for her fiancé to join her here. In September 1987, Miss C made an application through a solicitor. She sent the sponsorship forms over to her fiancé who took them to Islamabad and made an application there.

Back in Britain, Miss C, aged 18, started a Youth Training Scheme at a travel agents, where she worked for a year. The Company went bankrupt so Miss C finished her employment there in September 1988. She then found an clerical job in a Housing Association, and has been working there since then and has been promoted to a permanent position as a housing officer.

Mr D got an interview date for 11th of April 1989 in Pakistan and the interview took place in Islamabad. The questions he was asked included: what does your fiancée do for a living? Does she have a house? What is her income? And what is her education? At the time her fiancé was a student in Pakistan. On the 23rd of April he was refused a visa, the reason being the primary purpose rule. This rule states "The marriage must not be entered into primarily to obtain admission to the UK".[33] The officials clearly believed that gaining admission to the UK was the primary purpose of the engagement and proposed marriage. The visa was also denied because the officials were not happy with Miss C's wages and accommodation. Miss C was earning seven thousand pounds per annum. This concern about lack of financial support for the intending immigrant stimulated the suspicions about the primary purpose of the marriage.

Miss C's solicitor advised her to appeal against the decision through the Immigration Advisory Service, the organisation which has been looked at in detail in chapter 3. This is significant in that the solicitor felt he was not specialised enough in the immigration area. The solicitor's view supports the point made by an official from the Scottish Refugee Council in chapter 3 about the need to educate law firms on the immigration issue. Some ethnic law firms in Glasgow have subsequently advertised for clients faced with immigration problems.

The date of appeal arrived in December 1990. The type of questions Miss C was asked: "How did you meet him? How often did you meet? Did you meet alone?" The Home Office presenting officer asserted that Mr D had said at his interview in Pakistan he was not interested in Miss C. Rather he wanted to come to Britain for economic reasons. Miss C denied this and said this was a lie. They were also refused because of claims that Miss C said it was an arranged marriage and Mr D said it was a love marriage. The immigration official did not believe that the boy and girl were ever left alone because it is not normal for a Muslim family to allow this.

The official believed in the 'arranged marriage' interpretation which transgressed the primary purpose rule much more directly than the 'love marriage' interpretation. This is a vital point because there is a clash of cultures in respect of the nature of the marriage. The truth is that Miss C and Mr D were both right in their own way: the young man was a friend of the family so he knew the girl's relatives quite well, and yet the couple still fell in love without the parents being involved directly. Thus the way the couple met did not go against the tradition of arranged marriages while still involving a clear choice of partner by the two young people romantically attracted to one another.

Immigration officials asked questions like "if your other brothers are married to cousins - why not you"? The implication behind this question is that in the Indian sub-continent culture it is the norm to marry cousins.

In January 1991, Miss C got a letter announcing another refusal of a visa to her fiancé. The application was again rejected on the grounds of primary purpose. The girl could not believe it because she had a stable job, with a good income and had her own house. The IAS tried to appeal to the tribunal, but got a letter in June 1991, saying that there was no chance of the tribunal looking at the application.

Miss C then went to Labour MP Jimmy Dunnachie (Pollok) for assistance, informing him about the tribunal refusing to look at the application. The MP wrote to the Home Office on the 12th of July regarding the case. The Labour MP got a reply on the 16th of August that since Mr D did not satisfy the requirements,[34] the couple should make a fresh application. The requirements meaning firstly, "it must not be the primary purpose of the marriage to gain admission to the UK". Secondly, "the parties should have met within the meaning of the immigration rules"(see chapter 2, section 3.5). Thirdly, "there must be adequate support and accommodation available in this country for Mr D without recourse to public funds".

The MP gave Miss C advice on how to comply with these requirements. Firstly, he advised her to get a letter from someone stating her fiancé has a job to come to in Britain, and, secondly to provide a letter stating that if the couple needed security then there was someone, who would be named to help financially. Miss C carried out these instructions; then the MP wrote to the Home Office including the two pieces of information provided by Miss C. The MP wrote this letter on 18th of August (1991) and got a response from the Home Office on 27/9/91. The Home Office advised that a new application be made. Thus Mr D reapplied in Pakistan and got an interview date in November 1992. He was refused, mainly on primary purpose grounds yet again.

The senior councillor at the IAS now advised Miss C to go to Pakistan and get married to make her case stronger. In the past she had always refused to do so because she wanted to get married in Britain with her family and friends.

Miss C now needed time to think. Her fiancé had asked her to settle in Pakistan with him but she had refused. Nevertheless Miss C finally decided that she would have to get married in Pakistan. It was her only choice, otherwise she would have to give up her fiancé. In November 1993 she got married in Pakistan. She did not go in summer because of the heat wave. Both husband and wife went to Islamabad and made a fresh application, paying £75 each time to make an application. Miss C, now Mrs D, stayed there for three months and came back to Britain in January 1994. Her husband's interview date did not come until September 1994. Mrs D then went to Pakistan again, to be with him in Islamabad for the interview. Normally when a young person is interviewed in Pakistan, another person is also interviewed as his/her witness. In the past Mr D's uncle had been the witness. This time Mrs D went as the witness. Mr D was interviewed for over an hour, while Mrs D was interviewed for only 15 minutes. Her husband was asked questions such as - Why did you get married after such a long time? He answered; "because we were waiting for the result of the appeal and we were waiting for the weather to cool down, it is too hot in Summer". Mrs D said it normally takes a year to plan a marriage anyway.

Mrs D was asked similar questions, such as why did it take so long to get married? And she answered that her husband was a student. She was further asked whether her husband had female cousins in Scotland. Mrs D said yes, this favoured Mrs D because it meant the boy was interested in her and was not marrying just anyone to get into Britain. At the end of the

146

interview Mrs D asked the immigration officer if he would like to see the marriage video, wedding photos etc. The ECO said no, but Mrs D took them for safety purposes. In October 1994, Mr D received the decision that he was refused on the grounds of primary purpose.

Mrs D, totally disturbed by the immigration procedures, decided to go to another solicitor. The solicitor's company was called "Aurang Zeb Iqbal and Co", based in Bradford which she saw advertised on an Asian Sky channel. The solicitor was coming to Glasgow and thus Mrs D decided to contact him.

The solicitor's company were asked to visit the High Commission in Islamabad and sit in on some of the interviews. They were basically given approval to sit and re-open some of the cases. "To that extent their visit has the FCO's 'approval' or at least no 'objection', but they are not of course going solely on our behalf".[35]

During November 1994, the solicitor was doing interviews and Mrs D asked the solicitor to deal with the case at a cost of £350. The case was thus re-opened and the paperwork and the marriage video were taken to Islamabad. The solicitor came back to Bradford and the embassy said they would write back about the case.

The solicitor subsequently received a letter from the ECO which commented on the additional information provided by the sponsor's representatives i.e. Aurangzeb Iqbal and CO, regarding the couple's devotion to each other. It said

> This additional evidence consisted of 24 letters and cards allegedly sent by the appellant to the sponsor. However, my colleague noted that all were post-dated the most recent application and not one appeared to be from the six years between the engagement and the marriage.

Mr Fulton, the ECO, felt that the letters and cards did not constitute credible evidence and were only being used as a tool to strengthen the application. "This only further diminished the appellant's credibility and my colleague was not moved to alter his decision".[36]

On 13/11/94 the right of appeal was exercised and all aspects of the application were viewed. The ECO wrote "However no further evidence

147

has been produced and I am not persuaded to reverse my colleague's original decision to refuse this particular application".[37]

Mrs D appealed on December 1994 and got an interview date in June 1995. The interview took place but the case was adjourned as more intimate letters were needed between the husband and wife in order to establish the strength of the relationship.

The adjudicator gave the Home Office and Mrs D 4 weeks to get the letters back to court in July 1995. At the next interview Mrs D was in court for 2 to 3 hours and was subjected to a very extensive interview. The Home Office presenting officer asked more complex, ambiguous questions relating to seven years ago, that it was hard to remember in exact detail. The father was also interviewed as a witness. Mrs D got the decision in November, that they had finally got the visa. The adjudicator said in his determination "..the couple have not done themselves any favours by trying to paint the lily as to how the marriage came about, and...I am satisfied from the letters of 1989 that they kept in touch with each other". The adjudicator on the other hand thought the marriage was genuine as the appellant had other cousins in the UK whom he could have married but he chose to marry Mrs D. Taking into account the time factor which showed the couple had been in a relationship for a long time, he stated "I am satisfied on balance that the appellant's primary purpose in marrying the sponsor was not to gain admission into the UK".[38]

Unfortunately just when everything was succeeding the Home Office appealed against the adjudicators decision (the Home Office can appeal within 3 months). The Home Office appealed to the Tribunal. Mrs D had to wait from December 95 to 1st of February 96. Mrs D then received a letter stating the Home Office's appeal was dismissed by the tribunal.

This case shows how tiresome, mentally exhausting and expensive it can be for a person when applying for a husband/fiancé. There seems to be lack of privacy in the intimate details demanded for a person involved in immigration cases. It also shows the difficulties presented by the primary purpose rule. Couples find it difficult to prove the marriage is for genuine reasons and not just to obtain an entry visa to live in the UK. It also shows the need to get the evidence accurately reported to the interviewing officers. Mr Nabi a senior councillor in the Immigration Advisory Service located in Glasgow said, "a person finds it extremely difficult to satisfy the

'Primary Purpose' of his/her marriage".[39] This case also highlights the fact that if there are any discrepancies in a case then that is likely to have serious negative implications for an application, and is likely to lengthen severely the decision-making process, thus instilling more and more doubt in the minds of the authorities and feelings of discrimination in the minds of the applicants.

Case 6: Settlement Visa - Marriage

The sixth case is similar to the fifth[40] in that it emphasises the long drawn out nature of procedures provoked by the primary purpose rule. Miss E and her entire family including the mother, all UK citizens, went from Glasgow to Saudi Arabia and then to Pakistan for a 7 week holiday in January 1993. In Pakistan Miss E's mother fell ill. She was taken to all the best doctors there but her own GP over the phone advised that her mother should come back to Britain because he knew what treatment to give her. At the time there were many marriage proposals for Miss E but her father ignored them because of the mother's ill health. However, the elders (grandparents) advised the father to find someone suitable for the girl, since they were already in Pakistan and the elders being old wanted to be present at her wedding.

Miss E then said to me at the interview "If I was to get married in Britain, it's not as if my relatives would get a holiday visa very easily, in order to attend my wedding".[41]

Therefore with Miss E's consent, she got married to Mr F who was of her own choice on the 27th of March 1993. Unfortunately they had to return to Britain on the 29th of March as the mother needed to be admitted to hospital in Glasgow. Now married, Mrs F also flew back as her mother needed her. In Britain she helped to look after her mother who was in hospital but she also worked as a secretarial assistant. Most importantly Mrs F had health problems herself.

The couple kept in touch through phone calls and letters. Then Mr F, a farm labourer, made a visa application in Pakistan. Mrs F sent him the necessary documents including a copy of her passport, their marriage certificate, her bank statement and evidence that she had accommodation for him in the UK. The British High Commission in Islamabad sent Mr F an interview date and specified the documents he should bring along with him. The British High Commission also sent copies of general immigration rules from the Foreign and Commonwealth Office so the applicant would understand what was required.

After his interview in Pakistan on the 12th of August 1994, Mrs F was informed that she was to be interviewed at Glasgow Airport. She was also required to bring documents such as marriage certificate, proof of funds and accommodation, evidence of employment and evidence of correspondence.

At the airport Mrs F was asked questions such as: Had she consummated the marriage? How did she meet her husband? Where did he work? Why did she marry him instead of someone in the UK? Mrs F was also asked whether she would live in Pakistan if her husband did not get the visa. Mrs F replied no, that it was too hot in Pakistan. Mr F was asked similar questions in his interview.

However, the visa was refused on the basis of primary purpose. She was given a time limit of three months to appeal on her husband's behalf. She also thought that he was refused a visa because he was not 100% sure about where she worked, but she claimed that was mainly due to nerves.

Mrs F decided to appeal, with the Immigration Advisory Service (IAS) representing her appeal. The appeal date was 29/6/94 in Glasgow at the immigration appeals court. The IAS councillor prepared her for the appeal date by doing some role playing and by studying the evidence to be submitted at the hearing. The type of evidence to be submitted at the hearing included bank statements, affidavits with translation, land deed and medical report. The medical report regarding Mrs F's illness was provided as evidence. Since the appeal date was a long way yet, Mrs F flew back to Pakistan and stayed for three and a half months with her husband and only had to come back for the appeal date.

At the appeal the sponsor was asked the following questions:

1. Why did you marry this particular boy? Were there no others you could marry here?
2. Why did he marry you? Was there nobody in Pakistan for him?

3. Why did you come back 2 days after the marriage? Surely there are hospitals in Pakistan which could have treated you satisfactorily.
4. If you do not get the visa, what will you do?

Mrs F answered to the last question, that I am a British citizen and I do have a right to bring in my husband. If the worst comes to the worst, I will stay in Pakistan rather than destroy my marriage.

One can note from the above, that the type of questions the ECOs ask are tricky, ambiguous and can be confusing. Any simple person from a rural village in Pakistan would definitely have problems and especially if they had never been confronted by officials before.

The appeal was refused. The following reasons were given to explain why the adjudicator came to his decision. According to the wife (sponsor), her husband "the appellant would have a better life in Pakistan than he would have in the UK, yet he was prepared to come here". The point that Mrs F was trying to stress was that because her husband was willing to give up a better life in Pakistan to come and live in Britain was proof that the primary purpose of the marriage was *not* to gain entry to the UK. Therefore he should not be rejected on the basis of the primary purpose rule. The adjudicator found that Mrs F said that "She had never seen the appellant before 1993".[42] While the boy had said he had seen her before in 1986. Basically the appellant had said that he did not get married for a better life in the UK. However "the appellants family were all aware of his wife's condition and of her mother's health and they knew that they had to go back to the UK. The mother still had regular treatment for her condition".[43] This evidence was interpreted as signifying that Mrs F would definitely have had intentions to stay in the UK for treatment and her husband may have married her for this reason. The adjudicator found in the evidence the sponsor's father provided as a witness at the appeal, that "It is also evident from the family tree that there were other close relatives available in Pakistan for a match with the appellant". This finding implied that the young man could have married one of his cousins in Pakistan, and that therefore the primary purpose rule was being breached. The adjudicator went on to say "It was claimed at the hearing that those relatives are not on good terms. The appellant had made no mention of this difficulty and was in fact reduced to silence when asked about this at the interview".[44]

Another reason which seemed to cause doubt in the mind of the adjudicator was that the sponsor, must have mentioned to her husband after the marriage that she preferred to live in the UK because that was where she grew up. However, at the hearing the sponsor said the primary purpose of the marriage was to be with her husband, therefore she would live in Pakistan if she was forced to do so.[45] The adjudicator wrote in his determination "I do not find credible the evidence of the sponsor and her father that if the visa application were refused the sponsor would live in Pakistan". Yet the claim by Miss F that she was prepared to live in Pakistan was contingent upon her husband being refused a visa to enter Britain; living in Pakistan was Miss F's second choice which would be forced on her only if her husband was refused a visa.

The adjudicator believed that there was no reason to believe the couple were not devoted to each other i.e. seen through the use of intimate letters. In spite of this the adjudicator's final decision was "I am not satisfied on the balance of probability that the primary purpose of the marriage as far as the appellant is concerned is not to secure his entry to the United Kingdom".[46] The appeal was therefore dismissed, although it may have seemed obvious that the appellant was aware that due to this marriage, he may need to live in the UK. But the primary purpose rule does seem harsh if evidence exists that the couple are devoted to each other, yet the visa is refused on the probability of why the appellant got married to the sponsor.

The IAS wrote to Mrs F that the appeal was dismissed but "We have 14/42 days from the date of the decision to apply to the Immigration Appeals Tribunal for leave to appeal against the decision".[47]

There could be possible reasons to appeal to the tribunal if there is strong proof that the couple are devoted to each other i.e. the sponsor is willing to live in Pakistan if all else fails, yet the adjudicator does not believe this.

After the appeal was refused in June, Mrs F flew to Pakistan in September 94 to visit her husband. At the same time the process of appeal to the Tribunal was taking place. The IAS Tribunal Unit wrote to Mrs F that "the application that has been made is a request for leave to appeal, that is permission to take the appeal further". It went on to say "If leave to appeal is granted then we will be able to proceed with the case; however leave will only be granted if there is a point of law to be argued".[48]

The application for leave to appeal was refused on 29/11/94. The tribunal had read all the papers and decided: "....the adjudicator's conclusions are fully supported by the evidence, bearing in mind his findings on the credibility of the witnesses and his assessment of the oral evidence he heard".[49] The Tribunal Councillor then wrote to Mrs F "...it is my view that the tribunal may have been wrong in their decision...consider the possibility of challenging the tribunal's decision by making an application for judicial review in the High Court".[50]

In January 1995, Mrs F found out she was pregnant, thus there was a change in her (immigration) circumstances as the government had introduced a concession in the primary purpose rule:[51] i.e. if there is a child born after the marriage or the marriage is successfully subsisting for the last five years without a child, the entry clearance will be granted as long as the couple have evidence that they can maintain and accommodate themselves in the UK without depending on social security.

After finding out about her pregnancy, a close relative discussed her case with an official at the British High Commission who advised her to re-apply.

Mr F in July 1995, filled an IM2A form which is for long stay and short stay applicants and an IM2E form, which is basically a re-application form and a letter from Rutherglen Maternity Hospital confirming his wife's pregnancy. He took the documents to Islamabad where he was asked a few questions about where his wife lived and what she did. He was informed he would be sent a letter in Spring 1996. Now the baby was due at the end of August 1995. Mrs F gave birth to a son and informed me that she had a difficult birth and had a caesarean operation. Basically this was the time she really needed her husband at her side. After the birth, she wrote to Islamabad asking if they would bring the interview date forward as the baby was born and enclosed a copy of his birth certificate. Within two weeks, Mrs F received a letter asking for tax papers, housing accommodation, birth certificate. Mrs F then received notification that the Embassy had received the documents and would soon come to a decision. Six weeks later Mrs F received a letter asking for the exact same papers again. Thus the papers were sent again, but this time by hand. A Glasgow relative of Mrs F was visiting Pakistan and took the papers so that they reached Islamabad safely. Mrs F phoned from Glasgow ten to fifteen times to find out about the decision because a long time had passed. Then finally the husband was sent a letter telling him to collect the visa and that was without an interview. It had taken 2 years to obtain the visa.

Mrs F then said to me "why is it that my male relatives in the UK managed to secure entry visas for their wives within one year, while it normally tends to drag on for females"?[52] The point of men having more difficulties than woman to gain an entry visa has already been analysed in the previous chapter.[53] The Conservative government did use a similar ploy in 1980 where black British citizen women were prevented from bringing in their husbands and the European Commission on Human Rights declared this as discriminatory.[54]

Cases 5 and 6 were both at first refused on the primary purpose rule that "the marriage was entered primarily to obtain admission to the UK".[55] These cases emphasise how difficult a criterion it is to prove to the entry clearance officers the genuineness and the credibility of the marriage. Such decisions inevitably include a strong measure of subjectivity.

Case 7: Settlement Visa for a Wife

This case involving a man trying to get permanent stay for his wife in the UK is a little different from the usual spouse case but the theme of primary purpose is still seen as the root of the problem here. This case also reveals a significant conflict between British institutions implementing the immigration regime. A young wife had a difficult time with the immigration official because she tried to avoid the waiting queues to come to the UK and came on a visitor visa instead.[56] It is true that she did break the rules. The sad part is that she felt compelled to do so because the immigration rules led to families being separated for long lengths of time. Otherwise Mrs Kanabar would have probably come via the proper channels. Mrs Kanabar, a freelance journalist, was 23 when she got married in India. Her husband was an electrical engineer from Glasgow and a British passport holder. They got married in 1985 in India. The husband had to return to his job in Britain where he worked in the defence industry.

Mrs Kanabar first applied for an entry visa in 1985, after her marriage, at the British High Commission in India but they advised her to go to Britain as a visitor and apply from there. She said "If we applied from Britain it would not take as long and we would have been together".[57] She said it was not that difficult to come as a visitor in comparison to a spouse. In Britain Mrs Kanabar was refused entry at Glasgow Airport because "immigration officers believed she intended to settle".[58] The entry clearance officer in Glasgow told her to go back to India and apply for a visa there. Mr Kanabar took his wife's case to the Joint Council for the Welfare of Immigrants and to Mr Roy Jenkins MP for Hillhead and as a result his wife was given permission to stay for three months. Mrs Kanabar went back to India after the three months but said it was a mistake she regretted. It was now 1986 and from India Mrs Kanabar applied for a permanent visa. Their first child was due in December 1986 and she was called for an interview in March 1987 at the British High Commission in India. Mr Kanabar was worried because he wanted the baby to be born in Britain so he could be with his first child and his wife. His wife wrote to the embassy that she would like her interview date brought earlier as it would have been difficult to travel to Britain when she was so heavily pregnant. The embassy brought the interview date to October 1986. Later on the High Commission cancelled the interview in October saying the waiting list was too long.

Her husband, now in a dilemma, contacted the immigration officers in Glasgow for advice. The ECO advised him to bring her to Britain before October so that she could be interviewed in Glasgow. Mrs Kanabar came to Glasgow in September and was 7 months pregnant. The same immigration officer then turned against everything he said. He said there was no way he was letting her in and it was illegal to come into the country as a visitor, when the genuine reason is to stay in the UK permanently as a wife. He was saying that the husband had made the story up. Mr Kanabar a decent educated man was shocked at this false accusation. The ECO told her to leave the country.

The Herald had also covered the story the head line was "Asian couple faces split before baby's birth". To the *Herald* the husband said "I had two options...either return to India and lose my job or bring her over as a visitor again".[59] The husband and wife again contacted their local MP for Hillhead Mr Jenkins. The MP got an extension for the wife to stay three months, whilst Mrs Kanabar gave birth to a baby girl in December. When the baby was 1/2 weeks old the immigration officials contacted her to go back with or without the baby. At another time the immigration officers came to the house while the husband was away at work. The officers were saying they had papers that the wife had to leave the country. Again this story was reported in the *Herald* "Asian mother must leave baby behind".[60] Mrs Kanabar told the immigration officers that the baby was still very young, has not been keeping well and needed looking after. Luckily her husband came for lunch and was outraged. He told them to leave the house at once and that his lawyer would deal with them.

The doctor advised that the baby should not go to India until it had been immunised. Which would mean the baby should be around 9 months old.

From 1987 onwards it was a nightmare for the family; according to Mrs Kanabar, the immigration officers kept writing to her, her MP and her lawyer that she should leave the country. Mrs Kanabar said "I never said I won't go back, but I will go back when the baby is one years old and I will then apply for a visa from India".[61] Now it was 1987 and the problems still continued with immigration. The immigration officers informed the husband and wife that they would pay them a visit. The couple had contacted Janice Fox who worked for the Scottish Asian Action Committee (SAAC). Mrs Fox brought along with her two people from a Human Rights organisation to be present at the interview. Thus the SAAC representative and the two people from Human Rights waited for the immigration officers to show at the house. The immigration officers felt very uncomfortable and embarrassed. They never said anything but left a letter telling the wife to leave the country by the next day.

The Scottish Asian Action Committee started campaigning. The media became involved; Scottish Television, radio, the *Evening Times* and the *The Herald* all interviewed the couple. After the media attention the immigration officials had a change of heart. At the end of 1988 and beginning of 1989 Mrs Kanabar got a letter from Timothy Raison informing her to go to Glasgow airport and collect her visa allowing her to stay permanently. Mrs Kanabar told me "It nearly broke up my marriage. We owed £2,000 to the solicitor and I suffered from depression - why"? [62]

This case illustrates the fact that immigration rules may be applied as strictly to females as to males seeking permanent settlement. In this case what did not help was the fact that Mrs Kanabar tried to bend the rules by coming on a visitor visa. This gave the immigration authorities a plausible reason, if they needed one, to deny her permanent stay. Although she eventually got permission to stay permanently, it is arguable whether this would have been the eventual outcome had it not been for all the media attention which the case attracted.

Case 8: Visiting Visa for a Sick Person - Visa Refused to a Person who Needs an Operation

George Galloway MP told me of a case where he was trying to help a person in Pakistan who had a serious heart problem and needed a triple by-pass. [63] This man has six brothers all of them British citizens and all of them businessmen. The one who came for help to the MP had paid last year £14,000 pounds in tax. All the brothers got together 60,000 pounds so that their brother in Pakistan could go to the HCI hospital in Clydebank, which is almost empty, in order to get the triple by-pass. Unfortunately the brother was refused and was eventually treated elsewhere in Pakistan. The MP said "they are even turning down people who want to spend money in the private health sector - in case he stays here permanently and runs away from his family back home - I don't think so". [64]

Conclusions

This chapter has illustrated the various issues and conflicts that arise when individuals from the Indian sub-continent apply for visas to stay in Britain permanently or temporarily. There is clearly a significant clash of cultures at the heart of the conflicts arising out of the implementation of immigration control rules and procedures.

Immigration officials have a clear duty to perform. Firstly, they are required to ensure that individuals from the sub-continent applying for a short stay in the United Kingdom are not actually seeking to enter permanently. Secondly, the officials must satisfy themselves that individuals coming to Britain to get married or after they have just been are not merely using marriage as a device to settle in Britain. The prime reason for the marriage must not be to secure a visa to settle permanently in Britain.

This chapter suggests that the implementation of immigration rules and procedures by officials carrying out their duty has caused hardship, pressure and strain for many of those involved in the cases described in this chapter. Stressful and distasteful procedures include the intimate questions posed, the lengthy waiting time often imposed before the eventual granting of a visa after an initial rejection, and the experience of interrogation in appeal courts as if two people had committed a crime rather than getting married.

This chapter has also shown that there is very little difference in how the different types of applications are viewed and handled. For example whether you are applying for a visa to come for an operation or for a visa to attend a wedding you are likely to encounter similar problems. In fact no case that we have seen in this chapter has been straight forward. The difficulties in obtaining a visa are outlined by the cases. Cases 2, 3, and 4 illustrate how difficult it is to prove that someone is just wanting to visit temporarily. Cases 5, 6, and 7 illustrate the difficulties confronting couples attempting to prove their marriage is genuine.

Examining the immigration requirements in the case of settlement visas reveals conflict between the immigration rules and Indian sub-continent traditions. Salience is given to a couple's devotion as seen in case 6. However more priority seems to be given to the primary purpose of the marriage e.g. was it to enter the UK? Taking into consideration case 5, the ECO refused the visa on various grounds which do depict the basis on which settlement visas are allowed. The visa was not permitted on the grounds that the couple were not related whereas in Muslim tradition couples tend to be cousins. This is tantamount to claiming that a marriage not involving cousins cannot be genuine in the eyes of ECOs. Another reason for refusing a visa was that the majority of marriages in Indian sub-continent cultures are arranged; the marriage in case 5 seemed to be a love marriage which also aroused the official's suspicions. In reality it could be said it was a mixture of arranged and love. Another reason to refuse a visa was the length of time involved when the couple were engaged to the date they actually got married. This could however be interpreted as devotion on the part of the couple who have maintained a relationship for a lengthy period. In Asian culture the women generally stays with their husband's family and the ECO believed it was wrong for a husband to join his wife in the UK.

All the above refusals were based on subjective judgements based on stereotypical views of Asian culture. Nonetheless, these are the common arguments used by an ECO to refuse a settlement visa. The ECO's justification is derived from cultural reasons independently of economic facts. It is not the law of the land and neither a necessary requirement in religion that a couple before marriage must be related, or the marriage must be arranged, or the daughter-in-law must stay with her husband's family. In fact when the Conservative government under Thatcher tried to prevent the entry of husbands and male fiancés to the UK for economic reasons,[65] the same philosophy did not apply to wives entering the UK. In fact there is no religious or cultural writings which stress that women from the Indian sub-continent are not allowed to work. Overall, Asians born in the UK have very different perceptions being brought up in a Western society and it is not fair to assume that he/she adheres to the same customs of their forefathers. Asian women in the UK are not brought up thinking they will be living with their in-laws and these are the same women who apply for their husband or fiancé to join them in the UK. Neither are British Asian women destined to have arranged marriages. Yet ECOs seem to take it for granted that marriages are arranged and if a couple do not have an arranged marriage then the ECO is sceptical about the case. The whole procedure of interrogation, interviews, intimate questions, appeal courts, tribunals seem to treat a person as if they are committing a crime rather than entering upon the institution of marriage. The couples' devotion to each other is not seen as important a factor as the official evaluation of the primary purpose of the marriage.

From the evidence gathered, it does look as though the immigration rules are tied with customs but there is a contradiction when one of the requirements is: "..the parties to the proposed marriage have met",[66] when in arranged marriages the couple are not meant to meet. This example shows how the immigration procedure opposes the arranged marriage idea and yet the system still manages to create hurdles for British born Asians who are involved in the process, using culture as a tool.

In the cases mentioned dealing with settlement visas, all the sponsors and the appellant go through a long and laborious process to attain a visa but at the end of the day the government grants the visa anyway. The counter-argument to the lengthy waiting time for a visa is provided by an official from the FCO in chapter 6. In the opinion of Maria Fyfe (Maryhill) the Labour MP, the ECOs in primary purpose cases look for any tiny detail to refuse the visa.[67]

The appellate authority is good in the sense people are given a chance to appeal against a refusal decision. Regional Adjudicator Mr Deans believes adjudicators are fair in their decisions.[68] However the cases looked at do show appeals failing at the adjudicator level and chapter 3 illustrates the IAS having less success at representation than at the appeal level over the 1980-1990 decade.

The most common type of immigration case the IAS deals with are those concerning the primary purpose rule.[69] It is indeed a difficult task to prove a person is marrying for love rather than entry to the UK. In most cases the IAS councillors advise marriage rather than engagement. It is disappointing that most commonly a young woman from the UK has to get married abroad as seen in case 5, since it is very difficult for a fiancé's application to succeed in comparison to an application made for a husband's settlement visa. Many young women I spoke to wanted their own family and friends to attend their wedding but this was not possible since they had to marry in Pakistan, India or Bangladesh due to visa difficulties. The Home Office officials from the Immigration and Nationality Department acknowledged that people from the Indian sub-continent did not like the primary purpose rule.[70] The Scottish Labour MPs such as George Galloway, Mike Watson and Maria Fyfe also criticised the primary purpose rule.[71]

Another way to try to counter the primary purpose rule was for many women to have children. It is again deplorable that one has to plan a family in accordance with immigration policy. Women also complained about having to reveal intimate personal details to immigration officers e.g. marriage being consummated. In Asian culture one's sex life is seen as a very private matter yet in an immigration case one has to speak about it openly with strangers. The most common complaints I heard while interviewing women in primary purpose cases was the cost of flying a couple of times a year to see their husbands/fiancés. The fee paid each time an application was made, was also a common criticism mentioned by the interviewees and was even recognised by an official from the Migration and Visa Unit of the FCO.[72] This also affected their relationship with their employers. The number of visits made abroad were important as ECOs took into account the number of times a wife visited her husband.

However if tough immigration policies are to exist then at least on compassionate grounds, there should be some relaxing of the rules. When Labour came to power in 1997 the primary purpose rule was abolished, seen by many as a step in the right direction. Case 1 involved a woman and her family from Pakistan not being able to see their dying relative on time, because they had to satisfy the immigration requirements. In case 1, Mrs B was granted a visa before her grandmother's death but her husband was refused a visa even on compassionate grounds, except to attend the funeral. This case illustrates the attitudes of immigration officials when considering visa applications from men. Where does one draw the line between compassion and entry requirements? The reasons for denying a visa to the husband seemed to be valid till the 22nd of November but dropped later. It is true that there may well be many bogus cases from these countries but one cannot assume that every single person from the Indian sub-continent is attempting to gain entry by deception. This is a view shared by Layton-Henry in his work analysed in chapter 1. Layton-Henry stresses the fact that tough immigration procedures have meant that genuinely innocent individuals have been denied entry. A senior IAS councillor made the point about immigration policy "If the person is coming from Western countries, e.g. USA, Canada, Australia, they will have very little difficulty to get the entry clearance".[73] This is the view of a IAS Councillor who has been working in this area for 15 years. Immigration officers are given an difficult duty and they do get their instructions from the Secretary of State. A civil servant from the Foreign and Commonwealth Office admitted that people from the Indian sub-continent (Pakistan, India and Bangladesh) had more problems with the procedures than individuals from the white commonwealth countries i.e. Canada, Australia and New Zealand. His reason was that people living in these countries have a higher standard of living than people in the Indian sub-continent. Therefore it is assumed that the Australians are likely to return home after their visit to the UK, whilst people in the Indian sub-continent have a low standard of living and want a chance to better themselves in Britain.[74] This official confirmed that people from the white commonwealth countries are favoured by prevailing attitudes and assumptions in comparison to people from the Indian sub-continent. Nevertheless it is still a crude way to treat any human being since individuals in the Indian sub-continent also have some pride. This again raises the question of unfairness and discrimination. The immigration regime just like the rule of law in any other area must be implemented fairly and equally without any semblance of discrimination, be it racial or cultural discrimination. The immigration officials decisions are based on probability but at what costs?

Notes

1. *Interview* with Mike Watson MP (Glasgow Central), 2 February 1996.
2. Names have been changed to ensure confidentiality.
3. *Fax* from Neurosurgeon at Southern General sent to British High Commission. Islamabad, Pakistan, 15 October 1994.
4. *Fax* sent from Western Infirmary regarding the health of Mrs A, 11 November 1994.
5. *Letter* from Mike Watson MP to Entry Clearance Officer, British High Commission, Islamabad, 11 November 1994.
6   *Letter* to Mike Watson from Foreign and Commonwealth Office (FCO), Immigration and Visa Correspondence Unit, London, 15 November 1994.
7. *Ibid*, 18 November 1994.
8. *Letter* to Right Hon Douglas Hurd from Mike Watson, 25 November 1994.
9. *Ibid* to Mike Watson from Foreign and Commonwealth Office, London, 28 November 1994.
10. This was clearly stated to Mike Watson in a *letter* from the immigration authorities.
11. *Letter* from Mike Watson to the sponsor in relation to the outcome of the case, 12 December 1994.

12. *Statement of Changes in Immigration Rules*, para. 41, p. 8, 23 May 1994, (London: HMSO).
13. *Interview* with Mike Watson, 2 February 1996, who after the 1997 General Election is no longer an MP.
14. This was specified in a *letter* sent by the Entry Clearance Officer to the applicant.
15. *Letter* from Mike Watson sent to Foreign and Commonwealth Office, London, 4 July 1995.
16. *Ibid* to Mike Watson MP from FCO, 19 July 1995.
17. *Statement of Changes in Immigration Rules*, para. 317, p. 63, 23 May 1994.
18. *Interview* with Mr Raja, 15 June 1996.
19. Alan Stewart MP (Eastwood) resigned before the 1997 General Election and was replaced by Paul Cullen.
20. *Letter* to Mr Raja from Alan Stewart's private secretary, 14 October 1994.
21. See *Glasgow Herald*, November 9, 1994, p. 1.
22. *Ibid.*
23. *Ibid.*
24. See *ibid*, November 12, 1994, p. 14.
25. *Ibid*
26. *Ibid.*
27. *Interview* with Mr Raja, 15 June 1996.
28. *Ibid* with Councillor Sarwar, 15 June 1996, who after the 1997 General Election became Labour MP for Govan.
29. *Ibid*
30. *Ibid* with George Galloway MP (Hillhead), 19 April 1996.
31. *Statement of Changes in Immigration Rules*, op. cit. para. 41, p. 8, 23 May 1994.
32. *Interview* with Miss C, 2 December 1996, the names have been changed for confidential reasons.
33. *Statement of Changes in Immigration Rules*, op.cit. para. 290, p. 55, 23 May 1994.
34. *Letter* to the MP from the immigration authorities.
35. *Letter* to Keith Best, Immigration Advisory Service Chairman, from the Migration and Visa Department, 4 July 1994.
36 *Ibid* to Solicitors "Aurung Zeb Iqbal and Co" from Entry Clearance Officer M Dyson.
37. *Document* from M Dyson, Entry Clearance Officer to solicitors "Aurang Zeb Iqbal and Co" referring to the re-opening of the case still being unsatisfactory.
38. This view was laid out in a detailed recording of the hearing and sent later to the applicant's representative.
39. *Interview* with Mr Nabi, Senior Councillor, Immigration Advisory Service, Glasgow, May 1994.
40 *Ibid* with Miss E, names have been changed for confidentiality.
41. *Ibid* with Miss E, 10 January 1996.
42. *Adjudicators determination and reasons*, p. 4, 29 June 1994.
43. *Ibid*, p. 6.

44. *Ibid*, p. 7.
45. *Ibid*, p. 9.
46. *Ibid*, p. 12.
47. *Letter* from IAS to Miss E to lodge an appeal against the adjudicators decision, 11 August 1994.
48. *Ibid* to Miss E from the Tribunal Unit informing her that an application for leave to appeal has been made, 31 August 1994.
49. The decision is detailed in a *letter* to the applicant from the adjudicator.
50. The decision is detailed in a *letter* from the Tribunal counsellor to the applicant.
51. *Immigration Directorate Instructions 1997*, Concession intervene devotion introduced 1993, Chapter 8, Annex B, available House of Commons Library.
52. *Interview* with Miss E, 10 January 1996.
53. See *chapter 4*.
54. Paul Gordon and Francesca Klug, *British Immigration Control a brief guide*, p. 12, (Runnymede Trust, 1985).
55. *Statement of Changes in Immigration Rules*, op. cit. para. 281, p. 53, 23 May 1994.
56. *Interview* with Mrs Kanabar, 22 January 1996, the name has not been changed since the story was covered by the press.
57. *Ibid*
58. See *Glasgow Herald*, November 5, 1985, p. 5.
59. *Ibid*.
60. *Glasgow Herald*, March 17, 1987, p. 11.
61. *Interview* with Mrs Kanabar, 22 January 1996
62. *Ibid*
63. *Ibid* with George Galloway MP (Hillhead), 19 February 1996.
64. *Ibid*.
65. Satvinder S. Juss, *Immigration, Nationality and Citizenship*, p. 11, (Mansell, 1993).
66. *Statement of Changes in Immigration Rules*, op. cit. para. 290, p. 55, 23 May 1994.
67. *Correspondence* with Maria Fyfe MP (Maryhill), 1 April 1996.
68. *Interview* with Mr. Deans, Regional Adjudicator, Immigration Appellate Authority, Glasgow, August 2 1996; see also *chapter 6*
69. *Ibid* with Mr Nabi, Senior Councillor, Immigration Advisory Service, May 1994.
70. *Ibid* with Nick Troake, Policy Directorate, Immigration and Nationality Department, Home Office, 19 September 1996.
71. *Ibid* with George Galloway MP (19 April 1996), Mike Watson MP (2 March 1996), and Maria Fyfe MP (1 April 1996).
72. *Ibid* with Sean Lusk, Migration and Visa Unit, Foreign and Commonwealth Office, 20 September 1996.
73. *Ibid* with Mr Nabi, Senior Councillor, Immigration Advisory Service, May 1994.
74. *Ibid* with Sean Lusk, Migration and Visa Unit, Foreign and Commonwealth Office, 20 September 1996.

6 Immigration: The Official View

Introduction

Up till now this study has concentrated on one side of the debate on the issue of immigration, focusing on those who are affected directly and indirectly by the immigration regime and on those who provide help to the individuals and families who require assistance. This chapter will attempt to widen perceptions of the immigration issue by analysing the views of those who administer and interpret the contemporary immigration regime, i.e. civil servants, adjudicators, and immigration police. In other words it will balance the immigration debate by providing the other side of the argument. The chapter looks at how the authorities are involved, and how they themselves perceive immigration issues. Implementation is a vital feature of the immigration arena because this is the aspect which confronts would be immigrants directly. The views of various civil servants on the immigration policies and on the common complaints arising from implementation of the policies provide a different perspective on immigration issues.

This chapter is divided into sections on the basis of who was interviewed (see Appendix for the list of questions asked). For sections one and two the interviews were conducted in Glasgow, but since implementation of policy is mainly decided in the Home Office in London the interviews for section three took place in London. Section one deals with the Police and Nationality Department. Section two involves interviews with three adjudicators about their ideas on immigration procedures. In section three, civil servants in the Migration and Visa unit of the Foreign and Commonwealth Office and officials from the Immigration and Nationality Department at the Home Office give their response to public criticisms of their job.

Also since most of the policies and laws passed in the 1980s are still in operation, the immigration officials can give an opinion on the regime developed during the Thatcher era. The acts of legislation include: the 1981 British Nationality Act; introduction of visas in 1986; the 1987 Carriers' Liability Act; and the 1988 Immigration Act.[1] The adjudicators and the Police and Nationality Department all have a role to play today dealing with immigrants under the laws enacted in the 1979-90 period.

This chapter seeks to show how the immigration officials in Glasgow perceive the immigration policies and procedures, and how civil servants in London view the Conservative government's immigration policies of the 1980s. Organisations in Glasgow helping immigrants,[2] and immigrants themselves,[3] depicted the immigration regime as "tough" because of lengthy waiting periods, frequent refusals[4] and the harsh, discriminatory, and unfair procedures and criteria which had to be met. However, is that view shared by those responsible for making and implementing the regime?

Police and Nationality Department

The police have quite a few duties relating to immigration. The police are concerned with registering foreign nationals, and like the immigration officers, the police can arrest individuals who are suspected of being here illegally. The police may also be required to accumulate information on the personal circumstances of a sponsor making application for bringing in relatives into this country.[5]

The police involvement in immigration goes back to 1914.

..For the first time in the constitutional and legal history of Great Britain, aliens became liable for registration by the police and by 6th August 1914, the instructions were in the hands of all police forces and immigration officers.[6]

I interviewed a Detective Sergeant[7] from the Police Nationality Department in order to examine their involvement with immigration (see Appendix). He emphasised that the main objective of the Police and Nationality Department is to assist the immigration service.

The interviewee said the "Department was set up many years ago as a nation-wide system". He went on to give a small summary of immigration procedure. When an individual comes into the country the first people he meets are immigration officers at airports and seaports. It is the immigration officer who determines the length of stay an individual should be given based on certain circumstances e.g. here to study, work, or just for a holiday. The immigration officer may decide depending on the immigrant's nationality that he has to register with the police. Commonwealth citizens and citizens of the British Protectorate Territories do not need to register with the police so that includes Canadians, Australians, Indians and Pakistanis. The Detective Sergeant said "However at this present time Strathclyde police has around 2,800 individuals who register with them, from 67 different countries throughout the world". Once the immigration officer makes the decision that the individual must register with the police, he or she must thereafter go to any police office or headquarters, where the appropriate form is filled in and a fee is paid. He said that this is the police side of the immigration service. He went on to emphasise that the department worked on behalf of the Home Office but under the rules and guidance of the Chief Constable of Strathclyde Police. If the Immigration service wishes to carry out an operation to apprehend someone who is either an illegal immigrant or an 'over-stayer', or working in breach of the conditions in the country, then the immigration officers contact the immigration police who will arrange to provide personnel to assist the immigration service. The Detective Sergeant told me that "The immigration service no longer uses the powers of arrest". This is because a number of years ago the immigration service were told by their union they might get injured. So the immigration officers no longer enjoy the powers of arrest. Instead they now take the police with them if an arrest is to be made. The Immigration Service will contact the police; if they need to go to an address, a factory or a restaurant, the police will accompany them. If there is someone who is in breach of immigration law, "we will then effect the arrest and take them to our police office where they can be questioned by the immigration service".

When asked how many people were working in the department, he said there were five individuals; a Detective Sergeant, a Detective constable, and three civilian support staff. The civilians dealt mainly with registration procedures affecting foreign nationals.

When asked how the department deals with an individual case, he gave a brief description. Because the immigration service no longer enjoys the powers of arrest, the police work on their behalf "whether they are going to detain someone or whether they are going to release them to report later for an interview with them". This is usually when an individual has entered the country illegally. The Home Office decides when a person should go to prison. A good reason for such a decision is that he may have absconded in the past so the person has to go to his nearby police office every week to ensure he does not abscond. In a deportation situation the police would assist by taking the individual down to Heathrow and putting him on a flight direct to his homeland. If the person has absconded before or has been charged with a serious crime i.e. murder or rape, then the individual will be escorted back to his homeland which could be anywhere in the world.

Males in breach of immigration rules in the Strathclyde area are taken to Greenock prison and females are taken to Corntonvale prison in Stirling.

The rights they have according to the Detective Sergeant are the same right as any one else in police custody i.e. they are entitled to a solicitor, to be washed and fed, and to be provided with exercise facilities. They are only held for temporary purpose in a police office on behalf of the immigration service who will make arrangements for them to be transported to a prison, again depending on the situation. "The conditions are fair and I try to be impartial the way all police officers should be anyway". The Detective also made the point that they deal a lot with illegal immigrant cases from the Indian sub-continent as there are people living in the UK who tell on them i.e. "they send letters, they will telephone, just to tell of an individual working illegally". So why are there informers? The police official gave the reason that people do not like the other person, they want his job and those who just think it is morally wrong. Some of these informers are of British origin and some of Asian origin.

The thinking behind the need for such a department was really a government policy, "this would be the Foreign and Commonwealth section along with the Home Office. We are acting on behalf of the Home Office...".

The Police and Nationality Department is accountable to the Chief Constable. He went on to say "anything we do involving foreign nationals is under his guide-lines". The Chief Constable is accountable to the Home Secretary. The police official informed me that every chief officer of police for each force has the responsibilities to keep a register on behalf of the Home Office of all foreign nationals to be registered with the police.

The present structure, the Detective Sergeant said, was a national structure. Every police force in the whole of the UK has a nationality department.

He also released information as I interviewed him which shows that the immigration authorities have always had a link with people from the Indian subcontinent. He informed me of a time when people from Asia, India and Pakistan did register with the police. Now "all foreign nationals register with the police except for the Commonwealth countries, British Dependent Territories, EEC countries and now in 1994 the European free trade countries e.g. Iceland, Norway and Sweden" said the Detective Sergeant. Once people register with the police they have certain conditions to fulfil. If the address is changed, then within seven days the police must be informed. It is possible with this present identity card idea that people will be stopped in the street and asked for their identification if they look suspicious, which according to the Detective Sergeant is a good idea. Since in this way people could easily be caught by the police when in breach of immigration rules.

The immigration police also deal with nationality and naturalisation inquiries. "Persons who come into the country and have been given indefinite leave to remain in the country apply for British citizenship". That would mean husband, wives and children who have been here 5 years or more can apply to the Home Office for British Citizenship. There is also a fee of around £300. He said the file is sent from the Home Office and the police interview the applicant and his family. The process would include the interviewing of two referees, asking questions on birth and education, and examining marriage documentary evidence of the person wanting British citizenship. Then a report of suitability would be sent back to the Home Office. It is the Home Office that makes the decision on the citizenship. The police are the intermediary who do the enquiry.

When asked how many cases the department deals with annually, the police official told me they only dealt with a few naturalisation enquiries per year. Strathclyde Police does a dozen per year. An interesting point was "this has been decreasing per year, since 1979, we get less now than before. Ten years ago we were fairly busy with people wanting to become British Citizens". This could be due to the fact that there has been a tightening of the immigration laws during the 1980s, thus people found it harder to get into the country and therefore fewer cases of naturalisation arose. In general, another officer, a Detective Constable in the Nationality Department, informed me, Strathclyde Police deals with 90-100 operations concerning illegal immigrants.

When I asked whether the job of the department has been affected by Conservative immigration legislation, the Detective said 'no' and then, referring to asylum seekers, said "I don't think a person from a foreign country should be able to live on our handouts". He felt that it is the tax payers who should be getting the fruits of their labour not others i.e.

> I mean it's the people of the UK that includes Asian nationals who are paying into the system, they are the ones who should be able to get out of the system not people who have broken the laws to come here, and then want to take the money as well.

The detective said they should be housed and catered for "but not fancy hotels, maybe a camp style life for them... nothing further - this is a personal opinion".

He was asked if there had been any complaints, criticisms when handling individual cases. He told of an example where Maria Fyfe MP made a complaint and wrote that "while we were in a house checking for documents we stood on a prayer mat". The detective said "It just looked like a mat but now we know". He said "It is the only complaint I have ever received". The Detective Sergeant felt that immigration laws for people from the Indian sub-continent were fair and "..... we do have to have some way of stemming the flow of immigrants into the country, we can only carry so many, that's what the screening process is all about, you can't just throw open your doors". The police official felt they were needed because "you end up with all sorts of terrorists and unsuitable persons that nobody would like to live beside".

When asked about which organisations the department liaise with he said "We liaison with the Home Office and the immigration service". The Immigration Advisory Service contacts the police for advice which the police give unofficially.

The Police Immigration Department has no say on the implementation of an immigration rule, i.e. "all policy making is at a national scale, so that's done by the Home Office". The department gets the instructions from the "Home Office Immigration and Nationality Department in Lunar house".

The Detective Sergeant actually gives lectures on race awareness, "its called the policing in ethnic community". It is held in Ayr police office and lasts two days. It is run by Glasgow University's Professor Eleanor Kelly. The Detective Sergeant also lectures to police officers in the training college on nationality matters which covers culture and traditions of the Indian sub-continent. This shows that the police officials are given some form of training in the race arena, since there is no doubt the Nationality Department have a strong role to play within the immigration process. On the basis of what has been said in this section, the Police and Nationality Department would refute any criticism of immigration laws and procedures. It is clear that the department feels that the immigration regime is firm but fair, and any liberalisation of it would be a mistake.

Adjudicators

In 1966 a Committee on immigration appeals under the chairmanship of Sir Roy Wilson QC was set up and this committee led to the 1969 Immigration Appeals Act. The Committee was to find remedies or rights of appeal for those who are refused entry into Britain or for those who have to leave the country. Its report was published in 1967. The present appellate system was initiated by the Wilson Committee. It "..recommended a two-tier appeal system, compromising an Immigration Appeal Tribunal at one level and a number of single adjudicators at another lower level".[8]

The appeal at the first instance is heard before one adjudicator. If the Appeal is dismissed then the person can apply for leave to appeal to the tribunal. Individual experiences of immigrants with the appeals process was analysed in chapter five.

The Immigration Appellate Authority in Glasgow is in Portcullis House and was opened in Spring 1994. The appeals are heard at a lower level by the adjudicators. Before this, appeals were heard in the City Chambers and in Edinburgh.[9]

Adjudicators play a very important role in the immigration appeals, for once a person's immigration case is refused he/she can apply to the immigration appellate authority. We have already seen their role when looking at individual cases. In such cases the adjudicator decides if the appeal should be dismissed or allowed.

There are five adjudicators, one full-time and four part-time working in Portcullis House in Glasgow where the appeals are heard. The full-time adjudicator is Mr. Deans who is also the regional adjudicator. The regional adjudicator also has other duties, i.e. organising training and dealing with bails.[10] Only Mr. Deans and adjudicators A and B allowed me to interview them (see Appendix).

The duties of an adjudicator can be put into two categories according to adjudicator A. The first duty is: "To hear appeals against decisions by the Home Secretary, these concern applicants who are in the UK and who disagree with the Home Secretary's decision". Such cases would be e.g. refusing asylum, decide to deport, and refusing to extend the length of stay in UK. The second duty is to hear appeals against decisions by

> Entry clearance officers in Embassies/High Commissions abroad. These concern applicants who seek from abroad to gain entry to the UK and who have been refused e.g. applications from students, husbands, wives and fiancé(es).[11]

According to adjudicator B "we hold first instance hearings to try and establish the facts on the basis of evidence produced to us....to make a decision based on those facts by applying the regulation".[12] Mr Deans basically said "The prime duty is to determine appeals and the basic obligation is one of fairness".[13]

172

The types of cases adjudicators deal with are varied. Both adjudicators A and B agreed that the majority of cases they deal with are political asylum appeals. Adjudicator A said this, "involves people who are in the UK and claim that to expel them would be a breach under the Geneva Convention 1951". Many appeal to seek to stay in the UK after their engagement and marriage. Adjudicator A gave other examples such as "numerous appeals from students wishing to enter/remain in the UK. Occasional nationality/citizenship appeals come from applicants living abroad who claim the right of abode through descent".[14]

When the question of accountability arose they both gave slightly different answers. Adjudicator A said he was accountable to "My employer - the Lord Chancellor's department i.e. for conduct/competence". He then said in relation to his decisions, the immigration appeal tribunal can overturn him if he is wrong in the law. He said "They will not interfere with my findings on an applicant's credibility".[15] While adjudicator B said he was not accountable to anybody, i.e. "I hold an independent judicial appointment and was appointed by the Lord Chancellor". He did also take into account that if his decision is in error of law then it can go on to the Appeals Tribunal and then Court of Session in Scotland.[16]

Adjudicator A takes into account when considering his decision, the applicable law and whether the applicant is telling the truth about his claim. While adjudicator B "considers all the evidence...including oral and documentary...and comes to a view on what the correct facts are".[17]

Decisions are dismissed on the grounds of "credibility i.e. a failure to believe that I have been told the truth on material issues by witnesses". At times there maybe no problems with credibility but "the facts brought forward by a an appellant do not bring him within the rule so the appeal must fail". Adjudicator B gave an example of a case being refused on primary purpose, "when the appellant has not established that the purpose of the proposed marriage was not primarily to come to the UK". Mr B agreed that this was a very difficult area i.e. "..it's proving the negative and...a controversial area of the law". Nevertheless he went on to say "but we have to simply work our way through the rules and the guidance of the court and make the best decision that you can".[18]

When asked on what grounds a decision is granted, adjudicator A grants a decision when he believes the applicant is telling the truth about his claim and at the same time satisfies the legal requirements.[19] Adjudicator B feels that allowing one to appeal is a way to rectify the matter if a gross mistake has been made. That it is basically "establishing the balance of probability often that is a test which some appellants, and even presenting officers do not always understand, we are only looking for 51% certainty".[20]

The present structure of the appeals system in Scotland is illustrated in Figure 6.1 below.

Figure 6.1 Structure of the Appeals System in Scotland

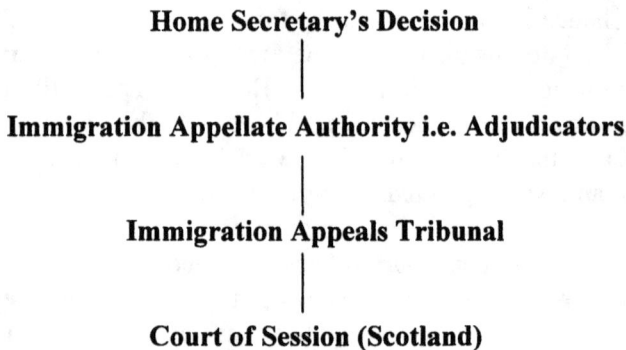

Home Secretary's Decision

|

Immigration Appellate Authority i.e. Adjudicators

|

Immigration Appeals Tribunal

|

Court of Session (Scotland)

The Immigration Appeals Tribunal "will not overturn an adjudicator's findings on an appellant's credibility". They are only concerned with mistakes in law said adjudicator A. If the Tribunal is wrong in matters of law, the case may end up in the Court of Session in Scotland (in England, the Court of Appeal).[21]

Adjudicators have very little liaison with other organisations. Adjudicator B stated that "we keep very informal ties with other bodies such as the Immigration Advisory Service and the Scottish Refugee Council".[22]

According to adjudicator A, "the proportion of appeals allowed in every area of immigration law remains about the same year after year", adding "although the total number of appeals increases year after year". He also mentioned that a higher proportion of student appeals are granted than other areas. The proportion of appeals granted in asylum is low i.e. 5%.[23] Mr. Deans said he did not have any statistics but "we are not concerned with appeals as a whole, we are concerned with an individual appeal".[24] He was thus emphasising that numbers do not matter as long as each case is dealt with fairly.

Adjudicator A did not think the immigration rules are more stringent towards people from the Indian sub-continent. He mentioned that the rules apply to applicants from every part of the world. He admitted that people from Pakistan/India do without a doubt have more problems in satisfying the rules than those applying from other countries. He stated "I do not believe that there is a policy of bias/racism designed to exclude Indian/Pakistani applicants". He also went on to say "the marriage rules are not incompatible with the arranged marriage system. It is also very easy to overlook how many applications are successful". Adjudicator A believes that applicants from countries such as India and Pakistan face problems because these countries are economically poor. Poverty may suggest that the "motives for the match are primarily settlement for economic reasons rather than the match itself".[25]

Adjudicator B simply accepted that there were problems for people from the Indian Sub-continent in comparison to Australians and Canadians. He blamed it on the arranged marriage idea i.e. "it is fair to say that there are problems facing appellants from the sub-continent not shared by those who are dealing with non-arranged marriages". He went on to say that this was a common view expressed by immigration law practitioners. That this is "really a political matter for our political masters to sort out".[26] While Mr. Deans as always tended to give a neutral answer, "as adjudicators we apply the rules that we have to apply regardless of a person's nationality or country of origin".[27]

Adjudicator A felt that the immigration rules over the years have not caused an increase in the number of appeals made. Adjudicator A said "by and large the rules have not become more severe causing increasing numbers of appeals from dissatisfied applicants". The reason for the increase in appeals in adjudicator A's views is that the "implementation of immigration law has made people aware that they should appeal when in the past they might not have done so".[28] However, adjudicator B to some extent thinks that immigration rules over the years have caused an increase in the number of appeals being made. He feels that parents/dependents have a very tough time i.e. "difficulty....on the basis that the dependent has no other relative to turn to in his/her country, it is quite difficult to satisfy".[29] The regional adjudicator Mr. Deans admitted that there was an increase in the number of appeals made but he said "..I don't know what the cause is and I don't know if it's immigration rules or not".[30] Again each adjudicator has his own opinion.

On the question of whether immigration rules over the years have prevented adjudicators from allowing appeals to succeed, adjudicator A did not think they have done so; i.e. "if an applicant is a credible witness (and satisfies the law) he will succeed. Appeals fail when applicants and witnesses are judged to have lied about their claim".[31] Whilst adjudicator B mentioned that it is a fair comment "that the appeal process now takes longer and maybe offers fewer chances of success. That makes it more important that those of us sitting on judgement consider the correct facts to make a proper decision". From adjudicator B's comments one is led to believe that he feels there is a problem for those from the Indian sub-continent but it is a matter for the politicians to solve.[32] Similarly Mr. Deans mentioned it is not an adjudicator's responsibility to make rules or to comment on them "..the rules are simply there as a given factor which we have to follow and that's our jurisdiction".[33]

If an appellant is refused a visa, the Entry Clearance Officer (ECO) "must prepare a written statement of the facts relating to the decision or action in question and the reasons for it, and serve it on the appellate authority and the appellant".[34] This statement is known as the "explanatory statement". When asked how much weight is given to the explanatory statement, adjudicator A said "considerable weight usually"; this is because when the applicant is abroad he/she cannot give evidence in front of the adjudicator. Therefore "the ECO's impressions of the applicant and his claim can be important". However, the ECO must act fairly and if he has reached conclusions without proper analysis the value of the explanatory statement as a case against the applicant is useless. He also stated that "many of these ECOs value interviews in formal settings with interpreters. Good care has to be taken in ensuring that the ECO has done his job properly". Adjudicator A seems quite satisfied that an ECO would not jeopardise anything by giving a false statement.[35] Adjudicator B believes that the explanatory statement "is evidence.. but it is not binding on an adjudicator and not necessarily of any greater weight than any other evidence". Although its sometimes the only major part of the evidence that is available for the respondent's case.[36] One is made to believe that adjudicator A gives quite a lot of importance to the explanatory statement. On the other hand adjudicator B gives equal importance to all evidence provided. The regional adjudicator does not even regard the explanatory statement as evidence. According to Mr. Deans the real evidence consists of interview notes, visa applications, copies of passports, birth and marriage certificate. The explanatory statement is essentially the ECO's interpretation of such evidence in particular cases.

In relation to the length of time it takes for an adjudicator to deliver his/her determination, Mr. Deans said it should normally take four weeks but could be six weeks depending on whether there is a long hearing or a great deal of documentary evidence.

Adjudicators do not have a say in policy making regarding the content of any particular rule or even its implementation. Adjudicator B believes that they can make observations through the chief adjudicator. The chief adjudicator, Judge David Peril, has the responsibility of training and updating adjudicators on immigration matters. Judge Peril is the co-ordinator and adviser, he is in charge of the appellate system. Judge Peril is based in Thanet House, London which is the head office for the Immigration Appellate Authority. Adjudicator B addressed the Chief Adjudicator's influence in the following terms: "His views are very carefully considered by the Secretary of State but at the end of the day he is only another Judicial officer".[37] Again, the emphasis from adjudicator B seems to be that it is the politicians who make the decisions on immigration policy and that adjudicators work only through these guide-lines. Likewise Mr. Deans said they cannot say anything to the Home Office about policy making as "..that would be a transgression of the judicial function".[38]

Normally to be an adjudicator it is now necessary to be a qualified lawyer with considerable practical and academic experience in immigration. Adjudicator A said "The minimum age for part-timers is 35 and full-timers 40".[39]

Adjudicators A and B said they do not get any training regarding race, culture and traditions of people from the Indian sub-continent. The two adjudicators agreed that having heard one or two of these cases, they learn very quickly about other cultures. Although adjudicator A does remember vividly handouts giving a general introduction on the area. Mr. Deans feels that adjudicators are given training on race issues. There are adjudicator conferences held time to time where a group of people from the Lord Chancellor's Ethnic Minority Advisory Committee deal with such issues. Mr. Deans also mentioned that Portcullis House has a library which has books on Muslim law and so on.

Interpreters are used very commonly at the appellate authority if the adjudicator does not speak the same language as the witness. Adjudicator B feels that some translators are good but some are bad, however one can detect a bad interpreter as he sounds confusing. Adjudicator A feels that interpreters are of a very high standard and like adjudicator B believes if they are bad it becomes obvious quickly and the interpreter will not last. Mr. Deans mentioned that Judge Peril the Chief Adjudicator was taking steps to improve the quality of interpreters by giving them more training.

One can say that the adjudicators are merely carrying out the duties fairly, they are independent and are there to help immigrants. They do not feel the need or the obligation to make detailed comments on how fair the immigration regime is. Moreover, as seen in this section there is some evidence to suggest that some of the adjudicators are aware of the special problems which arise in the case of Indian sub continent applicants.

The Role of the Home Office and Associated Institutions and their Response to Public Criticisms

The Home Office

This section looks at the response of the civil servants or policy makers to the criticisms people from the Indian sub-continent and some MPs have made about immigration procedures. The following are the functions of the Home Office Immigration and Nationality Department at Lunar House.

1. To conduct immigration control at the ports and airports;
2. To deal with applications from those here on a temporary basis for an extension of their stay;
3. To determine applications for asylum in the United Kingdom;
4. To enforce immigration law in appropriate cases, identifying and removing those who are in the United Kingdom unlawfully or whose removal is otherwise justified;
5. To grant British citizenship to eligible applicants;
6. To help Ministers set policy on immigration control and the granting of citizenship.[40]

Three people from the Home Office gave an opinion on the criticisms, Mr Troake from the Policy-making Directorate, an Assistant Director from the Immigration Service Ports Directorate, and Ms X from the Immigration Service Enforcement Directorate. The Head of Immigration policy section in the Visa and Migration Division at the Foreign and Commonwealth Office gave his views on the immigration issue.

Mr Troake[41] believed that immigration policies did not have to be justified to anyone. He mentioned that the Home Office receive letters from MPs and their constituents saying "why do you allow so many immigrants into the country?" The point made was that Britain is a very densely populated country and the number entering had to be controlled i.e "There is a vast pressure to emigrate from the third world, where some of the countries are becoming overpopulated, access to land is difficult and their social services...are not so well advanced as ours".[42] The official felt that in Britain domestic employment and the social services had to be protected. He argued that the policies are what a political party promises to the public in its manifesto commitments and if the government comes to power then they will carry the policies out.

Mr Troake accepts that there is strong public criticism about their job. He complained about not having enough resources. "The main complaint is delay and delay is caused because the resources are not there, we are competing with the police and prisons".[43] Normally constituents write to their MPs when they are unhappy about someone being deported but then again people from the extreme right wing also let their views be known to the Home Office. However, not many Scottish MPs write to the Home

Office because they do not have a large immigrant or immigrant descendent population in their areas, according to Mr Troake. However, George Galloway (Labour, Hillhead) and Archie Kirkwood (Liberal Democrat) have a tendency to write to the Home Office.

The civil servant admitted that the Home Office had been criticised for their policies on people from the Indian sub-continent. Not surprisingly Mr Troake discussed how people did not like the primary purpose rule, pointing out that its purpose was to prevent people from using marriage as a way into the UK. This dislike of the primary purpose rule was evident in the survey analysis of people from the Indian sub-continent.[44] He agreed that in the primary purpose rule effectively required that the couple should have met and liked each other but this goes against the Indian sub-continent culture of arranged marriages where people do not even meet.[45] Mr Troake also mentioned that some people are unhappy anyway about their marriage to a person from abroad i.e. 'reluctant spouse syndrome'. According to Mr Troake the Home Office "gets quite a lot of letters saying we are forced into this marriage...please refuse this application.."[46] However girls do not let the Home Office use this information at appeals as they are scared about the family's reaction, therefore the person enters the country because he has satisfied the requirements.

It was clear from the individual cases[47] and from the survey findings[48] that young women were unhappy that it was more difficult for men to gain entry into the UK as partners than women. The Home Office official responded by saying that "it is folklore amongst immigration department officials and the entry clearance officers that its usual for the wife to go to her in-laws rather than the other way around".[49] Although he mentioned this should not be a basis for decisions.

Mr. Troake agreed with the conclusion from my survey that having a good occupation if you are a sponsor or if you are the person coming from abroad can help a person's application.[50] He said, referring to doctors and lawyers, that "..you are more likely to work your way around the system and know what is required, your command of English will be a great deal better than somebody who is lower in the social or intellectual scale". Nevertheless they must still satisfy the requirements and "it's not intentional discrimination against people who are lower down the social scale".[51]

The "main aim of the Immigration Service Ports Directorate is to maintain an effective and efficient entry control which meets prescribed standards".[52] The Assistant Director (Mr X) from the Immigration Service Ports Directorate was available to give his views on public criticisms of immigration officers and immigration control.[53]

Mr X discussing the public criticisms said "political views range from we are discriminatory to we are not discriminatory enough and that depends upon which side of the political spectrum the person happens to be speaking from".[54] He felt that his directorate's functions had political implications but pointed out that "we try to depoliticise it by operating in the context of satisfying the immigration rules; those who don't meet them don't get in".[55]

The Assistant Director agreed that immigration officers were criticised for the type of questions they asked "some people feel that the questions asked of them are intrusive and personal and complaints are made of the manner and attitude...of staff and interpreters".[56] He said immigration officers try to balance and evaluate the facts that they have and hope to reach a sensible conclusion which is where some criticism arises. The main point he makes is that all they do is operate an immigration control regime legislated by parliament.

If people don't like the immigration control or the provisions of immigration control, then that is not a criticism of the immigration service. Rather it is an expression of dissatisfaction with the politicians who were responsible for its passage in parliament.[57]

Mr X did feel that the Immigration Service does try to help ethnic minorities. Officials do meet with groups, e.g. the West Indian Standing Conference. The meetings take place every five or six months and immigration problems are discussed. Also a part of the six-week training for immigration officers is race awareness according to Mr X. However the Assistant Director was not aware of meeting any groups representing people from the Indian sub-continent. This is an important point to note given that it is this group which has levelled some of the greatest amount of criticism against the immigration regime.

The Immigration Service Enforcement Directorate is concerned with tracking down people who are here illegally and with removing people who have overstayed their leave. The spokesperson Miss Y[58] admitted that they received criticism from all sides of the political spectrum. Miss Y said they received letters from people with opposing views on the immigration matter, as did the spokespersons from the Policy Directorate and the Immigration Service Ports Directorate. She said the Directorate was recently criticised by the Council of Churches which argued that people who have been here illegally for more than five years and now are married with children here should not be deported. The spokeswoman asserted that "we are operating immigration control firmly but fairly"[59] and that cases only reach them once they have been through a lengthy appeals process.

Miss Y said they were accountable to Ministers and ultimately to the Home Secretary for the decisions they made, i.e. "All the actions we take, such as refusing an application and issuing a deportation order, is done on behalf of the Home Secretary".[60]

The Immigration Service Enforcement Directorate and the immigration police as looked at earlier on in this chapter are concerned with detecting illegal immigrants. Table 6.1 below shows the number of removal from the UK of persons as illegal immigrants from 1980-1990 and Table 6.2 shows the removals from the United Kingdom of persons under the deportation process from 1980-1990. The tables include the number of those removed who are from the Indian sub-continent.

It is important here to emphasise the distinction between those who are removed as illegal entrants and those who are removed under the deportation process. The former includes persons who entered by illegal means. While the latter includes those who were given leave to enter or remain but breached those conditions. This includes overstaying, violating restrictions on employment, behaving in a manner which posed a danger to public security or for making a false statement to immigration officers.

Table 6.1 Removal from the UK of Persons as Illegal Entrants, 1984-1990

Year	Total Removed (all nationalities)	Numbers removed who were from the Indian sub-continent	% Removed who were from the Indian-sub continent
1984	425	94	22
1985	528	70	13
1986	704	122	17
1987	1044	238	23
1988	1639	351	21
1989	1820	298	16
1990	1976	244	12

Source: Control of Immigration Statistics United Kingdom, various years

Table 6.2 Removal from the UK of Persons Under the Deportation Process, 1984-1990

Year	Total Deported (all nationalities)	Total Deported who were from the Indian sub-continent	% Deported who were from the Indian-sub continent
1984	932	93	10
1985	897	107	12
1986	812	99	12
1987	946	151	16
1988	1047	231	16
1989	2019	292	14
1990	1786	210	11

Source Control of Immigration Statistics United Kingdom, 1988

Illegal entrants are defined by the Home Office as persons who entered the country by deception or clandestinely. Table 6.1 shows the number of removals from the United Kingdom of persons as illegal entrants. They can be defined as persons who were detected as illegal immigrants and were forced to leave the UK under the action of the authorities. It has to be noted that the figures in Table 6.1 refer to the total number of people who entered the UK illegally, were then detected and removed. The figures do not refer to those who entered through legal measures or through the standard immigration procedures but were subsequently found not to qualify for admission or breached their right to entry later, such individuals are classed as deportees and are subsequently removed under the deportation process as shown in Table 6.2. The immigration requirements needed to be satisfied were discussed earlier.[61]

The substantial increases in the total numbers of persons removed from the UK under the enforcement powers in the Immigration Act 1971, either as illegal entrants or under the deportation process, reflected more effective enforcement procedures, including the use of supervised departures which rose markedly in the latter part of 1988.

The figures in Tables 6.1 and 6.2 show that since 1984 the total number of persons removed by the Home Office has risen consistently, and is continuing to do so. If we consider the fact that the Home Office statistical department has divided the various nationalities into geographical categories to see the number from each part of the world removed (these geographical areas being: Europe, Americas, Indian sub-continent, remainder of Asia, Australasia, and other nationalities), we find that those from the Indian sub-continent who are removed form a considerable proportion. The percentage removed from the Indian sub-continent during the 1980s, either as illegal entrants or under the deportation process, has constantly been in double figures. This is startling when one considers that in comparison to other sources of immigration, the Indian sub-continent only comprises of three countries: India, Pakistan and Bangladesh. Better detection measures since 1987 have aided the authorities to track down, and enforce removal powers.

Some would argue that given the increasing numbers removed annually by the authorities the Home Office is justified in taking a tough line and operating strict rules. This is particularly true of the Indian sub-continent from which an increasing number who come are removed, and it is this group that has constantly argued about unfair practices by the authorities. As seen in chapter 1 writers such as Paul Gordon mentioned how black people, including those from the Indian sub-continent, were subjected to tough internal controls during the 1980s which included being subjected to passport raids by immigration officers and the police. The fact that an increasing number of nationals from the Indian sub continent are removed may also explain why they have developed a reputation in the eyes of the authorities for being 'bogus' applicants and are therefore treated more harshly. Evidence from interviews with individuals suggests that this is indeed the case. However officials interviewed in this chapter, not surprisingly, did not agree with this line of argument.

Entry Clearance Officers: Foreign and Commonwealth Office

The Home Office is concerned with control on entry and after entry. The Migration and Visa Unit of the Foreign and Commonwealth office is responsible for entry clearance work overseas. Mr Lusk the head of immigration policy section in the Visa and Migration Division gave his opinion[62] on public criticism of immigration policy and procedures as it affected his responsibilities.

The civil servant said that visas were imposed on a country for security reasons (implying terrorism etc.) or to tackle the growing number of immigrants from certain regions of the world such as the Indian sub-continent. Immigration from the Indian sub-continent created migratory pressures driven by political and economic factors. The hope was that the imposition of visas would tackle the growing number of immigrants from regions such as the Indian sub-continent. He went on to say "the advantage of having a visa is that you can be pretty sure that you are going to get through the immigration control on arrival quickly".[63]

Mr Lusk pointed out that people complain about the fees they have to pay every time they apply for a settlement visa or a visitors visa, this criticism was also made by people interviewed in the individual cases.[64] Presently the fee being £33 for a visiting visa and £215-245 for a settlement visa. The cost of providing entry clearance work overseas was £45 million and the cost of various visas is set at a level which allows the visa department to recover that cost, but the money goes to the Treasury not to the Foreign Office. According to Mr. Lusk this is why "we are always under the pressure to find ways of achieving the work more efficiently, ideally with fewer staff but trying to have a good standard of service".[65] There is a need to invest in good information technology. He said the biggest immigration post in the Indian sub-continent was Islamabad, with 26 entry clearance officers and 70 locally engaged staff (a mixture of British and Pakistani staff). The reason for such a large post at Islamabad was the high numbers of applications to settle permanently in the UK which requires intensive interviewing.

The head of policy making admitted that entry clearance officers are criticised for the types of questions asked but Mr. Lusk said the officer must often in order to clarify matters ask "are you feeling tired". People should feel free to say 'yes' but they don't and the entry clearance officer (ECO) could give another appointment. Nevertheless ECOs are given book exercises in interviewing techniques.[66] The booklet "focuses on the categories of information officers will need to be aware of, and the types of questions to be asked, in order to carry out interviews with applicants".[67] To give an idea of how immigration officers deal with visa applicants, the booklet contains various exercises and the Entry Clearance Officer must work out questions to gain knowledge on the applicants reasons for a visa. In the case of a scenario which involves an applicant hoping to settle in the UK the ECO would need to ask questions to find out the following information, such as where the fiancé lives, what does he do for a living and the funds he has. Concerning the relationship, the ECO requires information on how the couple met, how long they have known each other, how many times they have met, how they maintain contact, when will they decided to marry and where they will marry. Finally the ECO has to ask if any of them have previous marriages or children.[68] The type of questions resemble exactly those which individuals interviewed for the case studies said they were asked.[69]

In the case of an applicant wishing to enter the UK for medical help, the ECO would need to ask questions to gain the following information. Why does the applicant need treatment in the UK and in which hospital? When is the treatment and the length it would take the applicant to recover from the illness? What the cost of the treatment is and how will it be

186

funded? If the person has plans to return to his/her job and will the applicant be accompanied by family? The ECO must also ask to see "confirmed return air ticket, evidence of accommodation and acceptance by hospital".[70] The ECO must also know that the applicant has funds in his/her bank. Therefore evidence such as proving the applicant will return to his/her country after medical treatment can be linked to the case George Galloway MP for Hillhead described.[71]

In relation to accusations that ECOs are very rude, Mr Lusk said in defence "you do get people who are very rude or who can get aggressive".[72]

The immigration official agreed that they are indeed strongly criticised by the public. He mentioned cases such as those on compassionate grounds where a 65 year old lady becomes a widow, has two daughters in India but two sons in the UK. Now the sons have been supporting her financially and due to cultural reasons (in the culture of the Indian sub-continent it is the responsibility of sons *where possible* to not only support their parents financially but to stay with them) she cannot stay with her daughters. The ECO will ask the lady how long she is going to stay. And she will reply: "I don't know as long as they want me to stay". Then the ECO will ask if she is staying permanently and she will say no. Then the ECO will say how long will you stay and she replies how long can I stay? The ECO will say six months and the old lady will then say that she will stay for six months. The above is a very typical scenario and Mr Lusk says "The visa officer has got a real problem which is that very often these people are not going back to their country of origin".[73] Mr Lusk said all they can tell their Entry Clearance Officers is to weigh the evidence "has she got somebody to come back to in the Indian sub-continent? How likely is it she is going to come back? If there is very little chance of her coming back then the visa is refused".[74]

Another very critical area is the primary purpose rule. Mr Lusk tries to play down the controversy which this rule attracts by saying "All we can do is make sure our ECO's are as well trained as possible to deal with primary purpose cases as fairly as possible and are aware of the emotional pitfalls", and he goes on to say "I think by in large we succeed in that".[75]

Last but not least Mr Lusk said that his service is extensively accountable. The Migration and Visa Unit is accountable to Ministers, to Parliament and, recently, to the independent Monitor, who "monitors refusals in entry clearance cases where there is no right of appeal".[76] They are accountable to the appellate authorities and courts.

Mr. Lusk also mentions the 'reluctant spouse syndrome' where young people from the United Kingdom are forced to marry someone from abroad. Some people give such information to immigration officials but will not let them use it for fear of family rows. The fact the young people mention they are being forced does show they are unhappy. The Foreign and Commonwealth official said the boy or girl from the UK say "My father will beat me up, there have been death threats and in some cases even deaths".[77]

Therefore all the civil servants agreed that there were many areas of the immigration policy that gave people from the Indian sub-continent a very difficult time. However, criticisms came from both sides of the political spectrum i.e. from Conservative right wing people as well as from Liberal Left-wingers, so the point being, satisfying one group would mean getting criticisms from the other.

The Work of the Home Office: The Statistical Evidence

So far in this section we have seen the role played by the Home Office and its associated institutions in the immigration arena, and their response to criticisms. This brief sub-section will look at what impact the work of the Home Office has had on levels of immigration from the Indian sub-continent, in comparison to regions such as those comprising the countries of the Old Commonwealth.

Looking at the total number of admissions to the United Kingdom in 1980 and 1990, we find that in 1980 and 1990 only 5% of all persons admitted were from the Indian sub-continent. In comparison the total number admitted from the Old Commonwealth was higher, 6% in 1980 and 7% in 1990. There are significantly more applications from the Indian sub-continent than there are from the Old Commonwealth.[78]

Also if we look at the acceptances for settlement by nationality we find that in 1980, 32% of all acceptances were from the Indian sub-continent. This figure had reduced to 25% in 1990.[79] This reduction in the proportion of applications granted accompanied a rise in applications from the Indian sub-continent. In comparison there was a slight increase in acceptances for settlement from Australasia, from 9% in 1980 to 10% in 1990. Similarly there was an increase from 10% to 13% for the Americas for the same period. This highlights the fact that the policy of the government was getting harsher and that applications for settlement from the Indian sub-continent were more likely to be refused, as applicants found it much more difficult to meet the restrictive criteria.

The following number of people as shown in Table 6.3 were accepted for settlement in the UK between 1980 and 1990:

Table 6.3 Accepted Settlements for all Nationalities

Year	Number Accepted for Settlement (all nationalities)
1980	69,750
1981	59,060
1982	53,870
1983	53,460
1984	50,950
1985	55,360
1986	47,820
1987	45,980
1988	49,280
1989	49,650
1990	52,400

Source Control of Immigration Statistics UK, various issues

Table 6.4 Total Acceptances from the Indian Sub-Continent

Year	Number Accepted for Settlement From the Indian Sub-Continent
1980	22,220
1981	21,370
1982	20,180
1983	16,690
1984	14,840
1985	17,510
1986	14,550
1987	11,620
1988	12,180
1989	12,520
1990	12,980

Source Control of Immigration Statistics UK, various issues

There are essentially two types of acceptances as classed by the Home Office; a) Settlement on arrival and b) Settlement on removal of time limit. Acceptances for settlement comprise people accepted on arrival at ports and people initially admitted to the country subject to time limit which was subsequently removed on application to the Home Office. Category a) refers to those granted settlement as they enter. Category b) refers to those granted settlement for a specified time period which was later removed. This category would include someone here to work (employment, dependent relatives).

If we look at the figures for the number of citizens of the Indian sub-continent accepted for settlement between 1980 and 1990 (see Table 6.4) we can see that there was a steady decline between 1980 and 1984, followed by an increase in 1985 but by a further two years of decline and a small rise in 1988. Since 1988 the figure has stabilised around or between the 12-13 thousand mark. The decrease in acceptances since 1985 from the Indian sub-continent can be explained by the same factors which caused a fall in total acceptances, namely the changes regarding the right of abode, and the probationary year requirement for wives. These represent changes in laws and rules which as we have already seen in this book, affected the black countries such as those of the Indian sub-continent more than the white countries.[80]

Conclusions

The 'official' views on immigration were varied but most tended to believe the implementation of immigration policies and the policies themselves could in general be justified. Some officials from the Home Office and Foreign and Commonwealth office accepted that there were criticisms but believed that they were unjustified.

When interviewing the Police Nationality Department, the Detective Sergeant gave the notion that the Immigration laws were fair for people from the Indian sub-continent. Then again there might be some justification in their eyes since Strathclyde Police deals with 80-90 cases of illegal immigration annually and that is not counting the cases that escape their clutches.[81]

Of the three adjudicators interviewed only one agreed that people from the Indian sub-continent did have a more difficult time with the immigration laws in comparison to the Australians and Canadians, and that the primary purpose rule caused major difficulties for some applicants. The two other adjudicators believed that immigration rules were fine, as long as those who implement them give a fair, non-biased decision in accordance with the immigration rules. Indeed throughout the interview Mr. Deans an adjudicator tended to be very neutral and did not say anything to offend any party. Interestingly enough all adjudicators admitted that there had been an increase in the number of appeals made over the years but only one adjudicator admitted that the immigration rules were possibly the cause.

One can say that all officials of the various units working in the immigration field were satisfied with the immigration laws and the way they were practised. This included the Nationality Department of the police and the adjudicators all of whom played an important role to keep the system running. While those involved in the actual policy making had their own views on immigration policies.

The civil servants at the Immigration and Nationality Department, Home Office and at the Foreign and Commonwealth Office who help to implement policies agreed that they were criticised for the policies and the procedures in regards to people from the Indian sub-continent. However, every official interviewed claimed to have been on a race awareness course. The officials in London said that while many people criticised the policies for being too strict many people criticised the immigration laws/procedures for not being tough enough. Therefore criticisms are coming from both sides of the political spectrum.

According to all these officials lack of money in the Migration and Visa Unit of the Foreign and Commonwealth Office and in the Immigration and Nationality Department of the Home Office has caused delays in the implementation of immigration procedures. This coincided with the common complaints about the waiting lengths to attain a visa experienced by people from the Indian sub-continent.[82] Mr. Troake from the Policy Directorate of the Home Office said himself that the primary purpose rule and the concept of arranged marriages opposed each other. Mr. Lusk from the Migration and Visa Unit agreed that elderly people did face many difficulties to satisfy the entry clearance officers. This comment by Mr. Lusk was also illustrated by the experience of an individual who was trying to get a holiday visa for his parents but failed. The individual's argument was his parents had visited the UK before and they returned to their own country, so why was the Home Office suspicious? [83] Mr. Troake and Mr. Lusk had consensus on the issue that having a good occupation helps to attain a visa with fewer problems and that generally male spouses from the Indian sub-continent had more difficulties on getting an entry visa. Again this argument is supported by the findings in the survey chapter.[84] Mr Troake had made the case due to the common belief that in Asian culture women live with their husbands family rather than their husbands joining them in the UK. Now culture changes over time in every society, not all Asian women born and educated in Britain want to live in Pakistan or India just because they are married. Both men also mentioned the 'reluctant spouse syndrome' where British Asians are unhappily forced into arranged marriages with people from abroad. This should not be taken to mean that every British Asian in an arranged marriage is forced in it. Nor should some examples of 'reluctant spouse syndrome' be allowed to justify harsh policies and rules generally. People interviewed for the case studies were very happily married but had a tough time with the procedures.[85] Last but not least Mr. Troake, Mr. Lusk and an adjudicator believed people from the Indian sub-continent would very eagerly stay in the UK for economic reasons.

Overall, unsurprisingly the bodies involved in the immigration procedure in Glasgow were quite content with the procedures. An official who is an Home Office Presenting Officer in Glasgow, did mention that immigration cases were only covered by newspapers when the appellant's representative invited them to do so. She said "the media in order to get two sides of the story would have to sit and listen through the whole hearing and most of them do not do that. We are not allowed to talk to the press". This comment again can be regarded as a defence of some of the cases discussed in chapter 5.[86] The civil servants involved in policy-making could not deny the hardship caused by the immigration policies but agreed they were only doing what the Secretary of State and the government in power wanted them to do. The Home Office officials and the Foreign and Commonwealth officials tried to counteract the criticisms but their reasons were weak i.e. the primary purpose rule does cause hardship but the Entry Clearance Officers are told to handle the situation fairly. Others who strongly opposed the policies were the Labour party and of course those who suffer the long lengthy waiting time to attain an entry visa. Similarly contrary to what many people think, according to the officials interviewed in this chapter there is also considerable criticism from members of the public who feel that the immigration regime is not tough enough, and not just from those who feel that the regime is discriminatory and that some of its aspects are racist. The main line of defence noted in this chapter by officials in response to public criticism is quite simply: we are just doing our job.

Notes

1. See *chapter 2.*
2. See *chapter 3*
3. See *chapter 5*
4. See *chapter 4.*
5. Ian Macdonald and Nicholas Blake, *Immigration Law and Practise,* (Butterworths, 1995), p. 26.
6. Macmillan, J, *Historical Background of Aliens,* (Aliens registration department, 1952), p. 14.
7. *Interview* with Detective Sergeant, Police Nationality Department, 19 April 1996.
8. Ian Macdonald and Nicholas Blake, Immigration Law and Practise, op. cit. p. 562.
9. *Interview* with Mr Deans, Regional Adjudicator, Immigration Appellate Authority, 2 August 1996.
10. *Ibid.*
11. *Ibid,* Adjudicator A, Immigration Appellate Authority, 25 June 1996.
12. *Ibid,* Adjudicator B, Immigration Appellate Authority, 14 May 1996.
13. *Ibid,* Mr. Deans, 2 August 1996.
14. *Ibid,* Adjudicator A, 25 June 1996.
15. *Ibid.*
16. *Ibid,* Adjudicator B, 14 May 1996
17. *Ibid.*
18. *Ibid.*
19. *Ibid,* Adjudicator A, 25 June 1996.
20. *Ibid,* Adjudicator B, 14 May 1996.
21. *Ibid,* Adjudicator A, 25 June 1996.
22. *Ibid,* Adjudicator B, 14 May 1996.
23. *Ibid,* Adjudicator A, 25 June 1996.
24. *Ibid,* Mr. Deans, 2 August 1996.
25 *Ibid,* Adjudicator A, 25 June 1996.
26. *Ibid,* Adjudicator B, 14 May 1996.
27. *Ibid,* Mr. Deans, 2 August 1996.
28. *Ibid,* Adjudicator A, 25 June 1996.
29. *Ibid,* Adjudicator B, 14 May 1996.
30. *Ibid,* Mr. Deans, August 2nd 1996.
31. *Ibid,* Adjudicator A, 25 June 1996.
32. *Ibid,* Adjudicator B, 14 May 1996.
33. *Ibid,* Mr. Deans, 2 August 1996.
34. Ian Macdonald and Nicholas Blake, *Immigration Law and Practise,* op. cit. p. 598.
35. *Interview* with Adjudicator A, June 25 1996.
36. *Ibid,* Adjudicator B, 14 May 1996.
37. *Ibid.*

38.   *Ibid*, Mr. Deans, 2 August 1996.
39.   *Ibid*, Adjudicator A, 25 June 1996.
40.   Immigration and Nationality Department: Annual Report, p. 3, 1995.
41.   *Interview* Nick Troake, Policy Directorate, Immigration Nationality Department, Home Office, 19 September 1996.
42.   *Ibid*.
43.   *Ibid*.
44.   See *chapter 4*.
45.   *Interview* with Nick Troake, 19 September 1996.
46.   *Ibid*
47.   See *chapter 5*.
48.   See *chapter 4*.
49.   *Interview* with Nick Troake, 19 September 1996.
50.   *Ibid*
51.   *Ibid*.
52.   Immigration Service Ports Directorate, Operating Plans, p. 4, 1996-1997.
53.   *Interview* with Assistant Director (Mr X), Immigration Service Ports Directorate, Immigration Nationality Department, Home Office, 19 September 1996.
54.   *Ibid*
55.   *Ibid*
56.   *Ibid*
57.   *Ibid*.
58.   Interview with Miss Y, Immigration Service Enforcement Directorate, Immigration and Nationality Department, Home Office, 19 September 1996.
59.   *Ibid*.
60.   *Ibid*
61.   See *chapter 2* for immigration requirements and see *Statement of Changes in Immigration Rules*, 23 May 1994 (London: HMSO).
62.   *Interview* with Sean Lusk, 20 September 1996.
63.   *Ibid*.
64.   See *chapter 5*
65.   *Interview* with Sean Lusk, 20 September, 1996.
66.   *Foreign Language Skills for Entry Clearance Work*, (Training Department, 1995).
67.   *Ibid*, p. 1.
68.   *Ibid*, p. 59.
69.   See *chapter 5*.
70.   *Foreign Language Skills for Entry Clearance Work*, op. cit. p. 58.
71.   See *chapter 5*
72.   Interview with Sean Lusk, 20 September, 1996.
73.   *Ibid*
74.   *Ibid*
75.   *Ibid*
76.   Dame Elizabeth Anson, *Report by the Independent Monitor*, (Migration and Visa Division, July 1996).

77.   Interview with Sean Lusk, 20 September 1996.
78.   *Control of Immigration Statistics United Kingdom* 1990, p. 3.
79.   *Ibid*, p. 5.
80.   See *chapters 2 and 3*
81.   *Ibid*, Detective Constable, Police Nationality Department, 30 July 1996.
82   See *chapter 4*.
83.   See *chapter 5*
84.   See *chapter 4*
85.   See *chapter 5*
86.   *Private Communication* with a Home Office Presenting Officer, Immigration Appellate Authority, 1996.

Appendix

The following questions were put to the Police and Nationality Department:

1a   When was the Department set up?
1b   How many people are working in the Department and what do they do?
2   What are the main objectives of the Department?
3   How does the Department deal with an individual case?
4a   Where are individuals taken?
4b   What are individuals' rights?
4c   Are conditions fair?
5   What was the thinking behind the need for such a Department?
6   To whom are you accountable?
7   What is the present structure of the Department?
8   Apart from assisting the Immigration Service, what type of immigration cases do you deal with?
9a   How many cases does the Department deal with annually? How many has it dealt with between 1979-1991?
9b   Has the number of cases or workload changed considerably from the pre-1979 period?
10   How do you feel that the job of the Department has been affected by Conservatives' immigration legislation?

11a Do you feel that the Department has done its job fairly and effectively e.g. has there been complaints and criticisms of your handling of individual cases?

11b Who has made these criticisms e.g. what organisation, MP, paper etc.

12 What do you think about immigration laws? Do you feel that they are fair or too strict regarding people from the Indian sub-continent?

13 What organisation do you have liaison with?

14 Do you have any say in policy-making in relation to the implementation of any particular rule?

15 Which Department of the Home Office do you get your instructions from and under which specific legislation?

16 Do you also get training or awareness courses with regard to race and culture and traditions of the Indian sub-continent?

The following questions were put to the adjudicators at the Appellate Authority:

1a What are your duties as an adjudicator?

1b How many adjudicators are there working in Glasgow?

2a What type of cases do you deal with?

2b Who are you accountable to?

3 What factors do you take into account when you make or consider your decision?

4a On what grounds do you dismiss a decision?

4b On what grounds do you grant a decision?

5 What is the present structure of the appeals system in Scotland?

6 How much liaison do you have with other organisations, departments and institutions?

7 Do you think there has been an increase or decrease in the number of appeals allowed?

8 Do you think immigration rules are more stringent towards people from the Indian sub-continent?

9 Do you think immigration rules over the years have caused an increase in the number of appeals made?

10 Do you think immigration rules over the years have prevented you from allowing appeals to succeed?

11 What weight do you attach to the explanatory statement, as it is
    generally the only discriminatory evidence from the respondent's side?
12 What is your policy of adjourning the appeals hearing?
13a How long does it take for an adjudicator to deliver his/her
    determination?
13b Do you have any say in policy-making regarding the implementation
    of any particular rule?
14 What educational qualification and experience is required to be an
    adjudicator?
15 Do you also get training or awareness courses regarding race, culture,
    and traditions of the Indian sub-continent?
16 What are your general comments regarding court interpreters?

7 Political Perceptions of the Immigration Issue

Introduction

This chapter will look at the contrasting views of Scottish Conservative and Labour MPs before the 1997 general election by analysing their perceptions of immigration issues. The objective is to analyse opinions of MPs on immigration policies and to evaluate their assessments of immigration policies in relation to people from the Indian sub-continent. The MPs' opinions are significant because they are the ones who have a say in the passing of the legislation described in chapter two.[1] Also "by convention, Members of Parliament are duty bound to represent a whole constituency, not only those who voted for them. This work includes immigration cases because most people who seek the help of the Member of Parliament with an immigration problem live within the constituency, or at the very least a friend or a relative does".[2] One of the constitutional functions of Parliament is "procuring the redress of individual grievances"[3] which again emphasises the responsibility of MPs to all their constituents.

This chapter is divided into two sections. Section one deals with the limited number of Scottish Conservative MPs during the last government (ten of Scotland's 72 MPs for most of the period under review) and their attitude and experiences of dealing with immigration matters. Section two compares the views of Glasgow's Labour MPs on immigration policy regarding people from the Indian sub-continent with those of the Scottish Conservative MPs. The Conservative MPs were sent questions through the post and the response was varied. Most of the MPs were either not very keen to help or were too busy. The 11 Glasgow Labour MPs were more helpful. Some MPs allowed me to interview them in person, whilst the others completed my questionnaire. It can be said the Labour MPs were more co-operative when approached.

Although this research is on the immigration regime established in the 1979-90 period some MPs elected in 1992 were also MPs in the 1980s. Also since most of the policies or laws passed in the 1980s are still in operation, MPs during the last and present parliament can appropriately give an opinion on the laws associated with the Thatcher era. The acts of legislation include: the 1981 British Nationality Act; introduction of visas in 1986; the 1987 Carriers' Liability Act; and the 1988 Immigration Act.[4] It is necessary to find out whether Labour MPs differ from Conservative MPs in their views on immigration because it was a Labour government that first introduced immigration control, in 1977, on people from the Indian sub-continent.[5] It has to be pointed out here that although all the Tory MPs lost their seats at the May 1997 election they will still be referred to us MPs because they held office at the time they were interviewed.

Conservative MPs

Out of the 10 Conservative Scottish MPs during the last parliament, 4 MPs gave me an interview (see Appendix). The four MPs were Phil Gallie (Ayr), Hector Munro (Dumfries), Alan Stewart (Eastwood), and one other MP (MP A) who preferred to remain anonymous. I had given the MPs a choice of either filling a questionnaire or being interviewed in person. MP Ian Lang's (Galloway-Upper Nithsdale) secretary wrote that because he was a government minister, it was his rule not to complete any questionnaires.[6] While the Rt. Hon Michael Forsyth MP for Stirling wrote "I am unable to assist as I have had to make it a rule only to respond to questionnaires sent to me by constituents".[7] Malcolm Rifkind's (MP for Edinburgh Pentlands) secretary wrote "as the Foreign Secretary, it would not be appropriate for Mr Rifkind to respond to your questionnaire".[8] MP for Edinburgh West Lord James Douglas Hamilton wrote that it was not his policy to complete questionnaires, but he was only too happy to help his constituents if immigration problems arose.[9] These refusals illustrate the high percentage of government ministers who made up the small numbers of Scottish Conservative MPs under the last Conservative government. In addition two Conservative MPs never made any contact at all.

Constituents may make contact with Members of Parliament in a number of ways such as attending surgeries at the MP's local party office, through their constituency office or by phoning the MPs hot-line at the House of Commons. Other means of contacting members would be by telephoning their home and writing to the MP at the House of Commons.[10]

When asked if Asian constituents (Indian sub-continent) attended their surgery and wrote to them, Phil Gallie,[11] Alan Stewart[12] and MP A[13] answered in the affirmative. MP Hector Munro said they did not attend his surgery and "very seldom" wrote to him.[14] Phil Gallie (Ayr) said 2% of constituents attending his surgery were Asians,[15] MP A said less than 1%,[16] and Alan Stewart (Eastwood) said about 10%.[17] Significantly, the percentage of constituents from the Indian sub-continent in the constituencies of Conservative MPs is very low as one can see in Table 7.1. Only in Eastwood were more than 1% of constituents of Asian ethnic origin. It is therefore not surprising that the number of Pakistani, Indian and Bangladeshi people attending the surgeries of Conservative MPs is low. This fact helps to explain why Conservative MPs view immigration policies as non-discriminatory and why they tend to be basically unsympathetic, compared to Labour MPs, to constituents from the Indian sub-continent. A low level of exposure to Indian sub-continent constituents means that many Conservative MPs possibly think that everything is 'rosy' and that there is no problem with immigration policies. They do not experience on a large scale the grievances which Indian sub-continent constituents may have. It could also be that many Indian sub-continent constituents may be less willing to approach a Tory MP, given that he represents the government which is responsible for the tough immigration policies being discussed in this book.

Table 7.1   % of Indian Sub-Continent Constituents in Scottish Conservative Constituencies

Constituency	% Constituents from the Indian sub-continent	MP
Eastwood	1.7	Stewart
Edinburgh Pentlands	0.8	Hamilton
Edinburgh West	0.7	Rifkind
Aberdeen South	0.4	Robertson
Dumfries	0.2	Munro
Ayr	0.2	Gallie
Stirling	0.2	Forsyth
Deeside and Kincardine	0.1	Kynoch
Galloway and Upper Nithsdale	0	Lang
North Tayside	0	Walker

Source: 1991 Census, Monitor for Parliamentary Constituencies

Nevertheless the four MPs interviewed said that they had dealt with immigration cases in Scotland in recent years. When asked what comparison they could make of their workload/immigration cases dealt with in recent years and those dealt with prior to 1979, Phil Gallie said he was elected in 1992.[18] Hector Munro said "perhaps two cases a year, none before 1979".[19] MP A and Alan Stewart said nothing.

The four MPs believed that immigration procedures were not discriminatory. MP Hector Munro added they are complicated but there was no reason to believe they are unfair.[20] MP A felt they were fair.[21]

Not surprisingly when asked if there was any law they would like to see changed, the Conservative MPs, except for Phil Gallie, said 'no'. Phil Gallie, who lost his seat in 1997, said: "Where individuals come into the country following marriage, I consider that any rights of abode should be removed if marriage breaks down within 5 years depending upon level of fault".[22] This comment suggests that Mr. Gallie believes that people should never get the chance to use marriage as an excuse to gain settlement and if the marriage breaks down the person should be sent back. Then one may ask what happens if there are children involved, which one can imagine would bring a lot of controversy, especially since the Conservatives claim to be a party of the family.

When asked if they thought immigration officials such as immigration officers, immigration police and the nationality department are doing an effective job, all the four MPs said 'yes'. This is hardly surprising given that these are agencies and institutions working for the government, and the MPs are from the governing party.

The MPs did have the prerogative when helping individuals with immigration problems. Phil Gallie said "MPs seem to have access to key figures in immigration departments",[23] while Hector Munro made the comment that they could "Speed up replies, but not change decisions".[24] MP A gave a reply similar to Phil Gallie emphasising having direct access to the Minister responsible.[25] Mr. Stewart gave a list of the amount of prerogative an MP possesses when helping in immigration cases: the MP could "write letters of support to Entry Clearance Officers (ECOs) and the Secretary of State, ask the Secretary of State to review decisions of refusal, and submit questions in the House of Commons". He also mentioned how efficient the MPs help-line is: "The MPs help-line to the Home Office and Foreign and Commonwealth Office gets information quickly to me and helps get my correspondence to the correct official quickly".[26] This shows that MPs do write to the Home Office and Foreign and Commonwealth Office when the need is there.

The Conservative MPs did not feel the prerogative they have in immigration cases has changed over the years. MP Alan Stewart did think that the "MPs help-line has improved considerably over the years". Mr Stewart was the only one who thought that the prerogative he has in cases has increased his workload over the years.[27] MP A, Phil Gallie, and Hector Munro did not see any affect on their work. Gallie described dealing with immigration issues as "just normal day to day involvement."[28] Hector Munro said that each case did take time but that was a normal duty for an MP.[29]

When asked how successful the MP is when helping constituents with immigration problems, MP A said 100%.[30] This may be misleading given that very few cases of this nature are dealt with by the Tory MPs. Alan Stewart said "Usually fairly successful".[31] Phil Gallie said that he "has never felt that the correct outcome has not been achieved other than in cases where marriage has been used to obtain access ultimately unjustly". The MP seems to give the impression that (even) when he could not help that the refusal was justified.[32] Hector Munro did not answer at all.

The most common type of immigration problems Phil Gallie deals with are "Naturalisation, visas for fiancés and parents".[33] MP A has come across "the problem of obtaining verification of Indian divorce certificate".[34] Alan Stewart said the general visiting visa was the most common type of problem he dealt with.[35] While Hector Munro did not answer at all, possibly because, as he did say from the start, he seldom had immigration cases in his surgery.

Very rarely had the MPs contacted or enlisted the help of organisations such as the Immigration Advisory Service. MP A has never asked for help;[36] Alan Stewart had only made contact on one occasion,[37] whilst Phil Gallie said they have contacted him.[38] Again Hector Munro refused to answer.

When asked the type of criticisms the MPs have heard against Immigration Officers, Home Office and Immigration Police, Hector Munro said none.[39] Phil Gallie said "delays in processing cases",[40] MP A said "very few".[41] The most common type of criticisms Alan Stewart hears are that "immigration officers do not always appear to fully understand the different customs and culture of the people they interview". This is a very significant point in the context of the subject matter of this study, i.e. the government's immigration rules and procedures have failed to take into account or fully appreciate the culture of the Indian sub continent. Stewart went on to say "they do not take account of any lengthy trip or wait incurred".[42] Mr Stewart is basically saying he has heard such complaints from constituents. However, when interviewing the officials in charge of immigration officers and ECOs they said a part of the immigration officers training was race awareness.[43]

The MPs themselves did not have any criticisms about immigration officials, and Alan Stewart also said he only hears constituents' side of the story of what is said at interviews.[44]

MP A could not think of any cases which he felt strongly about and which involved failure of an attempt to attain an entry visa or took unnecessarily long for a decision to be made. Hector Munro said he could not think of any such cases and MP Alan Stewart said yes but did not enhance his point. Phil Gallie felt strongly about a case where the man, because he is married to a British citizen, is living in this country. This man "constantly threatens the wife that he will take off with the children at first opportunity, lives off state benefits but is known by associates to have business interests". One can assume that Mr Gallie feels the regime is not perfect and possibly the laws are still too lenient; he clearly feels strongly about letting such type of characters into the country.[45]

The last inquiry was whether the MPs had spoken in House of Commons debates, or asked oral or written questions. MP A did not answer, Alan Stewart said 'yes', Phil Gallie said he could not remember and Hector Munro said 'no'. The Conservative MPs tended to be quite neutral on the comments they made on immigration and found the policies reasonable. Phil Gallie was definitely one MP who made his views very clear about a need to toughen immigration laws in relation to one specific situation. In general the only real criticism the MPs heard was what they heard about immigration officers, other than that they had no criticisms themselves about the laws except for Phil Gallie. Overall the MPs felt satisfied about the government's policies, and approach to immigration, and suggested that no real changes were required.

Labour: The Opposition's Views on Immigration

The Labour party did not hold power during the period under review. It was interesting to see that their perceptions of the immigration issues were very different compared to those of their Conservative counter-parts (see Appendix). The Labour MPs were interviewed and contacted prior to the recent election, and will be treated in this chapter as opposition MPs. The eleven Glasgow Labour MPs were sent a letter asking for an interview, seven MPs agreed, two refused and the remaining two did not answer. However, the Labour MPs were more keen to help in the research than their Conservative counterparts. This could be linked to the fact that the Labour MPs know the Conservatives already have a controversial image regarding immigration and as an opposition party they probably feel it is their duty to scrutinise Tory policies, and at the same time make political capital out of it. It also reflects the presence of more immigrants in central city constituencies.

One of the MPs who refused was James Dunnachie who was an MP for Pollok (and wrote to me in person).[46] Donald Dewar, the Labour Chief Whip, (Anniesland) did not feel he was in the position to fill the Questionnaire because "..Glasgow Garscadden has a very small number of residents from the Indian sub-continent and I very seldom get immigration cases". Apparently the number of immigration cases he deals with are 1 or 2 a year. Normally Mr Dewar deals with other matters for ethnic minorities such as commercial matters i.e. applying for a Sub-Post office.[47] There were seven MPs who gave me an interview, they were: Mike Watson, MP for Central; Maria Fyfe MP for Maryhill; Michael Martin MP for Springburn; George Galloway MP for Hillhead; Ian Davidson MP for Govan; David Marshall MP for Shettleston; and finally MP for Cathcart, John Maxton. Mike Watson, George Galloway, Ian Davidson and David Marshall allowed me to interview them in person, while the rest sent me a completed questionnaire.

Glasgow Labour MPs are much more likely to deal with problems brought to them by Asian constituents than Conservative MPs. There is a link between immigrant issues brought to the attention of MPs and the proportion of Asians in the constituency. When asked whether Asian constituents attended their surgery, or wrote to them, four MPs said yes to both questions.[48] They were John Maxton, Mike Watson, Maria Fyfe and Michael Martin. Three MPs said 10% of constituents attending their surgery are Asian,[49] whilst Michael Martin said less than 10%.[50] David Marshall said "I am lucky if one Asian constituent visits the surgery in every two or three years". He told me there were very few Asians staying in the Eastend of the city.[51] MP George Galloway said about 10% of constituents attending his surgery were Asian but many also wrote to him.[52] Ian Davidson also mentioned that Asian constituents wrote to him but that less than 10% of all constituents attending his surgery were Asian.[53]

Table 7.2   % of Indian Sub-Continent Constituents in Scottish Labour Constituencies

Constituency	% Constituents from the Indian sub-continent	MP
Pollok	7.3	Dunnachie
Central	5.5	Watson
Maryhill	3.3	Fyfe
Hillhead	3	Galloway
Cathcart	1.7	Maxton
Govan	1.5	Davidson
Anniesland	0.8*	Dewar
Springburn	0.5	Martin
Shettleston	0.4	Marshall
Provan	0.2	Wray
Rutherglen	0.3	Macvoy

Source: 1991 Census Monitor for Parliamentary constituencies in Scotland, (* % for Anniesland taken from the 1991 Census Monitor for New Parliamentary Constituencies in Scotland, published in September 1996)

Table 7.2 shows the % of constituents from the Indian sub-continent in the Labour held constituencies. The table includes the constituencies of the MPs who never gave an interview and of the Labour MP who preferred to be anonymous. It is not at all surprising that the Labour MPs are more active about the immigration problems experienced by their constituents than their Conservative counterparts. The % of constituents from the Indian sub-continent living in Conservative constituencies is less than 1% except for Eastwood. In contrast in the Labour held constituencies more than half of the constituencies have more than 1% constituents from the Indian sub-continent living there, the highest being in Pollok (7.3%), followed by Central (5.5%), Maryhill (3.3%) and Hillhead (3%).

All the MPs interviewed or answering the questionnaires have dealt with immigration issues in recent years. John Maxton, Mike Watson, Maria Fyfe and David Marshall could not compare the immigration workload in recent years with the pre-1979 period because they were not MPs during that period. However, Michael Martin said 5% of his workload is to do with immigration.[54] Mr Davidson could not compare the workload since he was not an MP then,[55] whilst George Galloway said "I have been dealing with more and more immigration cases since 1987 when I was first elected". Mr Galloway feels that as the laws became tougher more people sought his help and advice.[56] David Marshall mentioned he had seen changes in the law but these did not affect his constituents as his constituents are predominantly white. David Marshall made the point that "different constituencies vary, the Asian population is concentrated in specific areas, thus MPs for Glasgow Hillhead and Glasgow Central would be more familiar with immigration cases".[57] Mr Marshall said the Eastend of Glasgow was a very poor area and thus most of the cases he dealt with were housing, social security, and law and order.

When asked if they thought immigration procedures were discriminatory, six of the seven MPs (excluding David Marshall) agreed. In more detail Mr Maxton said "they apply much more rigidly to immigrants from the Indian sub-continent than they do to those coming from other Commonwealth countries like Australia or Canada".[58] Mike Watson also made the same point by comparing the White Commonwealth with the Black Commonwealth countries, pointing out that "..although immigration rules apply to everyone, an assumption is made by Immigration Authorities at its crudest that black people will stay here and whites will not".[59] Maria Fyfe MP said immigration procedures were being clearly designed to make it easier for people from White commonwealth countries.[60] Michael Martin gave a broader answer; "Africans, Asians..... each get a hard time from immigration officers".[61] Although David Marshall believed he did not have much experience of immigration cases, when he did come across one the person normally gained entry on the first occasion or possibly after trying a couple of times.[62] The MPs except for Mr Marshall had the same views about immigration procedures being discriminatory. MP Ian Davidson also mentioned the idea of patriality in the 1971 Immigration Act being discriminatory.[63] The MP for Hillhead Mr. Galloway gave a more lengthy answer; he stated that "we do not have a colour blind immigration system and we do not have colour blind immigration officers". He criticised the 1968 Commonwealth Immigrants Act by saying that it "was within itself implicitly, inherently racist...it drew distinctions between the so called Old Commonwealth and so called New Commonwealth". The MP mentioned how the primary purpose rules "have been tightened, and tightened in a way which variably disadvantages black and Asian people". The final example Mr. Galloway gave was how he believed that there was a predisposition of immigration officials at Embassies, High Commissions and airports not to believe black and Asian people. He went on to say "While white people can sail through often without even the slightest, remotest challenge". Mr Galloway said the result was discrimination against people from the Indian sub-continent.[64]

All MPs believed that Conservative immigration laws/rules did not treat people from the Indian sub-continent fairly. Maria Fyfe mentioned that the primary purpose rule divided families. The authorities in Islamabad looked for every possible discrepancy between the information provided by the sponsor and by the intending immigrant.[65] Michael Martin MP said "those who marry a UK citizen are often asked very probing or personal questions".[66] George Galloway sarcastically mentioning the distinction of the white countries and black countries in the Commonwealth said "we should call it the Indo-Pak sub-continent".[67] Although MP Donald Dewar did not answer the questions sent to him as mentioned before, he did give his opinion on Immigration. The MP criticised the primary purpose rule and said he was aware of and has experienced "...the heartbreak that this can bring".[68] David Marshall said "I have not been made aware personally of unfair treatment".[69] The only time in which the MP for Shettleston did feel there was unfair treatment was when a Turkish boy was refused a holiday visa for the UK. Mr Marshall went on to say that the Conservative government laws have tightened up immigration across the board not just the Indian sub-continent, "but it is alleged" that they are more discriminatory towards people from the Indian sub-continent.[70] Basically most MPs disapproved of the immigration policies and gave reasons for their views. Whilst Mr Marshall having limited experience in the area did believe the immigration laws were tight for every nationality and not just the Indian sub-continent. The Labour MPs were not supportive of immigration policies, again not surprising since the Labour MPs represent a high number of Asian constituents in their areas.[71] This also relates to Mr Marshall's views on immigration since there are hardly any Asians living in his constituency "maybe twenty Asians out of fifty three thousand people".[72]

The MPs wanted to see the laws changed. John Maxton simply said that immigration policy would be "a matter for Labour Party's Home Affairs..... when we come to power".[73] Mike Watson mentioned that immigration laws should be relaxed, and referring to the issuing of visas said there was "a need for greater fairness".[74] Similarly Maria Fife wants to see equality when dealing with immigration cases. MP Michael Martin criticised the length of waiting time for an interview and that people in their own country "should not be subjected to such probing questions".[75] He also made the comment that people seeking political asylum should be given more help and sympathy. George Galloway would like to see an end to the distinction between the Old Commonwealth and New Commonwealth. This is similar to Dummett's argument, cited in chapter 1; she emphasises the need to focus on immigration from a wider global perspective rather than concentrating on the classification of immigration by region. Also in relation to the relaxation of the primary purpose rule in favour of a family policy, Galloway ridiculed the Conservative government, "this is a government that claims to be a party of the family...the truth is families are torn asunder by the immigration rules".[76] Ian Davidson was another MP like David Marshall who simply said he did not have enough expertise on the area to comment. This was a little surprising since the MP for Govan Ian Davidson has 1.5% of people from the Indian sub-continent residing, which is higher than constituencies such as Anniesland, Springburn, Provan, Rutherglen and Shettleston (see Table 7.2). Nevertheless regarding the need for any changes in the immigration laws, Mr Marshall did have a comment to make about the laws separating couples "I do not think it is right to separate a man and wife".[77]

I asked the MPs if they thought immigration officials i.e. immigration officers, immigration police, are doing an effective job. John Maxton said it depended on for whom they were doing an effective job. Mike Watson said 'yes' for the government (i.e. the previous Conservative government) but not for the immigrants i.e. asylum seekers and visa applicants.[78] MP Ian Davidson touched on the idea that immigration officials are doing an effective job if their job is to keep people out. Very importantly Mr Davidson seemed a little unsure about the subject. He himself said immigrants have even lied to him when he represents them. The Govan MP then said "I have taken up their cases and discovered that I've been misled, and that means you end up treating everybody as if they were lying to you".[79] Thus the point Mr Davidson was trying to make was he could understand when immigration officials accepted nothing at face value. This is in line with the previous chapter, where some officials claimed that there were many bogus applications made, and that there was a rise in the number of people being removed from the country as illegal immigrants and under the deportation process.

George Galloway also said the immigration officials are doing an effective job for the Conservatives. Maria Fyfe questioned the effectiveness of immigration procedures: "There are long delays in dealing with applications which are largely due to underfunding of the service".[80] This was a point made previously by the Home Office and Foreign Office officials. Michael Martin also did not agree that immigration officials do an effective job and complained about the length of time it took to deal with visa applications. David Marshall said the immigration officials simply do what the government tells them to do and are obliged to do it whether they like it or not. The MP for Shettleston did say that the lengthy waiting times some applicants experience can be due to an inadequate number of staff processing the large number of applications the Home Office receives. Mr. Marshall then went on to say "the government decides the staffing level so they can speed up applications if they want".[81] This comment made by Mr. Marshall suggests the government, rather than officials should be blamed directly for the hardship experienced by immigrants. Officials from the Foreign and Commonwealth Office and the Home Office did claim that lack of funding was a setback in dealing with applications quickly.[82]

Opposition MPs do have some power when helping individuals with immigration problems. Mr. Maxton said he could "contact directly the government minister which at least ensured the case is looked at again".[83] Mike Watson felt he had "a fair amount" of prerogative.[84] Maria Fyfe said she could not overturn a decision, however "..appeals on behalf of potential immigrants have sometimes been successful and sometimes not".[85] Ian Davidson and David Marshall gave a similar answer to Ms Fyfe. Michael Martin said he could approach the Minister when there was a problem;

George Galloway gave the impression that he was not happy with the prerogative MPs possess and that it could be improved.

John Maxton, Mike Watson and Maria Fyfe believed that their influence in respect of immigration issues has declined over the years. Mr Maxton says that "our ability to influence cases has been reduced",[86] Mike Watson mentioned deportation procedures where before "anyone threatened with deportation just phoned an MP and it was immediately stopped - 5 years ago". He went on to say "now this cannot be done which makes it more difficult to delay and overturn a decision".[87] George Galloway gave the same answer as Mike Watson, agreeing that not being able to stop deportations made his work very difficult. Maria Fyfe did state the laws had been made tighter: "I used to be able to take up a case with the relevant minister, but now if I want a relatively quick response I have to write to the Immigration and Nationality Department".[88] Michael Martin's views differed: he thought that the MPs prerogative had not changed over the years i.e. "no Ministers will listen to an MP".[89] Ian Davidson felt he could not answer this since he became an MP when all the main changes had happened. David Marshall also found it difficult to answer due to the lack of immigration cases and lack of experience on the issues and problems involved.

I asked the MPs how successful they were in helping people with immigration problems. John Maxton did not answer this question. Mike Watson felt he was fairly successful. Maria Fyfe explained she has had success in asylum cases but "in more routine arranged marriages cases, these tend not to be successful".[90] Mrs Fyfe, it can be assumed is referring to the rules related to the primary purpose of the marriage as mentioned in chapter 2. Michael Martin feels he has been quite successful. Ian Davidson implied that he was not particularly successful in helping people with immigration problems, he said "I can make sure cases are heard but if they don't meet the very tight rules/regulations then I cannot really help".[91] George Galloway believed he was not very successful "...but I am probably more successful than most people".[92] Mr. Galloway claimed "we are up against a really difficult enemy and that enemy is racism".[93] David Marshall said "it depends on what you define as successful since some cases may take up to two years to attain a visa".[94]

212

Maria Fyfe deals with various types of immigration cases, e.g. visas for parents, spouses, visitors and political asylum. Nevertheless the most common type of problems she deals with are visas for husbands and fiancés. Mike Watson said he generally dealt with all the above variety of visa applications. Michael Martin deals mainly with husbands denied a visa, students and political asylum seekers. Ian Davidson dealt with the usual visa problems but the most common category he deals with concerns "economic refugees". This refers to people who came here illegally many years ago and are financially settled here but are deported once they have been found out. Whilst George Galloway deals with a variety of visas for husbands, wives, fiancé, and political asylum cases. However, the most common is the refusal of visiting visas. Galloway has to deal with many primary purpose rule cases which tends to break-up families. In relation to visiting visa cases to succeed, he said "the success chances are pretty low - 1 in 10".[95] David Marshall deals with visas for fiancés, general visitors visas and has never had any political asylum cases.

The MPs replies indicate that there is some liaison between organisations and opposition MPs. When asked if the MPs had ever enlisted or contacted organisations like the Immigration Advisory Service (IAS) for help, John Maxton did not answer. Mike Watson said he regularly contacted the Immigration Advisory Service and the Scottish Refugee Council. Maria Fyfe said yes she did contact organisations, while Mr Martin said "not often, however they often refer cases to me".[96] George Galloway does not enlist the help of organisations like the IAS but they do ask for his help. MPs Ian Davidson and David Marshall do seek advice and assistance from the IAS, which is not surprising since they are not heavily involved in the immigration arena.

Five of the MPs have heard criticisms against the immigration officials; the exceptions are for Ian Davidson and David Marshall. Mr. Davidson feels that "its criticisms of the rules, rather than the officers".[97] Mr. Marshall said "I think if any individual is not granted what they want, then they feel unhappy and feel they have a grievance".[98] MP John Maxton did say that immigration officials "in the main do the legitimate job they are asked to do within the political restraint placed upon them by the Conservative government". He went on to say "sometimes they are over-zealous and official". However, Mr Maxton was pointing out that immigration officials are doing the right job for the Conservative government, not for the would-be immigrants.[99] MP Maria Fyfe felt that families were being divided due to the primary purpose rule, and that the British authorities in Islamabad looked for "every possible discrepancy between the details given by the sponsor and the intending emigrant".[100] However, Maria Fyfe did mention she had not heard any complaints against the police. MP Mike Watson gave a list of criticisms he has heard including "delay, discourtesy, lack of clear information and racism".[101] Michael Martin emphasised how bad or embarrassing the questions asked by the immigration officials can be. MP George Galloway believes that immigration officials have a one track mind in thinking all Asians are liars; he said the officials think "..anyone given a visitor's visa to come to Britain will immediately take off into the undergrowth of Birmingham and never be seen again, this also includes applicants that are 80 or 90 years old".[102] On the whole the response of the Labour MPs to Conservatives immigration policies tends to be hostile.

MP Maria Fyfe did mention a case about which she felt strongly but which did not bring success. The case involved the deportation of the father of a baby She said "he was living here for 9 years, working and living as a law abiding citizen - but he had been a illegal immigrant".[103] The main case Ian Davidson thought of was where a man had been living here for many years, well settled and contributing financially to the community. Although this man was married to a UK born wife he was an illegal immigrant; nonetheless, he was still deported. George Galloway gave the example of Councillor Sarwar's (now MP) sister being initially refused a visa in spite of his political profile (This case was studied when looking at individual cases).[104] Mr Galloway also told of a case where a woman was living in the UK with her three children fatherless "..because the government would not admit the primary purpose of her marriage. How many children do you have to produce that you can demonstrate that this is a genuine, valid marriage"? [105] According to the Hillhead MP this is a very common type of case he deals with. Mike Watson said there were several cases in his mind but he did not give any examples. David Marshall could only think of the Turkish boy who was refused a holiday visa because the immigration officers believed he would not return to Turkey after his holiday to the UK was over.

I asked if the MPs had spoken about immigration issues in the House of Commons debates, oral or written. Out of the seven Labour MPs interviewed, four had some involvement in immigration debates in the House of Commons. MP John Maxton very rarely spoke in the House of Commons debates. Mike Watson said he had asked parliamentary questions. Mr Watson went on to say "I was a member of the Committee which examined the 1993 Asylum and Immigration Appeals Act; I spoke in Parliament at all stages of the legislation".[106] Similarly Maria Fyfe had also spoken in the House of Commons debates but more recently she had spoken about the Asylum and Immigration Bill. In the debate Maria Fyfe was concerned about fraudulent immigration councillors whom may be inexperienced in this field. Such councillors may make promises of success in immigration cases even though it is well known how hard it is to gain settlement in the UK and that MPs provide the same service free of charge.[107] In another debate on the 1993 Asylum and Immigration Appeals Act, Maria Fyfe made the point about the unfairness involved if a person who has been in a common law relationship for many years is refused a settlement visa unless he/she can show they are engaged or have an intention of marriage.[108] George Galloway said he had spoken in the House of Commons and asked questions, oral and written. Michael Martin said no but due to the fact that people want their cases to be private and not to mention their business in public. Last and not least Ian Davidson and David Marshall said no because they feel it is not an area on which they have a great deal of expertise.

Labour MPs expressed considerable concern about immigration policies; they directly criticised the primary purpose rule, asylum bill, and the separation of families. They stressed the need to remove the distinction between the Old Commonwealth and the New Commonwealth.

The Labour MPs tended to be much more concerned than the Conservatives about the consequences of the immigration regime. Their attitudes reflect their constituency experience and an increase in the impact of the immigration regime in the 1980s. An official from the Public Section, Migration and Visa Unit of the Foreign and Commonwealth Office said MPs correspondence, representation, queries on immigration matters has increased over the years. In 1988 there were 3864 letters from MPs, in 1989 the annual figures for MPs correspondence were 4,111 and in

1990 there were 4,561.[109] This increase could mean that the laws were getting tougher, along with the fact that more people were applying to enter the UK.

This section has illustrated a considerable partisan division on the issue of immigration. The Labour MPs expressed much more sympathy for those affected by the immigration regime. The strong nature of the criticism by some Labour MPs expressed during interviews is indicative of the controversial nature of the immigration issue during the time of the previous Conservative government.

Conclusions

The views of Conservative and Labour MPs on immigration conflict significantly because of differences in the policies of their respective parties and differences in the ethnic composition of their constituencies. The majority of Labour MPs interviewed said 10% of constituents attending their surgery were Asian, while the Conservative MPs emphasised that much fewer attended the surgery. The most important partisan difference was that the Conservative MPs felt that the immigration procedures were not discriminatory. In fact Phil Gallie MP would like to tighten the immigration regime. He recommended that where if a person from abroad is married to a UK citizen and the marriage breaks down within 5, years then that person from abroad should be returned to his or her own country.[110]

The Labour MPs strongly agreed that immigration laws were biased and discriminated against people from the Indian sub-continent by giving good solid examples such as the whole concept of patriality.[111] The Tory MPs did not want to see any change in the regime while the Labour MPs were all in favour of changing the primary purpose rule and of having laws that apply equally irrespective of race, colour or creed. One Labour MP Ian Davidson took a more balanced view, feeling that it was all very well to criticise immigration officers but immigration officers have a very difficult task to perform because people from the Indian sub-continent tended to lie a lot even to him. He actually said that behind closed doors Labour MPs have discussed this problem, which would suggest that it occurs fairly frequently. One could also argue that if the laws were not so tough in the first place, then maybe people would not be tempted to lie. Women said that they had in fact told the truth in interviews yet they were being treated as if they had been lying.[112]

Even when the MPs were asked how successful they were in helping immigrants, the Tories gave a more optimistic view of being quite successful in contrast to Labour MPs who felt their success rate could be much improved. There was certainly an unsurprising partisan divide on how immigration policies were viewed. This partisan division/conflict on immigration has occurred throughout the 1980s in relation to all of the laws passed. Opposition to Tory policies on Immigration also came from organisations such as the United Kingdom Immigration Advisory Service[113] and even the British Society for Social Responsibility,[114] as well as from opposition MPs. The 1981 British Nationality Act was brandished as 'racist' by the Opposition.[115] The introduction of visas[116] had also created a row within the Cabinet with on the one side Home Secretary Douglas Hurd strongly favouring the visa scheme to deal with what he called immigration chaos at Heathrow, and on the other end Foreign Secretary Sir Geoffrey Howe who opposed the scheme on "...practical and diplomatic grounds", pointing to the delays in recruiting and financing the extra officers to administer the scheme abroad. Sir Geoffrey Howe also expressed the detrimental effect it would have on relations with the countries involved. In 1987 Labour brandished as 'racist' the Carriers' Liability Bill[117] which later became law. Home Secretary Hurd argued that "Britain could not give asylum to just anyone who came".[118] It is therefore not at all surprising that the Scottish Conservative and Labour MPs interviewed had conflicting views. Overall there has been a rise in the number of MPs' enquiries over the years to the Migration and Visa Unit which deals with the entry clearances in posts abroad, reflecting more visa refusals over the years.[119]

The Labour MPs have a higher concentration of constituents from the Indian sub-continent in comparison to the Conservative MPs which does make Labour MPs more sympathetic to the immigrants' cause. The Labour MPs made the point that people from White Commonwealth countries have no problems in gaining entry clearance or with the immigration officers attitude. This argument can be supported by Mr Lusk from the

Migration and Visa Unit, Foreign and Commonwealth Office who agreed that people from Australia are likely to have less problems than people from the Indian sub-continent.[120] The Tory MPs admitted to hearing some criticisms from their constituents about immigration officers i.e. bad attitude of immigration officers and length of waiting time. They however had no criticisms themselves about the immigration officers. The Labour MPs heard criticisms about the procedures and claimed that ECOs were doing an effective job for the Conservative government. The Labour MPs wanted to see fairer immigration laws, and removal of the primary purpose rule in order to defend family unity. Again it can be stressed that the Labour MPs' criticism of Conservative government immigration policy is not wholly surprising given that the majority of black and coloured people vote Labour at general and local elections While one cannot question the commitment and understanding that Labour MPs portray towards the cause of immigrants, the need to keep black voters on their side must play some part in Labour denunciation of immigration policy. Being on the other end of the political spectrum Labour criticism of Conservative policy in this area is to be expected. Having said that, if there was any doubts about the motives behind Labour's commitment to the cause of ethnic minorities then these have to some extent been dispelled by the present Labour government's abolition of one of the most hated, discriminatory, and controversial aspects of the Conservative immigration regime: the primary purpose rule.[121]

This chapter also demonstrates that a greater level of exposure to constituents' grievances from constituents makes MPs sensitive to immigration issues and problems. Tory MPs have fewer immigration queries to deal with due to the fact that their constituencies contain fewer voters who belong to the immigrant community. As a result they have little to say on the matter. As government backbenchers they tended to be naturally more defensive of party policy when making any comments. The Labour MPs have more to say not just because they were the opposition but also because their constituencies have many more citizens who are of Indian sub-continent origin, and they are able to build a bigger picture of the situation and the prevailing mood regarding immigration.

Labour MPs felt that they have very little power in changing the course of events. While they could provide support and advice, and intercede on behalf of constituents, their powers were limited.

Notes

1.   See *chapter 2*.
2.   Cosme Morgado, *The Role of Members of Parliament in Immigration Cases*, p. 4, Policy Paper in Ethnic Relations No 14, Centre for Research in Ethnic Relations.
3.   S.A. de Smith, *Constitutional and Administrative law*, (Penguin, 1987), p. 247.
4.   See *chapter 2*.
5.   Zig Layton Henry, *The Politics of Immigration*, (Blackwell, 1992), pp. 154 & 189.
6.   *Letter* from Ian Lang MP (Upper Nithsdale), 30 May 1996.
7.   *Ibid*, Rt. Hon Michael Forsyth (Stirling), 29 May 1996.
8.   *Ibid*, Malcolm Rifkind (Edinburgh Pentlands), 3 June 1996.
9.   *Ibid*, James Douglas-Hamilton (Edinburgh West), 30 May 1996.
10. Cosme Morgado, *The Role of Members of Parliament in Immigration Cases*, op. cit. p. 27.
11. *Interview* with Phil Gallie (Ayr), 28 May 1996.
12. *Ibid*, Alan Stewart (Eastwood), May 1996.
13. *Ibid*, MP A, June 1996.
14. *Ibid*, Hector Munro (Dumfries), June 1996.
15. *Ibid*, Phil Gallie (Ayr), 28 May 1996.
16. *Ibid*, MP A, June 1996.
17. *Ibid*, Alan Stewart, May 1996.
18. *Ibid*, Phil Gallie, 28 May 1996.
19. *Ibid*, Hector Munro (Dumfries), June 1996.
20. *Ibid*.
21. *Ibid*, MP A, June 1996.
22. *Ibid*, Phil Gallie, 28 May 1996.
23. *Ibid*.
24. *Ibid*, Hector Munro, June 1996.
25. *Ibid*, MP A, June 1996.
26. *Ibid*, Alan Stewart, May 1996.
27. *Ibid*.
28. *Ibid*, Phil Gallie, 28 May 1996.
29   *Ibid*, Hector Munro, June 1996.
30. *Ibid*, MP A, June 1996.
31. *Ibid*, Alan Stewart, May 1996.
32. *Ibid*, Phil Gallie, 28 May 1996.
33. *Ibid*.

34. *Ibid*, MP A, June 1996.
35. *Ibid*, Alan Stewart, May 1996.
36. *Ibid*, MP A, June 1996.
37. *Ibid*, Alan Stewart, May 1996.
38. *Ibid*, Phil Gallie, 28 May 1996.
39. *Ibid*, Hector Munro, June 1996.
40. *Ibid*, Phil Gallie, 28 May 1996.
41. *Ibid*, MP A, June 1996.
42. *Ibid*, Alan Stewart, May 1996.
43. *Interview* with officials, Home Office and Foreign and Commomwealth Office, 19 September 1996 and 20 September 1996.
44. *Ibid*, with Alan Stewart, May 1996.
45. *Ibid*, with Phil Gallie, 28 May 1996.
46. *Letter* from James Dunnachie MP (Pollok), 27 May 1996.
47. *Ibid*, Donald Dewar MP, (Anniesland), May 1996.
48. *Interview* with John Maxton MP (Cathcart), April 1996 and Mike Watson MP 2 March 1996 and Maria Fyfe MP (Maryhill), I April 1996 and Michael Martin MP (Springburn), April 1996
49. *Ibid*, John Maxton, April 1996 and Mike Watson, 2 March 1996 and Maria Fyfe, 1 April 1996.
50. *Ibid*, Michael Martin, April 1996.
51. *Ibid*, David Marshall MP (Shettleston), 21 March 1997.
52. *Ibid*, George Galloway MP (Hillhead), 19 April 1996.
53. *Ibid*, Ian Davidson MP (Govan), 18 May 1996.
54. *Ibid*, Michael Martin, 10 April 1996.
55. *Ibid*, Ian Davidson, 18 May 1996.
56. *Ibid*, George Galloway, 19 April 1996.
57. *Ibid*, David Marshall, 21 March 1997.
58. *Ibid*, John Maxton, April 1996.
59. *Ibid*, Mike Watson, 2 March 1996.
60. *Ibid*, Maria Fyfe, 1 April 1996.
61. *Ibid*, Michael Martin, April 1996
62. *Ibid*, David Marshall, 21 March 1997.
63. See *1971 Immigration Act* and see also chapter 2.
64. *Interview* with George Galloway, 19 April 1996.
65. *Ibid*, Maria Fyfe, 1 April 1996.
66. *Ibid*, Michael Martin, April 1996.
67. *Ibid*, George Galloway, 19 April 1996.
68. *Letter* from Donald Dewar, May 1996.
69. *Interview* with David Marshall, 21 March 1997.
70. *Ibid*.
71. *1991 Census Monitor for Parliamentary Constituencies in Scotland*, Scottish Office 1994.
72. *Interview* with David Marshall, 21 March 1997.

73.   *Ibid*, John Maxton, 16 April 1996.
74.   *Ibid*, Mike Watson, 2 March 1996.
75.   *Ibid*, Michael Martin, 10 April 1996.
76.   *Ibid*, George Galloway, 19 April 1996.
77.   *Ibid*, David Marshall, 21 March 1997.
78.   *Ibid*, Mike Watson, 2 March 1996.
79.   *Ibid*, Ian Davidson, 18 May 1996.
80.   *Ibid*, Maria Fyfe, 1 April 1996.
81.   *Ibid*, David Marshall, 21 March 1997.
82.   *Ibid*, Sean Lusk, Migration and Visa Unit, Foreign and Commonwealth Office, 20 September 1996.
83.   *Ibid*, John Maxton, April 1996.
84.   *Ibid*, Mike Watson, 2 March 1996.
85.   *Ibid*, Maria Fyfe, 1 April 1996,
86.   *Ibid*, John Maxton, April 1996.
87.   *Ibid*, Mike Watson, 2 March 1996.
88.   *Ibid*, Maria Fyfe, 1 April 1996.
89.   *Ibid*, Michael Martin, April 1996.
90.   *Ibid*, Maria Fyfe, 1 April 1996.
91.   *Ibid*, Ian Davidson, 18 May, 1996.
92.   *Ibid*, George Galloway, 19 April 1996.
93.   *Ibid*.
94.   *Ibid*, David Marshall, 21 March 1997.
95.   *Ibid*, George Galloway, 19 April 1996.
96.   *Ibid*, Michael Martin, April 1996.
97.   *Ibid*, Ian Davidson, 18 May 1996.
98.   *Ibid*, David Marshall, 21 March 1997.
99.   *Ibid*, John Maxton, April 1996.
100.   *Ibid*, Maria Fyfe, 1 April 1996.
101.   *Ibid*, Mike Watson, 2 March 1996.
102.   *Ibid*, George Galloway, 19 April 1996.
103.   *Ibid*, Maria Fyfe, 1 April 1996
104.   See *chapter 5*
105.   *Interview* with George Galloway, 19 April 1996.
106.   *Ibid*, Mike Watson, 2 March 1996.
107.   *Parliamentary Debates, Commons (Hansard)*, vol. 272, cols. 381-382, 21 February 1996.
108.   *Ibid*, col. 540, 22 February 1996.
109.   Communication over the phone with an official from Public Section, Migration and Visa Unit, Foreign and Commonwealth Office, 23 September 1996.
110.   *Interview* with Phil Gallie, 28 May 1996.
111.   See *1971 Immigration Act*, also see Satvinder S. Juss, *Immigration, Nationality and Citizenship*, (Mansell 1993), p. 46, and chapter 2.
112.   See *chapter 5*

113.   *The Times*, July 5, 1983. The UKIAS now known as the IAS was complaining that the Conservative government was intentionally keeping immigrant figures down. This was achieved by providing a lower number of vouchers for entry to the UK to East African Asians holding a UK passport in India.

114.   *The Scotsman*, June 19, 1979, p. 4. In June 1979, the Conservative government published figures of Coloured Commonwealth and Pakistan citizens living in Britain. The government claimed that the number of such immigrants was set to arise to 3 million by 1991 representing a projected increase of about 81% from 1976. The British Society for Social Responsibility attacked the government about the figures being "misleading and potentially inflammatory".

115.   See *Glasgow Herald*, October 31, 1981, p. 3.

116.   See *ibid*, September 1, 1996, p. 1.

117.   See *ibid,* March 17, 1987, p. 11.

118.   *Ibid.*

119.   *Communication* with Official from Public Section, Migration and Visa Unit, Foreign and Commonwealth Office, 23 September 1996.

120.   *Interview* with Sean Lusk, Head of Immigration Policy, Migration and Visa Unit, Foreign and Commonwealth Office, 20 September 1996.

121.   See the *Guardian*, 28 May 1997, p. 5.

Appendix

The following questionnaire was compiled for the purpose of analysing the views on immigration of both Conservative and Labour MPs. In the case of those MPs who were unwilling to give me an interview they were sent a copy of the questionnaire and asked to fill it in and send it back. Those MPs who were willing to give me an interview in person, the questions in the questionnaire were simply put to them.

These questions concern only immigration and people from the Indian sub-continent.

1   Do Asian constituents ever:
a   attend your surgeries?
b   write to you?
2   If yes to 1 (a):
    what % of constituents attending are Asian?
3   Have you dealt with any immigration cases in Scotland in recent years?

4 What comparison can you make of your workload, and cases you have dealt with in recent years, and those dealt with prior to 1979 (If you were an MP at that time)?

5 Do you think immigration procedures are discriminatory?
Could you explain in detail?

6 Do the Conservatives' immigration laws/rules treat people from the Indian sub-continent fairly? Could you explain in detail?

7 Are there any laws you would change or would like to see changed?
Could you elaborate?

8 Do you think immigration officials such as Immigration Officers, Immigration Police and the Nationality Department are doing an effective job?
Could you elaborate?

9a How much prerogative do you have in helping individuals with immigration problems?

9b Has this changed over the years?

9c How has this affected your work?

10 How successful are you in helping people with immigration problems?

11 What are the most common types of cases regarding immigration do you deal with?

12 Have you ever made contact or enlisted the help of organisations such as the IAS in helping individuals?

13 What type of criticisms do you hear against Immigration Officers, Home Office and the Immigration Police Department?

14 What type of criticism do you have about immigration officials?

15 Are there any cases in your mind which you feel strongly about that did not succeed or took unnecessarily took long for an outcome?

16 Have you spoken in the House of Commons in debates related to immigration issues or asked Parliamentary questions, oral or written?

8 Conclusions - Conservative Immigration Policy 1979-1990: Reconsidered

Conclusions - Conservative Immigration Policy 1979-1990: Reconsidered

This book has analysed the nature and impact of the immigration regime developed by the Conservative government under Thatcher. It has demonstrated that the immigration policy of the Conservative party under Thatcher had a negative impact on would-be immigrants into Britain from the Indian sub-continent, and was characterised by unfairness and considerable harshness. The regime was perceived by those affected by it as unfair and discriminatory. A number of significant findings of this study provide clear evidence of the tough nature of the immigration regime and of its discriminatory impact. The principal 'victims' of the regime were males seeking to join wives and fiancées already established as citizens of the United Kingdom. The Glasgow survey revealed that only 29% of husbands and 22% of male fiancés applying for entry visas were successful in the first instance. In the case of applications for visitors' visas 74% of males were turned down in the first instance. In sharp contrast, the success rate of wives and fiancées applying for permanent stay visas was 76% and 78% respectively.

At the heart of these findings is the primary purpose rule. A majority of males, 63%, denied visas on first application claimed that the primary purpose rule was responsible for such discriminatory outcomes. This rule is framed in a negative form in that it requires would-be immigrants to prove that the primary purpose behind applications to enter the United Kingdom on a permanent or on a temporary basis was *not* economic in nature. Where a spouse or spouse to be seeks entry in order to join the British partner on a permanent basis the marriage or the forthcoming marriage should *not* have been entered into for economic reasons. The marriage should not be a 'marriage of convenience'. The primary purpose rule was perceived by respondents to the survey, many of whom had direct experience of its application, as unfair and discriminatory. The principal impact of the primary purpose rule was the rejection on first application of the great majority of males seeking to enter the United Kingdom in order to join partners or partners to be on a permanent basis.

The operation of the primary purpose rule and its consequences highlight a clash of cultures between Britain and the Indian sub-continent in relation to the institution of marriage. In Indian sub-continent culture it is commonplace for parents to arrange marriages for their children. The culture dictates that a couple should not be courting before marrying. In many cases such a tradition leaves no room for 'romantic love' in the Western sense as the principal reason for a particular marriage. In such cases the immigration authorities are unable to establish 'love and romance' as the primary purpose of the marriage. Rather the primary purpose is the satisfaction of the objectives of the families arranging the marriage. For the participants the primary purpose will usually be finding a partner. For *some* families and for *some* potential spouses the primary purpose of the marriage may be to enter the United Kingdom in pursuit of more favourable employment and other opportunities.

It would appear from the survey findings and from the individual case studies that immigration officers assume that an arranged marriage or engagement offends the primary purpose rule unless the *male* applicants for an entry visa can prove the contrary. The onus of proof that the primary purpose of marriage or engagement to a British national is not economic gain or the achievement of British citizenship is placed on the applicants.

How is the primary purpose of the marriage to be determined? This is a profoundly difficult question to answer. But it is essentially the question which British immigration officers stationed in British consulates abroad and at points of entry into Britain have to answer in particular cases. Both the enactment of the rule and its implementation have led to accusations of cultural insensitivity, especially in the light of changing customs in the Indian sub-continent. Today the arranged marriage system is more liberal and it is no longer uncommon for a man and woman to have met and to have fallen in love before entering the institution of marriage.

Another intriguing finding was that would-be immigrants with low status occupations had considerably less success in gaining an entry visa. The thinking here on the part of the authorities was that if one's occupation is not of a high status then the primary reason for marriage can be perceived as a desire to gain entry into the UK. This was once again viewed as unfair because the Indian sub-continent is dominated by low status professions such as farmers and farm labourers. Furthermore it was noted that occupation of the would-be immigrant was viewed as more significant than that of the sponsor in the decision-making of entry clearance officers. Therefore in some cases even when sponsors had good occupations they were still unsuccessful in securing a visa for the would-be immigrant. Once again it was males who suffered as a consequence of the connection between occupation and immigration. Females entering as wives or fiancées had little difficulty securing an entry visa even if they had low status jobs or no job. This was a direct result of the fact that females are not perceived as a threat to the British employment situation as they tend to perform the role of housewives when they settle in Britain.

This concluding chapter will review the impact that Conservative immigration policy under Thatcher had on people from the Indian sub-continent. Section one will look at the immediate background to Thatcher's tough stance on immigration and the thinking which prompted the pursuit of a strict immigration regime. Section two will review the rules and procedures adopted in pursuit of such a regime. Section three will review the overall evidence from the chapters in this work in order to make a final judgement on whether the Conservative immigration regime can be labelled as unfair and harsh in view of the impact it had on Indian sub-continent nationals. A final section will look at the future of the Conservative immigration regime now that a new Labour government has come to power.

Necessity for Stricter Immigration Control

At the political level the Conservative party was a strong advocate of strict immigration control. One of the reasons why the Thatcher government was elected in 1979 was the race issue. In the context of this issue some reasons were economic[1] and others nationalistic; many would view the nationalistic ones as examples of a racist attitude.[2] The Tory party under Thatcher's leadership adopted a tough policy towards immigration controls but despite this there were still further calls during 1979-1990 from those who were on the extreme right-wing section of the Conservative party for even stricter controls on immigration. The Conservative Party Manifesto had a list of specific commitments to reduce immigration[3] and this is what its leaders promised the electorate and the extreme right-wing section of the party. No one illustrated the advocacy of a even stricter immigration regime than Enoch Powell, described by the *Herald* as the "champion of immigration controls".[4] He was clearly a champion of the nationalist theory of immigration discussed in chapter 1, which advocated a virtual end to all immigration. In August 1979, speaking to a group of young Conservatives, Mr Powell outlined his argument that the proposed new Nationality Act, which would more clearly define entitlement to British Citizenship, should be used by the Government to end "the dual nationality[5] currently enjoyed by immigrants in Britain".[6] His remarks were directed largely against immigrants from the New Commonwealth and Pakistan who he claimed were citizens of their country of origin and not of Britain. In October 1979[7] the government once again came under right-wing pressure from within the party to get tough on immigration. Hard-liners on immigration had become increasingly concerned that the government appeared to be backing down from its pre-election pledge that it would introduce a quota system, would ban male fiancés, and would set up a register of dependants. They were keen to force the pace on the issue, reminding the government that they would battle all the way on this question. Therefore it is clear the Thatcher government was under pressure from its own members to tighten immigration controls.

The Conservative party was very keen to reduce immigration. Margaret Thatcher had claimed that the British character was being swamped by people with a different culture. Thatcher was interviewed on

Granada Television's World in Action in 1978,[8] when she discussed how Britain was being swamped by people from a different culture. She also pointed to a need to relieve the British public's anxieties about the number of immigrants. That this view was supported by the British public was suggested by the fact that Thatcher received 10,000 letters supporting what she said and by the Conservatives winning the Ilford North by-election in 1978. The National Front[9] had been prominent in this constituency. Such developments gave the government a reason to placate those voters who supported the Conservative party's 1979 Manifesto.

Officials administering the immigration control regime echoed many of the Conservative arguments when they explained why immigration control was necessary. An official from the Police and Nationality Department[10] who is concerned with finding illegal immigrants made it clear that the immigration laws were needed because there had to be some way of restraining the flow of immigrants into Britain which was just a small island. One very clear argument put forward by all officials interviewed was that people from the Indian sub-continent were using marriage as a tool to gain entry into the UK. One adjudicator argued that countries such as Pakistan, India and Bangladesh are economically poor and people would basically do anything to better themselves by entering the UK. Such attitudes suggest a strong predisposition to implement the primary purpose rule strictly.

All immigration officials interviewed at the Home Office mentioned they received many letters from MPs and their constituents demanding a reduction in the number of immigrants as well as letters from those who opposed the immigration laws. Mr. Troake from the Immigration and Nationality Department at the Home Office[11] stated that Britain was already overcrowded and that therefore the number of people entering had to be restrained. Mr. Troake believed that employment and the British welfare state had to be safeguarded because the third world was overpopulated; the absence of a welfare state meant that many people from the third world were desperate to live in Britain. Therefore immigration officials are more suspicious about the intentions of would-be immigrants from the third world since they are perceived as more likely to want entry for economic reasons.

Tight immigration control has been justified by many as necessary since many illegal immigrants enter the country.[12] The numbers removed as illegal entrants and under the deportation process from the Indian sub-continent is quite high. In 1984 a total of 94 persons from the Indian sub-continent were removed as illegal entrants (see chapter 6, Table 6.1). By 1990 this figure had increased to 244. Throughout the 1980s the Indian sub-continent accounted for over 10% of all those removed as illegal entrants. A similar picture can be seen when looking at the removal of persons under the deportation process. Throughout the 1980s the number of persons from the Indian sub-continent removed under the deportation process was 10% or more of total deportations.[13] The number of individuals removed as illegal entrants and under the deportation process during the 1980s was constantly on the increase.[14] This shows that quite a few people did enter illegally, and this was causing concern to the UK authorities. Naturally as a result of this the government opted for stricter controls.

Adjudicators and Home Office officials clearly believed that people from the Indian sub-continent wishing to enter permanently used marriage as an excuse to stay in the country. This belief influences their implementation of the primary purpose rule. Consequently immigration officials strictly applied the primary purpose rule by seeking to ensure that economic motives were *not* the primary reasons for marriage.

Rules and Procedures Adopted to Tighten Immigration Control

The government has a solid institutional base from which to control immigration. There is a strict hierarchical set up controlling immigration at the point of entry and after entry, i.e. British Embassies abroad dealing with immigration applications, and, in the United Kingdom itself, immigration officers, ECOs, Nationality Police and the appeal courts. The system is complicated; certain requirements for permanent stay in the UK and even a simple holiday must be satisfied.[15] Such Rules include: 1) in marriage/engagement cases the couple must prove they have met each other; 2) the primary purpose of the marriage must not be to enter the UK; 3) the couple must have the intention to live together permanently as

229

man and wife; 4) and applicants must have evidence that they are able to maintain and accommodate themselves without being a burden on public funds. In the UK the spouse is on a 12 month probationary period and will be granted stay over the 12 months if the couple have stayed together as man and wife.

In the case of visitors it is the sponsor in the UK who must prove that he/she can accommodate and maintain the visitor. In the case of visitors, a visitor must be able to prove that he/she has a stable job or home in their own country and are bound to return before or as soon as their 6 month period is over. The sponsor must also show that he/she can accommodate and maintain the visitor. Elderly parents wishing to settle in the UK must show that they are 65 or over, they are mainly dependant upon their sponsor in the UK, and that they have no close relatives in their own country to support them. These requirements are not easy to satisfy. The IAS senior councillor in the Glasgow office said elderly parents tended to be refused unless they could prove that they were fully dependant on their UK sponsors, having no relatives to turn to and living in compassionate circumstances.[16]

One can readily see the strictness and complexity of such requirements and the difficulties inherent in efforts to satisfy entry clearance officers. The survey results in themselves show that 40% of visa applicants felt they were refused a visa in case they stayed permanently in the UK; 32% said they were refused a visa because of the primary purpose rule; 7% said they did not satisfy the requirements. Case studies of individuals have shown how stringent the immigration officials have been with applicants, e.g. elderly grandparents have been refused a visiting visa to attend their grand-daughter's wedding in case they stayed permanently in the UK. A gentleman needing a triple by-pass operation was refused a visiting visa, although he was going to spend his money in the private health sector. He was refused in case he stayed permanently. The Conservative government throughout the 1980s was doing its utmost to limit immigration from the Indian sub-continent.

The Conservative government under Heath may have introduced virginity tests[17] but the Thatcher government continued to pursue it. This was to ensure that women from the Indian sub-continent who said they were coming to the UK for marriage purpose were not lying (i.e. could have been already married but wanted an excuse to live in the UK) and this was done by testing to see if they were virgins. In 1980 the government introduced rules which permitted only women who were UK citizens or who had a parent born here to apply for their husbands/fiancés to live in the UK. The European Court of Human Rights judged this to be discriminatory. Consequently all British women irrespective of where they are born now have the right to apply for their fiancé/husband to join them. The 1981 British Nationality Act introduced 3 categories of citizenship and the third category 'British Overseas Citizens' carries with it no right of abode in the UK. This category included people from the Indian sub-continent. One important change was that after the 1st of January 1983 a person born in Britain is only British if one of his/her parents is British or settled here at the time they were born. This meant being born in the UK was not enough to make a person British. The effect of the 1981 Act was to increase the numbers of applications made for registration and naturalisation. In response to this increase in the number of applications the government increased the application fees. This increase in fees prevented many people from applying for citizenship.

In 1986 the Conservative government imposed visas on citizens of India, Bangladesh, Pakistan, Ghana and Nigeria. The excuse given was that in early 1986 the unexplained large number of refusals and the increase in passengers had led to disruption at Heathrow airport for staff and passengers. The results were that detention centres were over-full with people refused entry. Several MPs had an enormous work load as they tried to prevent people from being sent back immediately to their country of origin. The Immigration and Service Union in 1985 discussed this issue with civil servants and ministers with a view to cutting down the numbers entering the UK from the above mentioned countries and to stop MPs from intruding when people were refused a visa. Visas were introduced and MPs could not automatically stop deportation temporarily as they could before. The removal of the right of MPs to stop deportation had also been a setback in the work of Labour MPs George Galloway and Mike Watson.[18]

To show how committed the government was to the visa scheme, Mr. Lusk from the Migration and Visa Unit of the Foreign and Commonwealth Office said "the cost of providing Entry Clearance Services overseas this year was 45 million pounds".[19] The visa system caused problems for family and friends visiting the UK from these countries.

The 1987 Carriers' Liability Act made it illegal for shipping companies and airlines to bring in people without proper documentation i.e. visas and passport. A fine of £1,000 (later increased to £2,000) was imposed on any airline or shipping company bringing into the country a person without proper documents. This was to prevent bogus asylum seekers entering the country.

One of the effects of the 1988 Immigration Act was to take away the right of immigrants who had settled before 1973 to be automatically joined by the their family. Since then their dependants have had to go through the entry clearance procedures like anybody else. The Act also meant that men were no longer allowed to bring in more than one wife into the UK, which would affect the Muslim practice of polygamy.

The introduction of DNA testing allowed immigration officials to make sure that people who were trying to bring in their children into the UK were actually their own children as they claimed. This also meant bogus family members were identified by the immigration service.

All these laws and rules were used by the Conservative government to reduce immigration into the UK over the 1979-90 period. Figures do show that from 1980-1990 there was a reduction in the number of acceptances from the Indian sub-continent for settlement. In 1980 there were over 20,000 acceptances from the Indian sub-continent (representing about 32% of all acceptances; see chapter 6, Table 6.4). But by the end of Thatcher's reign the number accepted had fallen to just over 12,500 (representing 25% of all acceptances). In fact since 1985 the number of acceptances from the Indian sub-continent has never reached the 15,000 mark. While in comparison the number from Australasia rose from 9% of total acceptances in 1980 to 10% of total acceptances in 1990. Although this is a very small rise it is nevertheless significant given that Australasia is much less densely populated than the Indian sub-continent, and the number of applications from Australasia is much less than from the Indian sub-continent. [20]

Whether Conservative Policy Under Thatcher was Justifiably Regarded as Tough and Unfair with Regard to its Impact: The Evidence before Us

The Conservative party's policy on immigration was brandished by opponents, including people who were affected by it, as racist, unfair, discriminatory, and unjust. The overwhelming evidence in this book suggests that the Tory immigration regime did indeed have a negative impact on nationals from the Indian sub-continent. Quite clearly the parties affected by the immigration regime had no doubts that the charge of discriminatory and racist is justifiable. However, the aim of this book is not to examine whether the Conservative immigration regime was discriminatory or racist. Instead the aim of the study is to analyse the consequences of the immigration regime on those who came into contact with it.

There is no doubt that the Conservative party adopted the centrist theory of immigration discussed in chapter 1, which advocates a balanced approach to immigration, rejecting the virtual end to particularly black and coloured immigration supported by the nationalist theory, but neither adhering itself to the liberal theory's call for an end to immigration controls. Instead the Tory's middle ground approach would make sure that immigration was allowed within reason, with significant controls remaining. However, in practice the Tory's were guilty of applying very strict controls, and for moving dangerously close to the nationalist view, with policies which had a negative impact on black and coloured immigrants. It has to be stressed at this point that a simple numerical measurement, which looks at the number of immigrants granted entry and the number refused entry, will not suffice as the only yardstick for assessing whether immigration policies were tough and unfair. In addition to the statistics we have to take into account the nature of the legislation and rules, and the procedures used, to see if they contain any unfair aspects.

The Thatcher government's policy on immigration was seen as discriminatory by those who were affected by immigration laws, by the Labour MPs and by the organisations which exist in Glasgow to help in these issues such as the Immigration Advisory Service (IAS), Community

Relations Council (CRC), Scottish Asian Action Committee (SAAC) and Scottish Refugee Council (SRC) all of whom were very active throughout the 1980s.

However, were the government's laws and motives unusually tough and unfair? Were they aimed deliberately towards the Indian sub-continent?

The survey conducted in Pollokshields and Hillhead showed how the immigrants themselves experienced and perceived immigration. A very important point noted was that out of the 201 people with an immigration experience, 148 were allowed to enter, which suggests a success rate of 74%. However, the length of time and worry experienced by the applicants was stressed by those who had experienced the process. Over half (56%) of the interviewees felt that the ECOs treated them or their family fairly, whilst 44% alleged the contrary. The complaints included personal and ambiguous questions, and the attitude of the ECOs. The accusations were very similar to those the Scottish Conservative MPs had mentioned they heard. The advice given by the Training Department of the FCO, to ECOs is:

> Aim at all times to be courteous and fair, bearing in mind that the entry clearance system is operated without prejudice of any kind, and the decisions you make can have a profound impact on the lives of others.[21]

The impact of the decisions made by ECOs was in evidence in the cases examined in detail in chapter 5. In particular, applicants were made to wait for years to attain a visa. The waiting process disrupted peoples lives, imposed financial burdens such as the cost of flying back and forth between Britain and the sub-continent, and strained relationships. British women experienced emotional stress because they did not know where they were destined to live.

Of all of those interviewed, including those with no immigration experience 32% found the immigration procedures racist, while 31% found them unfair but not racist. This once again illustrates the view of interviewees that immigration control should not be so tough. When asked if the interviewees had heard from others about immigration procedures,

44% said they had heard they were racist and 36% said unfair, again revealing dissatisfaction of the procedures.

One of the most significant findings of the survey was that men were discriminated against in comparison to women when trying to attain a visa either for permanent settlement or for a temporary stay in the UK. Women tended to have fewer problems and gained a visa more easily than men who tended to be refused more often and had to wait longer for the visa. This finding is supported by the view expressed by the Head of the Policy Unit, of the Migration and Visa Unit, Foreign and Commonwealth Office[22] that woman were more favoured than men because they were more easily believed. This finding is unsurprising in the light of the Conservative government's 1980 decision not to allow British women to be joined as of right by their fiancés/husbands in the UK.[23] The European Commission of Human Rights declared this as discriminatory, and the British government was informed that the economic argument against entry was invalid.

The survey also revealed another vital finding which was that having a higher status middle class occupation as the person entering and/or as a sponsor can improve the chances of attaining a visa successfully or with less hassle. This was a particularly significant finding. Results of the survey revealed that while having a good occupation does not guarantee a entry visa the chances are nevertheless significantly greater for those with high status occupations than for those with low status occupations. Since most men seeking entry to Britain in the sample were farmers or farm labourers, they had little success on first application. It is no coincidence that in the survey all of the 14 male fiancés refused an entry visa were in low status jobs such as farm labourers. In addition 22 out of the 27 husbands refused entry visas were also in low status occupations. In comparison the 4 who were granted entry visas had jobs which fell in high status categories such as salariat/intelligence and petty bourgeoisie.

Similar problems were encountered by males when they applied as visitors. Their experiences brings to mind what Mr. Troake from the Immigration and Nationality Department said, viz. that an educated person can obviously give a better interview and thus make a better impression on the ECO.

The survey also indicated that the occupation of the would-be immigrant is more significant than that of the sponsor in the decision-making process of ECOs, e.g. in some cases sponsors had good status occupations but were still unsuccessful in attaining a visa for their partner.

The refusal of the visa for males on the grounds of the primary purpose rule was related to the fact that they had low status occupations. If ones' occupation is not of a high standard then the reason for marriage is more likely to be seen as a desire to gain entry into the United Kingdom in order to improve one's income and wealth.

In contrast females entering as wives and fiancées had markedly fewer problems even when they had no job or low status occupations. In such instances it is the occupation of the sponsor, i.e. the husband or fiancé, which is crucial in determining the outcome of an entry application. If the husband or fiancé has a high status job then there are fewer difficulties which confront females seeking to enter as wives or fiancées. The reason why it is easier for females to enter is because they are not viewed by the immigration authorities as a threat to the British employment situation. This is related to the culture of the Indian sub-continent where females commonly perform the role of housewives and therefore would not be expected to put pressure on the British labour market. Despite the fact that most of the women in the survey seeking to enter had jobs in their country of origin, the culture of the Indian sub-continent dictates that the husband or fiancé is the 'breadwinner'. As a result hardly any females from the Indian sub-continent entering into marriage in Britain take up employment. In addition the fact that most women in the survey had jobs in the Indian sub-continent is related to the fact that it is common in third world countries for everyone to work in order to make ends meet.

The head of the policy unit in the Migration and Visa Unit of the Foreign and Commonwealth Office stated that a person from Australia is bound to have fewer problems than someone from India because the standard of living in Australia is very high and there is no need for the immigration officers to be suspicious about Australian applications. This in itself illustrates how an Australian and an Indian are compared by the ECO when applying to the UK. Mr. Lusk also mentioned that in the culture of the Indian sub-continent, girls live with their husbands' family and the ECOs have this in their minds. For this reason ECOs are more wary of applications involving husbands seeking to join their wives in Britain because they expect wives to live with their husbands in the husbands' country. This itself is unfair since an Asian girl brought up in the West is not going to have the typical Indian sub-continent traditions of living with the in-laws and yet the immigration officers are inclined to think in the former way. The level of difficulty experienced by males when applying as husbands, fiancés, or visitors was demonstrated by statistics in the survey (see chapter 4, Table 4.10) which highlight the fact that a smaller proportion of them were successful in obtaining a visa in the first instance in comparison to females. Subsequently more males had to go through the lengthy and at times tedious appeal process that was analysed in detail in chapter 5 - the case studies.

One can argue the organisations which helped immigrants and their sponsors were very critical of immigration procedures and the laws. Evidence of unfairness and extreme harshness was also offered in their annual reports. The Community Relations Council in its 1982 Report was strongly critical of the 1981 Nationality Act which caused uncertainty for ethnic minorities: the virginity tests were embarrassing and disconcerting for women: questions of a highly personal nature about sexual relations were degrading. The Scottish Asian Action Committee (SAAC) lobbied the Scottish Office on such issues and contacted Scottish MPs in an effort to seek redress for the humiliating procedures of the immigration regime. The SAAC was convinced of the discriminatory nature of the regime, stating in one of its reports that "white people do not suffer the same delays although in principle the rules apply to all".[24]

The IAS had also complained about the long delays involved for attaining visas, criticisms levelled at ECOs on their conduct and how the government was turning away people who were genuine and accredited to enter the UK, so the government could control immigration. The success rate of the IAS in presenting appeals has been very poor, again possibly revealing the toughening of the procedures. The fact that the organisations exist in Glasgow shows the need for their service. The IAS office in Glasgow holds surgeries in other parts of Scotland, e.g. Dundee. While SAAC which is based in the West end of the city of Glasgow holds surgeries in the Southside of the city. The survey conducted revealed that the IAS was the most used organisation in terms of application for an entry visa and for help when the visa was refused.

The Glasgow Labour MPs argued that there was discrimination when the experiences of would-be immigrants from White Commonwealth countries and the Indian sub-continent are compared. They emphasised the need for equality when dealing with applications, the primary purpose rule dividing families, the waiting time and how the ECOs looks for any contrariety in the application made. The MPs felt that it was commonly believed that all people from the Indian sub-continent are liars and are not coming to the UK for the intended reason. The Conservative MPs themselves heard criticisms about delays, immigration officers not understanding the Asian culture. Nevertheless unlike the Labour MPs they were not critical themselves about the immigration procedures or the Laws. The Glasgow Labour MPs were more in touch with the organisations in Glasgow in comparison to the Scottish Conservative MPs.

One of the three adjudicators interviewed believed that people from the Indian sub-continent were prone to have a more difficult time than people from the Old White Commonwealth countries. The adjudicator, focusing in effect on the primary purpose rule, emphasised that people from the Indian sub-continent have arranged marriages as part of their culture and do not even have a chance to converse with their partner to be. In sharp contrast, ECO expects the couple to have met and liked each other. Thus there is an inevitable clash between the expectations of the ECO and the cultural background of those seeking to enter Britain from the Indian sub-continent. The fact remains that the primary purpose rule was itself discriminatory to the arranged marriage culture that people have in the countries which make up the Indian sub-continent. This itself highlights a lack of understanding of the culture of the Indian sub-continent on the part of the Conservatives (although the Labour government at present has taken steps to remedy this by abolishing the primary purpose rule). Some officials also divulged that it was a very difficult task to prove that a person was not marrying a UK citizen to gain entry into the UK only. There is definite discrimination for those from the Indian sub-continent as the immigration rules are designed to oppose the culture of the Indian sub-continent.

Overall the results of this study, which has analysed the immigration policy of the Conservative government under Thatcher (1979-1990), has shown that Tory policy was unfair and had an adverse effect on people from the Indian sub-continent. This is more evident if we use a non-measurable yardstick such as the nature of the laws passed, and the actual exercise of authority by ECOs in terms of their conduct, and interviewing techniques, for assessing the thrust of Conservative immigration policy, which reveals the ferocity of the policies and procedures. It has been seen that persons from the Indian sub-continent not only suffered in terms of numbers accepted and refused, the actual execution of policy, and the criteria laid down was also unfair and very stringent. The actual practices adopted e.g. interviewing style and techniques; wording of questions, and the presence of an unfriendly environment and making people wait very long periods before granting visas only encouraged to antagonise the Indian sub-continent nationals. One element of this harshness and unfairness, as we have noted, was cultural. Therefore nationals from the Indian sub-continent suffered through the manner of processing applications, and establishing the credibility of an applicant was made more difficult. It appears as though the Thatcher government's philosophy on immigration directed at individuals from the Indian sub-continent was although "you might get in eventually providing you meet the criteria, we will make absolutely sure you will have to work for it". Even those who did eventually achieve entry many of them had to endure long and nervous periods of waiting. Unfortunately in a few cases this policy ended up excluding or denying entry to genuine people. In addition the rise in the number of male applications from many black countries also hardened the Conservative stance to such an extent that everyone was viewed from those countries with suspicion.

The Thatcher government made no secret of the fact that it felt that there were too many people entering Britain, and that this was proving to be a burden which financially or economically, and even from a political point of view (threat to jobs) could not be supported. It wanted to be more selective in those it allowed in.

However in practice it found that while it could take steps to be more strict e.g. more interrogation of applicants, it could not prevent the entry of many because they had genuine applications which fell within the guidelines set out by the government.

The argument of this study that Conservative immigration policy was unnecessarily restrictive and unfair is also sustained by a large majority of writers as seen in the review of literature in chapter one. Indeed many writers have gone a step further and accused Conservative immigration policy for being discriminatory. Writers such as Dummett, Gordon, Spencer and others make no secret of their unequivocal hatred of the Conservative immigration regime.[25] Furthermore, in line with what is argued by many contemporary writers on immigration, at no time does this study argue that immigration controls should be totally removed. What is disputed is their nature, the manner in which they are implemented, and the unjust and unfair impact they have.

The Future of the Conservative Immigration Regime and Towards a New Immigration Policy

Recent developments suggest that the controversial Conservative immigration regime in place since 1979 which had a very adverse effect on immigrants from the Indian subcontinent, is going to be dismantled by the new Labour government. Evidence of this can be seen in the fact that only 5 weeks into office the Blair administration abolished the much detested primary purpose rule.[26] This action demonstrates the fact that the Labour government acknowledged the discrimination and unfairness inherent in previous Tory rules and procedures, in particular the hardship that this rule caused many Indian sub-continent nationals. Indeed the Labour party manifesto clearly stated "we will, however, reform the system in current use to remove the arbitrary and unfair results that can follow from the existing primary purpose rule."[27] The abolition of the primary purpose rule means that the burden of proof will fall on immigration officers in contrast to before when the applicant had to prove a negative: that the purpose of marriage was not principally to gain entry to the United Kingdom. One of the arguments developed in this book was precisely the adverse effect which the primary purpose rule had on applications from the Indian sub-continent.

While acknowledging and understanding the need for an effective immigration policy, it is also important that such a policy passes certain tests such as those of fairness, equality, non-discrimination and non-racism. This is once again echoed by Labour's manifesto which points out that "every country must have firm control over immigration.... all applications, however, should be dealt with speedily and fairly".[28] These are precisely the tests that the Conservative immigration regime failed. Legislation was drafted in such a way that it did not apply to all races. Laws and rules favoured white people. The criteria for entry were wholly unfair. It can also be argued that the unequal application of laws and the unfairness inherent in the regime were deliberate. We only have to look at the reasons given for the adoption of tough immigration laws. Thatcher herself made no secret of the fact that she was concerned about alien cultures threatening traditional British culture. No attempt was made by the Conservative government to remove the unfairness and injustices of its policies. It is also useful at this point to note that the impact of the Conservative immigration regime were also felt by other groups of blacks. Many of the laws also discriminated against for example Afro-Caribbean immigrants. Nevertheless it is true that some of the key areas of contention such as the primary purpose rule affected the Indian sub-continent more since it is related to the concept of arranged marriages which are part of the cultural tradition of the Indian sub-continent. In addition we have to remember that our greater emphasis on the Indian sub-continent stems from the fact that the book is about the impact on immigrants from that region.

Perhaps under the present Labour government[29] we should witness a firm but fair immigration policy, which will remove cultural stereotypes and promote better race relations. Such a policy could be developed along the lines of that supported by Dummett, and analysed in chapter 1. Dummett supports a middle ground approach to immigration which states that while there should be some restrictions on immigration it is important that these are applied fairly and equally, and black and coloured groups should not be singled out as special cases requiring control.

Notes

1.   Ann Dummett, *Immigration How The Truth Got Swamped* (Action Group on Immigration and Nationality, 1978), p. 9.

241

2.   Michael Dummett, *Where The Debate Goes Wrong* (Action Group on Immigration and Nationality, 1978).

3.   *Conservative Party Manifesto*, 1979.

4.   *The Herald*, September 10, 1979, p. 4.

5.   The term *dual nationality* is used when an individual has two nationalities e.g. those born in India and those who came to Britain in the 1950s or 1960s were Indian nationals but under the rules at the time also acquired the status of British nationals if they so desired.

6.   *Glasgow Herald*, August 16, 1979, p. 1.

7.   See *ibid*, October 10, 1979, p. 8.

8.   *World in Action*, Granada television, 30 January 1978.

9.   Wapshott and Brock, *Thatcher* (1983).

10.   *Interview* with Detective Sergeant, Police and Nationality Department, 19 April 1996.

11   *Ibid*, Nick Troake, Policy Directorate, Immigration Nationality Department, Home Office, 19 September 1996.

12.   *Ibid*; see also *Control of Immigration Statistics United Kingdom* (London: HMSO), various years.

13.   *Ibid.*

14.   *Control of Immigration Statistics United Kingdom*, various years.

15.   See the *1971 Immigration Act*.

16.   *Interview* with senior IAS councillor, Mr Nabi.

17   *Which Half Decides? A Contribution to the debate on sex discrimination, British Nationality and Immigration Laws*, (National Association for Asian Youth, 1979), p. 25.

18   *Interview* with MP George Galloway; interview with MP Mike Watson and see chapter 6.

19.   *Ibid*, Sean Lusk, Migration and Visa Unit of the Foreign and Commonwealth Office.

20   *Control of Immigration Statistics United Kingdom, 1990*

21.   *Foreign Language Skills for Entry Clearance Work*, (Training Department, 1995).

22   *Interview* with Sean Lusk, Foreign and Commonwealth Office, 20 September 1996.

23.   Paul Gordon and Francesca King, *British Immigration Control. A brief guide*, (Runnymede Trust, 1985), pp. 12-13.

24.   SAAC *Annual Report*, 1987-88, p. 8.

25.   See *chapter 1*

26.   On this see the *Guardian* , 28 May 1997, p. 5

27.   *Labour Party manifesto 1997*, p. 35.

28.   *Ibid*

29.   See *ibid* according to which a more *fairer* immigration system will be put in place.

Bibliography

Documentary Sources

Central Office of Information, *Immigration into Britain: 1971 Immigration Act - notes on the regulations and procedures,* (1981).

Central Statistical Office, *Regional Trends,* no. 22, (London 1987).

Conservative Central Office, *Our first Eight Years: The Achievements of the Conservative Government since May 1979,* (1987).

Conservative Party, *Conservative Party Manifestos, 1979, 1983, 1987, 1992 and 1997.*

Court Service, *Standards of Service for Tribunals.*

European Parliament, *Report of the Committee of Inquiry into the Rise of Fascism and Racism in Europe,* (December 1985).

European Parliament, *Report of the Committee of Inquiry into Racism and Xenophobia,* (23 July 1990).

Home Office, *British Nationality Administration and Fees,* (London: HMSO, 1984).

Home Office, *Immigration and Nationality Department,* Annual Report, 1991-1992.

Home Office, *Immigration, Nationality, and Passports: a Report on the Work of the Departments,* (Croydon: 1987).

House of Commons, *Administrative Delays in the Immigration and Nationality Department: the government reply to the fifth report from the Home Affairs Committee, session 1989-90,* (London: HMSO, 1990).

House of Commons, *British Nationality Fees, third report, 1982-83.*

House of Lords, *Select Committee on the European Communities, Community Policy on Migration,* (London: HMSO, 1992).

Immigration Service Ports Directorate, *Operating Plans.*

Labour Party, *Labour Party Manifestos, 1979, 1983, 1987, 1992 and 1997.*

Memorandum of evidence - Submitted to the Race Relations and Immigration Sub-committee (SCORRI) of the Home Affairs Committee by UKIAS in connection with their inquiry into immigration from the Indian sub-continent, June 1985.

Memorandum on the Work of the Immigration and Nationality Department submitted by the UKIAS to SCORRI, March 1985.

Migration and Visa Division, Report by the Independent Monitor, 1996.

Parliamentary Debates, *Commons (Hansard).*

Scottish Office, *1991 Census Monitor for Parliamentary Constituencies in Scotland*, (Edinburgh, 1994).

Training Department, *Foreign Language Skills for Entry Clearance Work*, (1995).

Laws and Legislative Measures

Commonwealth Immigrants Act 1962, (London: HMSO, 1962).
Commonwealth Immigrants Act 1968, (London: HMSO, 1968).
Immigration Appeals Act 1969, (London: HMSO, 1969).
Immigration Act 1971, (London: HMSO, 1971).
British Nationality Act 1981, (London: HMSO, 1981).
Immigration (Carriers' Liability) Act 1987, (London: HMSO, 1987).
Immigration Act 1988, (London: HMSO, 1988).
Asylum and Immigration Appeals Act 1993, (London: HMSO, 1993).
Race Relations Act 1968.
Statement of Changes in Immigration Rules, (London: HMSO, 1994).

Official Statistics

General Register Office for Scotland: Population Statistics Branch.
Home Office, Government Statistical Service, (London: Annual).
Home Office, *Control of Immigration: Statistics United Kingdom*.

Organisational Publications

Commission for Racial Equality, *The Asylum and Immigration and Immigration Act 1996: Implications for Racial Equality*, 1996.
Commission for Racial Equality, *Immigration Control Procedures: Report of a formal investigation*, 1985.
Commission for Racial Equality, *Race, Housing, and Immigration, 1989*.
Ethnic Minorities Directory, (Hasib Publications, 1993).
Glasgow City Council: Town Clerks Office, *A Directory of Black and Ethnic Minority Organisations in Glasgow and Strathclyde*, 1994.
Joint Council for the Welfare of Immigrants, *The New Immigration Rules and the European Convention on Human Rights, 1980*.

Joint Council for the Welfare of Immigrants, *Out of Sight: The New Visit Visa System Overseas, 1987.*

National Association for Asian Youth, Which Half Decides? A Contribution to the Debate on Sex Discrimination, British Nationality and Immigration Laws, 1979.

Release Publications, *Immigration: How the Law Affects You,* 1978.

Runnymede Trust Bulletin, *Race and Immigration,* No. 167 May 1984.

Scottish Asian Action Committee Reports (annual).

Scottish Refugee Council Report (annual).

South Manchester Law Centre, *A Hard Act to Follow: The Immigration Act 1988.*

Strathclyde Community Relations Council Report (annual).

United Kingdom Immigration Advisory Service Report (annual).

Newspapers and Journals

A. English Language

Asian Age.
Asian Times.
Asian Voice.
Economist.
Financial Times.
Glasgow Herald.
Guardian.
Immigration and Nationality: Law and Practise.
Scotsman.
The Times.

B. Urdu and Punjabi

Daily Jang
Des Pardes

Interviews and Meetings

During the period 1993-1997 I conducted a large number of interviews, and attended a number of meetings with officials from government departments, and

MPs from the two major Political Parties - The Conservatives and Labour - and members and officers from various organisations. There were a small number of individuals, mostly Asian citizens, whom I interviewed but most of whom wished to remain anonymous.

Interviews and meetings are divided into a number of categories, and where possible dates have been supplied.

A. Interviews with Officers from Organisations in Glasgow

Mr Masood Nabi, Senior Counsellor, Immigration Advisory Service, May 1994.

Dr Singh, Interpreter, Strathclyde Interpreting Service, July 1994.

Jean McFadden, Officer, Strathclyde Community Relations Council, November 1994.

Lynne Barty, Chairperson, Scottish Refugee Council, May 1994.

Stan Crook, Case worker, Scottish Refugee Council, Glasgow Office, June 1994.

Danusia Zarembe, Refugee Support Worker, Community Relations Council, Glasgow Office, August 1994.

B. Interviews Conducted with Immigration Officials in Glasgow

Detective Sergeant, Police Nationality Department, 19 April 1996.

Private Communication, Detective Constable, Police Nationality Department, 30 June 1996.

Mr. Deans, Regional Adjudicator, Immigration Appellate Authority, 2 August 1996.

Adjudicator A, Immigration Appellate Authority, 25 June 1996.

Adjudicator B, Immigration Appellate Authority, 14 May 1996.

Private Communication, Home Office Presenting Officer, Blythswood House, Glasgow, March 1996.

C. Interviews Conducted in London

Nick Troake, Policy Directorate, Immigration and Nationality Department, Home Office, 19 September 1996.

Assistant Director, Immigration Service Ports Directorate, Immigration and Nationality Department, Home Office, 19 September 1996.

Senior Official, Immigration Service Enforcement Directorate, Immigration and Nationality Department, 19 September 1996.
Sean Lusk, Head of Policy Making, Migration and Visa Unit, Foreign and Commonwealth Office, 20 September 1996.

D. Interviews with MPs

The following key applies
C = Conservative, L = Labour
Davidson, Ian (L) (Govan), 18 May 1996.
Galloway, George (L) (Hillhead), 19 April 1996.
Gallie, Phil (C) (Ayr), May 1996.
Marshall, David (L) (Shettleston), 21 March 1997.
Munro, Hector (C) (Dumfries), June 1996.
Stewart, Alan (C) (Eastwood), May 1996.
Watson, Mike (L) (Central), 2 March 1996.

E. Interviews with Individuals

Kanabar, S, 22 January 1996.
Raja, Hanif, 15 June 1996.
Sarwar, Mohammed, 15 June 1996.

Completed Questionnaires

The following MPs completed questionnaires:

MP A (C) (June 1996).
Fyfe, Maria (L) (Maryhill), 1 April 1996.
Gallie, Phil (C) (Ayr), 28 May 1996.
Munro, Hector (C) (Dumfries), June 1996.
Martin, Michael (L) (Springburn), April 1996.
Maxton, John (L) (Cathcart), April 1996.
Stewart Alan (C) (Eastwood), May 1996.

There was also correspondence in the form of letters from the following MPs:

Lang, Ian MP (C) (Upper Nithsdale), 30 May 1996.
Forsyth, Michael (C) (Stirling), 29 May 1996.
Rifkind, Malcolm (C) (Edinburgh Pentlands), 3 June 1996.
Douglas-Hamilton, James (C) (Edinburgh West), 30 May 1996.
Dunnachie, James (L) (Pollok), 27 May 1996.
Dewar, Donald (L) (Anniesland) May 1996.

In addition there were letters sent from opposition MPs to government ministers and official institutions in support of various individuals or on behalf of constituents, and also letters received by themselves in reply to their initial correspondence.

Letter from:

Mike Watson MP to Entry Clearance Officer at the British High Commission, Islamabad, 11 November 1994.
Mike Watson MP to Right Honourable Douglas Hurd, 25 November 1994.
Mike Watson MP to Foreign and Commonwealth Office, London, 4 July 1995.
Alan Stewart MP to High Commission, Islamabad in support of Mr Raja's request, 14 October 1994.

Letter to:

Mike Watson from FCO, Immigration and Visa Unit, London, 15 November, 1994 and 18 November 1994, 28 November 1994, 4 July 1995, 19 July 1995.
Jimmy Dunnachie from FCO, London, 16 August 1991.
Keith Best, IAS Chairman from Migration and Visa Unit, 4 July 1994.

Books

Akram, Mohammed, (1974), *Where do you keep your string beds? A Study of the Entry Clearance Procedure in Pakistan*, Runnymede Trust.
Akram, Mohammed and Eliot, Jan, (1976), *Firm but Unfair? Immigration Control in the Indian sub-continent, A Preliminary Report*, Runnymede Trust.
Anwar, Mohammed, (1986), *Race and Politics*, Tavistock Publications.

Bevan, V. (1987), *The Development of British Immigration Law*, London.

Cohen, Robin and Layton-Henry, Zig (eds), (1997), *The Politics of Migration*, Edward Elgar Publishing Limited.

Coleman D. A. (1982), *Demography of Immigrants and Minority Groups in the United Kingdom*, Academic Press.

Cornelius, Wayne, Martin, Philip and Hollifield, James, (1984), *Controlling Immigration: A Global Perspective*, Stanford: Stanford University Press.

De Vaus, D. A. (1986), *Surveys in Social Research*, London.

Dummett, Ann (ed.), (1978), *How the truth got swamped*, Action Group on Immigration and Nationality.

Dummett, Ann (ed.), (1986), *Towards a Just Immigration Policy*, London: Cobden Trust.

Dummett, Ann and Nicol, Andrew, (1990), *Subjects, Citizens and Others*, London: Weidenfeld and Nicolson.

Dummett, Michael, (1978), *Where the debate goes wrong?* Action Group on Immigration and Nationality.

Farinto, Solomon-Saul, Jibowu, Muyiwa, (1997), *Practical Solutions to UK Immigration and Nationality Matters*, Turnaround : 2nd edition.

Geddes, Andrew, (1996), *The Politics of Immigration and Race*, Baseline Book Company.

Gordon, Paul, (1984), *Deportations and Removals*, Runnymede Trust.

Gordon, Paul, (1985), *Policing Immigration*, London: Pluto Press Limited.

Gordon, Paul, (1989), *Fortress Europe? The Meaning of 1992*, London: Runnymede Trust.

Gordon, P. and Klug, F., *British Immigration Control: A brief guide* (London: Runnymede Trust, 1985).

Goulbourne, H. (ed.), (1990), *Black Politics in Britain*, Aldershot: Avebury.

Heath, Anthony, Jowell, Roger, and Curtice John, (1985), *How Britain Votes*, Pergamon Press.

Hiro, D., (1991), *Black British, White British: A History of Race Relations in Britain*, London: Grafton Books.

Juss, Satvinder, (1993), *Immigration, Nationality and Citizenship*, Mansell.

Knowles, Caroline, (1992), *Race, Discourse and Labourism*, London; New York: Routledge.

Layton-Henry, Zig and Rich, Paul, (1992), *Race, Government and Politics in Britain*, London: Macmillan.

Layton-Henry, Zig, (1992), *Politics of Immigration*, Blackwell Publishers.

LeMay, C. Michael, (1989), *The Gatekeepers: Comparative Immigration Policy*, Praeger Publishers.

Macdonald, Ian, (1992), *The New Immigration Law*, London : Butterworths.

Macdonald, Ian and Blake, Nicholas, (1995), *Macdonald's Immigration Law and Practise*, London; Butterworths.

Macmillan, J. (1952), Historical Background of Aliens, Aliens Registration Department.

Martin, Ian and Grant, Lawrence, (1985), *Immigration Law and Practise: First Supplement*, London.

Messina, A. (1989), *Race and Party Competition in Britain*, Oxford: Clarendon Press.

Miles, Robert and Phizacklea, Annie, (1984), *White Man's Country*, London: Pluto Press.

Morgado, Cosme, (1989), *The Role of Members of Parliament in Immigration Cases*, Coventry: Centre for Research in Ethnic Relations, Warwick University.

Saggar, Shamit, (1992), *Race and Politics in Britain*, Harvester/Wheatsheaf.

Solomos, John, (1993), *Race and Racism in Britain*, London: Macmillan.

Solomos, John and Wrench John (ed.), (1983), *Racism and Migration in Western Europe*, Berg.

Sondhi, R. (1987), *Divided Families: British Immigration Control in the Indian sub-continent*, London: Runnymede Trust.

Spencer, Sarah (ed.), (1994), *Strangers and Citizens: A Positive Approach to Migrants and Refugees,* London: Rivers Oram Press.

Storey, H. (1983), *Immigrants and the Welfare State*, London.

Vincenzi Christopher and Marrington David, (1992), *Immigration Law: The Rules Explained*, Sweet & Maxwell.

Walvin James, (1984), *Passage to Britain*, Penguin Books.

Articles

Anwar, M, (1979), 'British Voters Reject the National Front', *Impact International*, 27 July-9 August.

Baldwin-Edwards, M, (1991), 'Immigration after 1992', *Policy and Politics*, vol. 19, no. 3.

Bovey, Mungo, (1990), 'Judicial Review of Immigration Cases: The Scottish Dimension', *Immigration and Nationality Law and Practice,* July.

Bulusu, L. (1986), 'Recent Patterns of Migration to and from the United Kingdom', *Population Trends*, no.46, Winter.

Cohen, S, (1984), 'From Aliens Act to Immigration Act', *Legal Action*, September.

Collinson, Sarah, (1995), 'Migration, Visa and Asylum Policies in Europe', *Wilton Park Conference Paper 107*, September.

Dixon, D. 'Thatcher's People: The British Nationality Act, 1981', *Journal of Law and Society*, vol. 10, pp.161-180.

Gillespie, Jim, (1987), 'The New Immigration Rules', *Immigration and Nationality Law and Practice*, vol. 1, no.4, January, pp. 26-27.

Gordon, D, (1987), 'Arranged Marriages: For Entry or for love?', *Family Law*, vol. 17, July.

Grant, Lawrence, (1987), 'Applications by Husbands, Wives and Fiancés', *Immigration and Nationality Law and Practice,* vol. 2, no. 2, July, pp. 25-52.

Layton-Henry, Zig, (1979), 'The Report on Immigration', *Political Quarterly*, vol. 50, no.2.

Leighton, J. (1980), 'How Britain Helps to Create Broken Homes', *New Statesman*, May 9.

LeLohe, M. 'Voter Discrimination against Asian and Black Candidates in the 1983 General Election', *New Community*, vol. 11, nos. 1-2, pp.101-184.

LeLohe, M. (1982), 'The Participation of the Ethnic Minorities in the British Political Process', *report submitted to the Commission for Racial Equality.*

Miles, Robert, (1990), 'The Racialisation of British Politics', *Political Studies*, vol. 38.

Nicol, A. (1981), 'No Hope of Justice for Illegal Entrants', New *Statesman*, October 16.

Solomos, John, 'Trends in the Political Analysis of Racism', *Political Studies*, vol. 34, no.2, pp.313-324.

Studlar, D. (1978), 'Policy voting in Britain: The Coloured Immigration Issue in the 1964, 1966, and 1970 General Elections', *American Political Science Review,* vol. 72, pp.46-72.

Studlar, D.T. and Layton-Henry, Z. (1990), 'Non-white Minority Access to the Political Agenda in Britain', *Policy Studies Review*, vol. 9, no.20.

Webb, David, (1987), 'Village Enquiries in the Indian sub-continent', *Immigration and Nationality Law and Practice*, vol. 1, no.4, January, pp. 16-23.

Wilson, A. (1980), 'Immigration Policy and the Police State', *New Statesman*, 11 July.

For Product Safety Concerns and Information please contact our EU
representative GPSR@taylorandfrancis.com
Taylor & Francis Verlag GmbH, Kaufingerstraße 24, 80331 München, Germany

www.ingramcontent.com/pod-product-compliance
Lightning Source LLC
Chambersburg PA
CBHW050705280326
41926CB00088B/2572